The
Second
Coming

The Archangel Gabriel Proclaims A New Age

Dear Rose + George

Hope you enjoy the

book !

Love Joe

JOEL D. ANASTASI

The Second Coming
The Archangel Gabriel Proclaims A New Age

iUniverse books may be ordered through booksellers or by contacting:

iUniverse
1663 Liberty Drive
Bloomington, IN 47403
www.iuniverse.com
1-800-Authors (1-800-288-4677)

ISBN: 978-0-595-49405-7 (pbk)
ISBN: 978-0-595-49346-3 (cloth)
ISBN: 978-0-595-61086-0 (ebk)

Printed in the United States of America

TO:

ROBERT BAKER
One of the great spiritual messengers
and teachers of our time.

PHILLIP COLLINS
Who first suggested this book and
encouraged me when I needed it.

and

THE ARCHANGEL GABRIEL
Who lovingly and patiently used the
simplest questions for profound teaching.
This is your book.

CONTENTS

Introduction   1

Chapter 1:

Hello, Gabriel! Who are You?   11

Chapter 2:

Gabriel/God/Creation   31

Chapter 3:

New Spiritual Age/Divine Plan/Man's Origins and Journey   49

Chapter 4:

Ascendant Masters/Evolution/Awakening of the Soul   83

Chapter 5:

USA/Democracy/Geopolitics/September 11, 2001   129

Chapter 6:

Religion/Scripture/Spirituality   159

Chapter 7:

Jesus and Mary/Christianity   173

Chapter 8:

Love/Creating Reality   195

Chapter 9:

Health/Healing/Living/Immortality   211

Chapter 10:

Death/Spiritual Realms/Guidance   231

Chapter 11:

Abortion/Homosexuality/Death Penalty   245

Chapter 12:

August 30, 2003: Martin Luther King, Jr. /John F. Kennedy/Middle
East/World Government/Democracy Revisited   251

Chapter 13:

April 25, 2004: A New Creation Story/Gnostic Gospels/Jesus and the
Early Church/Sacraments and Rituals   263

Chapter 14:

October 21, 2004: Redemption/World Management Team/Ecosys-
tem Imbalances/God's Messengers   283

Chapter 15:

November 29, 2004: Election 2004/2012/God and Religion/Two-
Thousand-Year Cycles/Root Races/Polar Shift   295

Chapter 16:

December 10, 2004: Duality Versus Unity/Secret Orders–Modern
Organizations/Power Of Consciousness And Intention   303

Afterword   315

Energetic Exercises   327

Glossary   333

About the Author and the Channel   343

Introduction

More than six billion human beings inhabit a small planet called Earth, a tiny warm Eden circling endlessly around an ordinary star at the edge of a galaxy, light-years from any other.

Who are we? Why are we here? Where did we come from? Do our lives here have any meaning or value? What is the purpose of this vast universe filled with giant galaxies and stars? Did some great God create all this?

Age-old questions. From where and whom will the answers come?

From us, claim religious leaders, citing the authority of ancient scripture although they know little of its authors or how it was assembled, and even less about how it may have changed or evolved through translations, transcriptions, or politics. Still, we are told to accept it as truth as many religious fundamentalists try to make their cultures and laws conform to their beliefs.

From us, say scientists, who tend to dismiss religion as so much superstition, instead searching for answers through technology and scientific enterprises such as NASA's Genesis Project—many perhaps agreeing with the late astronomer Carl Sagan's contention that he would be willing to believe in God if he could find any evidence to support that belief.

We may have progressed from a time when religious authorities could order the imprisonment or death of a Galileo. Nonetheless, science and religion are still locked in battle over whose views of creation will prevail.

Yet, why should we cede the quest for answers to either group? Both are constrained by limited belief systems that try to define for the rest of us what is possible or acceptable. Followers have repeatedly demonstrated a willingness to censor or punish their own who challenge their orthodoxy. No wonder so much innovation comes from outside organized disciplines where people are free to think outside the box of orthodoxy.

But what of the rest of us? How open are we to new information that challenges our beliefs?

How open, for that matter, am I?

That was the question I faced in August 2002 when I first encountered the Archangel Gabriel.

That summer I had learned of an energetic healing practice called Reiki that supposedly was related to the ancient healing arts practiced by Jesus. Curious, I tracked down a Reiki Master in Manhattan and began studying with Robert Baker, who I soon learned "channeled" the Archangel Gabriel. Gabriel of course is the archangel who the Bible says announced to the Virgin Mary that she would give birth to a child called Jesus who was the Son of God.

Gabriel is a sacred figure in the Catholic Church in which I was raised. Even if I might accept such a thing were possible, the idea of Gabriel communicating through some obscure person outside any recognized church seemed highly unlikely and somewhat irreverent to me. Why would Gabriel be communicating through Robert Baker, and why to a small group of people who gathered weekly in Baker's home rather than to someone of spiritual prominence and reputation? (Though I realized heavenly messengers in the Bible usually visited the poor and obscure, including the Virgin Mary.) In time, Robert's intelligence and gentle, unassuming demeanor along with the credibility he created in his Reiki classes sparked my curiosity, and I decided to attend one of his Sunday evening channeling sessions.

Some twenty people were spread over the furniture and floor in Robert's living room. Robert, slim, fifty-something but looking somewhat cherub-like with curly blond hair and blue eyes, sat in a comfortable armchair. He lowered his head and appeared to quietly meditate. Then he bolted upright and began twisting his arms and body as though invaded by some powerful force. With eyes closed and a slight smile, he slowly surveyed the room, observing the audience. Suddenly, as though propelled by a great force of energy, he announced himself as Gabriel and declared, "It is a joy to be in your divine presence." To my surprise and disappointment, I soon realized I was not feeling the same way.

Perhaps I was expecting a comforting spiritual message from the divine realm. Instead, Gabriel launched into a chilling warning that the democratic societies of the world were being undermined by powerful worldwide networks of wealthy institutions and families that dominated the financial, energy and pharmaceutical industries, among others, as well as most of the governments of the world—including our own. He said the ancestral roots of these networks went back hundreds of years and were connected to the Freemasons and something called the Illuminati. They were seeking to create a new world order in which the super-wealthy few controlled the many.

I am a trained journalist (Columbia Graduate School of Journalism), served as a vice president of a major financial services organization, and consulted for twenty years with many Fortune 500 companies trying to separate fact from fiction. I have little tolerance for deceit or misrepresentations. Gabriel was making darkly sinister charges about organizations and institutions of enormous prestige and influence, warning that their motivation was to create and control a world economy and government—in other words, us. "Wake up," he warned. And do what, I wondered? Write my congressman? Call the New York Times? Was Gabriel an archangel or an eccentric conspiracy nut?

Nonetheless, I was intrigued by much of what he discussed and returned to the Sunday sessions. Although Gabriel occasionally revisited the dark subjects of international conspiracy, he most often gave fascinating talks about God, creation, and the "divine plan," including man's role in it. He explained incredibly complex concepts with great authority and, occasionally, a dry wit that tempered their seriousness. He also gave personal counsel in an open questions segment after his lectures.

My confidence in Gabriel's authenticity grew along with my relationship with Robert during the Reiki training. Robert and I agreed that Gabriel's teachings were too important to be limited to the small numbers attending Robert's spiritual center that he headed with his business partner, Ronald Baker, in Manhattan. I proposed we do a book in which I would interview Gabriel as a journalist, asking questions anyone would want to ask a heavenly messenger. I felt encouraged when Gabriel told me in private session that I had been preparing for this work over "many incarnations," but that I had the right to choose according to my free will.

On April 11, 2003, we began the first of a series of interviews that were completed in December 2004. Gabriel counseled me to

3

proceed "as a little child," which I found both comforting and easy as I am no theologian and simply wanted answers to questions I've always pondered. As the interviews progressed, Gabriel's responses sometimes led into subjects I hadn't anticipated, and I occasionally felt Gabriel was guiding the interviews, not me. A number of subjects were developed over several interviews, thus permitting me to ask follow-up questions to clarify his answers. So you may find that questions arising in your mind at certain points get answered as you continue reading.

Invariably, the material seemed clearer each time I reviewed it. When I made that observation to Gabriel, he explained the material was given in "energetic layers" and is revealed gradually as we review it so we are not overwhelmed. If some passages seem too difficult, rereading may clarify them. Alternatively, skip them and return after you have covered more of the material, as they may then seem clearer. I believe this is more a book to study than to read.

Gabriel suggested I organize the book by subject. As one subject naturally flowed into another, I sometimes found it difficult to separate them, much like pulling apart a tightly woven tapestry. Chapter One presents the first interview in its entirety because it sets up the discussions that follow. The middle chapters are loosely organized by subject, though some topics reappear in several chapters as they are developed and may appear somewhat repetitious. (To me the repetition builds understanding.) The final chapters (all dated) present complete interviews because they develop subjects covered earlier.

So what has Gabriel come to teach us? As I reviewed hundreds of pages of transcribed interviews, I realized Gabriel was essentially retelling the creation story. The creation stories that man believes, he says, are largely "fairy tales." In telling his version, Gabriel discusses a wide range of subjects from great spiritual themes such as man's origin and journey to more personal issues such as healing and death. However, it seems to me his core teachings relate to the questions: Who or what is God? What is the nature and purpose of creation? Who are we? Why are we here? And he tells us very specifically why he is communicating with us now. Here are some of his key teachings:

God is all there is. Each of us is a part of God, an individuated expression of God. As part of the energy of God, everything is connected. Therefore, we are all one. God uses the vast universe to experience its infinite diversity through all the countless expressions of creation, including us. Therefore, God is experiencing itself (God has no sexuality) through each one of us.

Everything is composed of energy vibrating at vastly different frequencies, most of which we cannot perceive. The lowest vibration—what we perceive as matter—constitutes a tiny fraction of all creation. As we attempt to understand creation in the narrow range of what we can perceive, we are barely scratching the surface of all that is—much like a radio that can receive only one signal, unable to detect the countless frequencies around it.

In the realm of matter, mankind on earth is part of a divine experiment, which Gabriel says is unique in the universe. He indicates the earth was seeded millions of years ago by twelve star systems that created the human form (humans are unique in the universe) as a vehicle to allow God to experience the ascension of the soul, with twelve archetypes of the divine being represented by those twelve star systems. The ascension is an evolutionary process of discovery of the God within each one of us (our souls) that gives God the opportunity to "experience twelve aspects of the divinity of the force of love."

Each of us as a soul has chosen to come here from one of the twelve star systems to participate in this experiment. Many spiritual masters have come to help in that process, including Jesus whose birth Gabriel announced two thousand years ago. Jesus, Gabriel says, demonstrated the pattern of self-mastery that produces the awakening and the ascension of the soul in man through a series of "initiations," the seven stages of soul evolution (birth, baptism, transfiguration, renunciation, crucifixion, resurrection, and ascension) that Christian religions recognize but don't completely understand.

Now Gabriel is proclaiming a new two-thousand-year age, the age of spiritual unity of all mankind. This new age was born on January 23, 1997, signaled by a configuration of planets aligned to form a six-point star—the same configuration Gabriel says announced the birth of Jesus two thousand years ago.

In this new age, mankind will follow the pattern Jesus demonstrated to awaken the soul, the Christ Consciousness, in each one of us. This, he says, is the Second Coming. It is not "the Christ, the man, coming to rescue and save you. That is a fallacy. What he was telling you was that the Christ lies within you. You are the Christ. The time in evolution has come for the Christ Consciousness, the soul, to awaken in all humankind. We come to give you the step-by-step process for the awakening of the Christ Consciousness in all humanity."

Central to this process is the preparation of our body, the temple of the soul, by "raising its vibration to a vibratory rate where the vibratory rate of the physical body matches the vibratory rate of the soul." The chapter "Energetic Exercises" contains the exercises Gabriel has given to help each of us prepare our body, the temple, for our soul's awakening and ascension in this new age.

Preparation for this new age of unity of all mankind began centuries ago. A key component was the creation of the United States, which was to be the New Jerusalem, the promised land, the "land of the awakening of the new spirit," signified, Gabriel says, by the fact that the letters USA are the central letters in the word Jerusalem. "Its original intention was to be a synthesis of all the people of the world who have lived under oppression and have come here to find spiritual freedom and expression of their individual being. In its original intention, it was supposed to have been a collective of that democratic idea of the freedom of speech, freedom of religion, freedom of individual social construct, so that every person and every group can live together in harmony and peace.

"That creates a collective consciousness that brings together a synthesis of all the peoples around the globe to begin to synthesize all the belief systems into a new world of spiritual development. A new world that takes bits and pieces of everything and creates a synthesized whole to lead the world into a new level of unity, oneness, communion and freedom, spiritual freedom." The United States, in essence, is the prototype of the unity that is to develop in mankind in this new two-thousand-year age.

But "that has been distorted," Gabriel warns, because our democracy is now dominated by huge global concentrations of wealth and power that have greatly reduced the power and influence of the individual, which is fundamental to the success of democratic societies. It is the few "seeking through their greed to control and dominate the many, rather than creating for the many an experience of equality and provision, support, compassion, love and prosperity." These powers are working to undermine mankind's unity by fostering conflict, separation, and disunity and by gaining control through fear. "Create that war on terrorism, keep them fearful," he says, is a current manifestation of this strategy. He tells us to "wake up" because our leaders have been "bought and sold" by these powerful international consortiums. We must take back our democracy through the power of one—first alone, and then together in unity.

This unity will happen, he says, whether it happens on planet or off because it is "God's evolutionary plan." We are given the gift of free will. We have the power to create a "new golden age or a nuclear holocaust." It is up to us.

In the course of telling this story, Gabriel proves to be an equal opportunity offender, including religion, scripture, global corporations, government leaders, and many of the rest of us. He tells us religions that have done much to shape the cultural norms of most contemporary societies were created by men, not God, and that most of what is judged as moral or immoral simply reflects ancient tribal customs and cultural values that were taught and became accepted as God's word. "God had nothing to do with it," he says.

As for his warnings about the international power brokers that could easily be dismissed as "conspiracy theories," Gabriel insists they are not theories but dangerous realities that not only put our freedoms and democracies at risk, but seek to undermine the spiritual mission of this new age. "We are not interested in harboring your sacred cows to make you feel good. It is not our job to make you feel good. It is not our job to support your vanity. It is our job to reveal the truth as it is. Ye shall know the truth and the truth shall set you free!"

Most challenging for me is accepting and practicing the spiritual context Gabriel creates to help us respond to the information and challenges he presents to us, some of which I admittedly find quite disturbing. Rather than judging his warnings as issues of justice and injustice, right and wrong, he says we should "approach them from the point of view of redemption. Redemption is about bringing things into conscious awareness. From that you can receive the learning it offers you and, in that, uncover greater parts of yourself.

"Look at the history of the human experience as an experience of coming into a place of awareness and consciousness that allows you to see and experience reality in a conscious way. That then allows you to use that reality to discover and to grow and become more of the potential that you are. Challenges reveal your potential. They reveal those places where potential is blocked or thwarted or unconscious. In what you call the negative experience or the frustration of the challenge lies the redemption because in it lies the answer to what you're looking for. Behind every negative experience is redemption, revelation, and inspiration."

Ultimately, Gabriel is bringing an age old message found in metaphysical literature to this new age: Life is a journey of self-discovery, of expanding awareness and consciousness, as we remember our God selves, using all the circumstances of life—what we perceive as good and as bad—to help us. On this journey, Gabriel says each of us serves as "the discoverer and the uncoverer for God of all the parts that God gets to experience itself through. The fact that you've been given freedom of choice is not without a purpose where the divine is concerned. It is a brilliant choice … because through freedom of choice God gets to experience through experience, itself, the fulfillment of its beingness. It gets to experience it as if it were itself going through a process of evolution and discovery…."

Clearly, Gabriel is telling a very different creation story from those taught by most religions or science. Whether you find that Gabriel challenges your beliefs or confirms them, it may be wise to consider the counsel of spiritual teacher Ram Dass:

"Trust only those teachings that feel intuitively right in our deepest heart is to me the final criterion and protection that we must apply in regard to any system whatever its source. Cosmologies, by the nature of the metaphysics with which they deal, have no scientific or empirical base. We really must seek ultimate validation in our deepest being."

I began this journey as a skeptic. The intuitive truth and rightness of Gabriel's teachings have found their way into my "deepest heart," my "deepest being." It is my wish that Gabriel's teachings find that place in you and that all mankind may one day join in peace, love, and unity in this new two-thousand-year age.

Addendum (April 2008)
This manuscript is being published approximately five years after my
first interview with Gabriel, which occurred three weeks after the start
of the U.S. war with Iraq. Though Saddam Hussein is long gone and
the presidency of George W. Bush is nearly complete, I believe Gabriel's
observations about both leaders as well as political and economic
events and the Iraq War are timeless and contain important lessons for
citizens and their governments everywhere.

Chapter 1:
Hello, Gabriel! Who are You?

G: We are most joyous to be in your divine presence at this time on your planet as you move into this new year, this time of change where your world is concerned. At this time we understand that we are to work with you, if you will, to begin answering questions for the putting down of the "golden words of Gabriel" and the book and all that sort of thing. Therefore, we will then open the session to your questions, answers, and points of discussion so we can pursue this and not waste your time. How may we, Gabriel, help you at this time, dear one?

J: First of all, I want to tell you what a joy it is to be working with you.

G: Well, it is a joy for us too to be in your divine presence.

J: Thank you. I'm Joel, of course, and I'm here with my friend Phillip who will be listening to us. He might even pipe in once in awhile.

G: Oh good. Tell him to pipe in any time he wishes.

J: [Laughing] You're relaxing me already because in all honesty, I'm feeling a little nervous about this.

G: Well, breathing is good.

J: We talked about doing this together last year if you remember.

G: Yes.

J: I thought we might begin by putting together a general book that introduces you and addresses many of the metaphysical and spiritual questions that many people wonder about.

G: Well, that's perfectly fine, dear one. Let's do that and see where it leads us.

J: Before I propose my questions to you, I wonder if you have any observations or issues you suggest that we address?

G: What you are contemplating is a good idea because it is right on track with where the evolution of the planet is concerned. You are entering into a new two-thousand-year cycle that involves the development of a new spiritual root race of human kind. All of the spiritual development of the past, and particularly of the past two thousand years, has been based on duality, the separation between the divine and the physical. This two-thousand-year cycle is about bringing that together. Mainstream spiritual practices and religions have been based, more or less, on the idea of a division between man and God and that man must in some way make himself worthy of that connection. That is a fallacy because it is based on man's own illusion that he is separate.

What you propose is important from the point of view of allowing mankind to see they are not separate, that they are a part of all things. If we simply go to physics and science, we will understand that nothing is divided from anything else and nothing is separate. Everything is interdependent, interwoven. And everything, from the cell or the atom on up to the densest physical material, is all part of the same thing. It's very important to convey this idea. Let us pursue your questions so that we can together hopefully come to some clarity and some simple conclusions that can be available to all.

J: One of the points you made when we talked last year, and I strongly agree, is that everything has to be expressed as clearly and simply as possible to address the widest possible audience so they can understand what we are talking about.

G: Yes. And one of the main reasons for that is because the human consciousness, the collective consciousness, is so caught up in their illusion of division. So you don't want to threaten them with extreme esoteric concepts that are terribly complex because the nervous system will simply shut down and reject it.

J: I'm approaching this as someone who doesn't know a whole lot about you, which actually is true.

G: Good.

J: And I'm wearing the skeptic's hat that most people would wear, I think, if they were confronted with the idea that a spirit such as Gabriel is speaking to them. So I'll ask you first off one of the most basic questions: Who are you, Gabriel? Are you the Gabriel we've heard about in scripture, the Bible, the Annunciation?

G: Yes, we are the Gabriel who has been described in all the various doctrines, if you will, and all the various religious practices of evolution. But we have been much misinterpreted as to what we are. It is important to understand that what you call the angelic realm is really a hierarchy of consciousness. Therefore, what you call an angelic presence or angel is really a level or a hierarchy of consciousness—each of us, Gabriel, Michael, Uriel, Raphael—you name it, the names are your own. You've given us the names to identify us and label us as you do all things. And you have also sought to personify us in your image and likeness.

Man also tries to create God in his own image and likeness. And that is not a fallacy in the sense that you are all a part of God. Physical expression is simply a form of Godly expression. However, the angelic realm is not an expression of the physical. In other words, we have never retained physical form as you know it—even though you have depicted us in physical form with all those lovely wings to be able to personify us, to make us real, in order to connect to us in that sense. And for that purpose we have taken our consciousness many times, and through the refraction of light and the reflection of light upon atomic structure, we have created the density to create a form to appear to you in your own form so that you could believe or realize you have a connection there.

Now, would you say that Gabriel is an individual? Well, in the sense that we are a specific hierarchy of consciousness, we suppose you could say that. We embody, in consciousness, a certain hierarchy of information, knowledge, and experience that allies the physical and spirit.

J: You have never been physical?

G: No, we have never been physical, although, as we have said, we have created a holographic presentation of form in order to appear to you on occasion.

J: Are there many archangels, because there are only four referred to in scripture that I know of?

G: There are many. But you must think of them as levels of consciousness. See, there is a hierarchy of guidance. What you call God is also what you call spirit. God consciousness, or spirit consciousness, is unindividuated. It is not separate. It contains all consciousness. It is divine consciousness in a never-ending, infinite evolutionary cycle of realization of itself. Therefore, it is all of itself in the process of ever realizing itself in the aspects of its beingness, in all the individuated forms that make up its whole, whether they be physical or nonphysical.

We are a part of the nonphysical forms that make up its whole. Our hierarchy or level of consciousness is specific to a specific purpose or intention where that divine mind is concerned. It is called by you Gabriel. We always refer to ourselves as we. Why do we do that? We do that because we are not an I. We are not individual. Within the level of consciousness we represent are many levels of consciousness. In those levels of consciousness, one end, the high end, the highest frequency, has the direct connection to the divine plan and its intention. The lower end of our frequency, where the "we" of Gabriel is concerned, is connected to the physical world. So we interpret the information from the unindividuated consciousness of God and the divine plan as it refers to physical matter. We interpret that divine plan in the relationship of mankind to God and God to mankind to create the connection, to create the oneness.

J: So that is why you are called a messenger.

G: Exactly. We are the messenger of the truth of the relationship of humankind to the divine and the divine to humankind. We act as the interpreter of that portion of the divine plan, which is one tiny portion of the divine plan. You are, in your individual experience, one tiny infinitesimal part of creation as a whole. One experience. Within that one experience are all kinds of levels of evolution and development.

J: When scripture says that someone has communicated with God, is that possible? Because you said that God is not an individuated consciousness. If God is not individuated, what consciousness would we be communicating with?

G: You are always in communication with God because you are God and God is you. But the form of God that you represent as an individual expression is one infinitesimal part of that divine consciousness. Therefore, yes, you have absolute direct communication with God. But you do not have the conscious knowledge of that because of the density of your part of God that you represent and experience.

J: The author of the Conversations with God books, which were best sellers, claims to have been talking with God, and his books seem very credible.

G: He was. You see, the individual aspect of God that is your direct connection is your soul. It is often referred to as your higher self.

If you are in touch with your higher self, your soul, and your soul is speaking directly to you, then you are in direct relationship with the consciousness of God. God is talking to you. But God is talking to you through the soul fragment that you are in this lifetime. In other words, the soul consciousness that lies within you in this lifetime is one infinitesimal part of your whole soul.

Your whole soul exists in another realm or dimension of being which is called oversoul consciousness. Oversoul consciousness is the wholeness of all of your lifetimes in the physical: past, present, and future. So it contains all of the soul fragments that make up the whole of you as a physical being in your evolution through all of your incarnations—all of your physical experience from the beginning to the end, because physical experience has a beginning and an end.

J: You were explaining your role as the messenger of truth between God and man.

G: Yes. Our function is, quite simply, the truth of the development of the relationship between humanity and God. It is to inform you of your relationship by revealing how to awaken the doorway to that relationship, which is the awakening of the soul. This is why, for instance, we announced what you call the birth of Christ to the one Mary because Christ, the Christ Consciousness, is the consciousness of the soul.

The word Christ in its original meaning, means "of soul." The soul is the divine part of you, the God part of you that is individuated. So Jesus the Christ means "man of soul." The virgin birth is representative of the fact that the soul is not dependent upon procreation where physical matter is concerned in order to find its existence or to be born—therefore, the symbol of the virgin birth. Mary's purpose was to bring light into consciousness for humankind to realize that they are a soul, a divine being in the physical. And Jesus the Christ, man of the soul, is symbolic of man's awakening to his soul consciousness in the womb of matter. The word Mary means womb of matter.

J: I was raised in the Catholic Church. The birth of Jesus and the Annunciation are considered to be sacred teachings. Christmas and Easter are two of our most sacred holy days. For those who have been raised in the Christian churches, how might you explain the meaning of the birth of Jesus and what it represented in a way that they can understand and relate to?

G: First of all, the birth of Christ represents the birth of love, quite simply. And the birth of love represents the birth of the divine in the physical. And the birth of the divine in the physical is only possible

Anastasi

through the awakening of the soul. The soul is the container of the divine in the physical. Now what is important to understand is that you're going to shake up some sacred cows because the Bible as you know it is not entirely accurate. It has been translated many times.

J: Yes, I know.

G: You see, man has sought to use religion as the earliest form of government of the people to control the people. And just as man has given his power to God as something separate from himself, as a father figure that he must look up to but not be a part of, he has done the same thing in giving the power and control to the priests and ministers to interpret God for him. So he still keeps the relationship separate. And then the minister or priest or God, the old man with the beard sitting on the cloud, is the daddy who is judging me and is telling me I will be rewarded if I am a good little boy or girl, and I will be punished if I am a bad little boy or girl. I deserve to be connected to God only if I am good and I do as God says, or I am punished of God and separate from God if I do bad, and I go to hell.

So that is man's creation because man created duality—God didn't. And man created duality in his religions and that eventually has to be faced. You see, you're going to shake up some sacred territory. What is sacred is not so much sacred, but it represents control and limitation. So you are going to take the risk of making some people angry.

J: I'm only concerned about the truth. Whether the truth shakes people up is not important. However, at the same time, I don't want to be insensitive to people's feelings. But I think what you're saying is that the significance the Christian churches give to Jesus is valid.

G: Yes. You are now entering the time of the revelation of the Christ Consciousness. You are entering the time of the resurrection. You are entering the time of the Second Coming.

J: Whoa! Let's stop a minute because now you're announcing a momentous spiritual idea. Would you clearly state what Jesus' coming represented and what these times now represent in relation to that as directly and clearly as possible?

G: Jesus simply represents the awakening of soul in matter, the awakening of the divine in the physical experience. In order to experience that, you must take responsibility for it. As long as mankind remains as children in their ability to take responsibility for their own evolution and their own consciousness and their own choices, as long as they give that power away to something outside of themselves, they will always be separate from the God within. They will always be separate from the Christ within them.

J: The Christian churches tend to teach that Jesus is the only begotten son of the Father, and he was sent to us to save us from our sins. They also say we have to go through Jesus in order to get to the Father.

G: Well, that's true. They're absolutely right. But what they don't understand is that they're focused on Jesus, the man, and making him a separate divine being who is above them. If you read the Bible, you will find Jesus himself said, "Do not worship me, but worship the Father who is in heaven." He also says he leaves a promise for mankind in the new millennium. He gives a prediction of prophecy for this time. He says, "The works that I do ye shall do and greater than I have done." He also said, "Go into the city and find the man with the water pitcher, the water bearer, and follow him to the upper room and there make ready the feast."

The man with the water pitcher is the ancient symbol of Aquarius, representative of this new age. The city represents the masses. The upper rooms represent the connection to the higher chakras, the awakening of the soul, and the gateways of the heart. The bread and the wine represent the physical and the spiritual coming together, the soul awakening. Wine is representative of the flow of the blood force, the life force through the body that is nonphysical, that is representative of the soul awakening. The soul can only awaken when the emotional body of mankind has transcended from its separation of individual negative and positive feelings (duality) into the stillness of the direct line of communication to the soul, which is the intuition and the knowing.

J: If that was the meaning of what he was saying, I can't imagine anyone would have understood any of it because it's all symbolic.

G: The reason it was written symbolically was to hide the meaning until the time came that man had reached the stage of vibration and evolution that he could understand it and respond to it responsibly. Otherwise, he would misuse it.

J: If all this was hidden in scripture until the right time, who was going to uncover the meaning? How was that supposed to happen?

G: Well, you're one of them. You are sitting here right now uncovering the meaning, and you are thinking of putting it out as a book. So you are in the process of bringing the mysteries into the light. And many like you and the one who wrote Conversations with God. He has brought his piece of it to bring it into light. Do you see?

Back in 1994, an event took place in the heavens in which the Shoemaker/Levy Comet hit Jupiter with twenty-two fragments, and it exploded the emotional body of Jupiter. Some of those comet fragments were almost the size of the earth. That's a tremendous impact. The surface of Jupiter is gaseous. That gaseous surface is the emotional body of Jupiter. Its moon Io contains the secret codes of your solar system that are related to the codes of the ascendant mastery. When that explosion took place, it released the spiritual codes into your solar system.

That cosmic experience, that explosion of the Shoemaker Levy comet into the body of Jupiter, represented on an etheric level the birth of the divine child, the birth of the Christ Consciousness in your solar system. Eventually the vibrations began to trickle down into the density of the earth plane interpreted through the DNA band and are now coming into consciousness gradually, and have been since 1994.

As their influences grow, they raise the vibration of the earth, raise the consciousness of the earth. On a quantum physics level, it creates a high frequency vibration of energy, a sacred vibration. At the same time the density of the magnetic field of earth is decreasing and has been for the last two thousand years. That release of density of the magnetic field allows the density of consciousness to begin to awaken to that information that is coming in. It allows you to become channels for that information. It allows the soul consciousness to begin to awaken.

Where the law of physics is concerned, when you have a high vibration that maintains itself within a field as a dominant vibration, it begins the law of entrainment. It begins to raise the vibration of everything of a lower density to its higher vibration. When that happens, it shakes everything up. You create a spiritual crisis. And that's what you're in on your planet, a spiritual crisis—all the dualities coming to the surface, into the light. The shadow is rising from the subconscious to be brought into balance, to be healed. It's a healing crisis. If you cut your finger and your finger starts to heal, you begin to feel more pain. That's part of the healing crisis. So what you are experiencing now on your planet is a healing crisis. You're seeing the dualities everywhere.

J: Well, it sure feels like a crisis. Crises seem to be breaking out all over the world. Turn on the television like I did last night, and you're confronted with all the issues of the Middle East, North Korea, terrorism, and all the rest of it. It feels like we're being shaken to our roots.

G: Exactly. That's exactly what's taking place, shaken to the core. All the defenses are being shaken up so the core can reveal itself. Integration is taking place. But in all integration, what happens with duality is you see the extremes of the two sides first. At the same time in this new two-thousand-year cycle you're moving out of the sixth ray of consciousness, which is the ray of duality that controlled the Piscean age during the last two thousand years. As that moves out, it creates a crisis. And the seventh ray is moving in, which is the ray of the unified field, which is the spiritual ray that restructures everything in the physical that is out of sync or out of balance. It begins to destroy all systems that are in duality.

J: What do you mean?

G: What that means is all the old systems you have known are beginning to break down. They're going into crisis.

J: What kinds of systems?

G: Your corporate systems, your economic system, your capitalistic system as you have known it, your governmental political systems. Anything that is in separation or duality now will be in the extreme of its duality as it begins to break down. Civilization as you have known it has reached a point of crisis. Now it's beginning to break down. It's beginning to crumble. Whenever anything begins to crumble, when it reaches a point of crisis, it fights to maintain its reality. Just as an animal is cornered in the forest by a couple of other animals, it will fight like crazy to survive.

J: So what's coming?

G: What is coming, ultimately, is the breakdown of the system as you have known it and its transformation into a system that is not divided upon itself. A kingdom divided against itself cannot stand. So it must fall apart before it can be rebuilt.

J: So are you suggesting that our economic, political, and all the other structures you referred to are …

G: Breaking down.

J: Does that mean that civilization as we know it is going into chaos?

G: Yes, more or less.

J: That's pretty worrisome.

G: Of course it is. It is worrisome to those who try to keep it in place. But it is not worrisome to the awakening soul that exists in the truth that lies outside of duality. What you are talking about here that you fear is the breakdown of the veil of illusion, of separation. That's all. And what is taking place will bring, in the crisis, humanity together to build something anew, a new system, a new form that will embrace the good of the whole. But first you must develop an awareness of the other side, how extreme that other side of duality has gone.

J: What do you mean by the other side?

G: The side that is in separation, the side that is in control, the side that seeks to conquer, the side that seeks to dominate. Because basically you have developed a consumer culture in the Western culture, and it has permeated the world. That consumer culture is consuming itself. There isn't enough to go around any more because the focus has all been on the outside, in the physical, to get a sense of satisfaction and gratification by consuming all your resources, by consuming one another's spirit.

J: Well, I can't argue with you. I've worked in many organizations as a management consultant, and I've seen firsthand what motivates so many of these organizations. It's all about the bottom line.

G: It's all money and consumption. And what it creates is alienation. It creates more and more isolation, alienation and aloneness, protection and defense. When only a few people are controlling everything, they have to do everything they can to defend that control. Everything that opposes their control becomes their enemy. And so what you're seeing is the extreme of the fear of survival of a little wounded child inside who feels separate, unsafe, and defended.

The war on terrorism happening out there is simply a distraction because the real terrorist is within. And the terrorist within is that wounded child who has not been addressed, who has never grown up, has never grown up beyond the infantile stage of development of give me, feed me, take care of me because I am incapable of doing it on my own. I don't know who I am.

J: So we are in the process of dismantling all of the existing structures.

G: That's correct, in one form or another. All you have to do is look at your religions. Look at the Catholic religion last year, all of the duality coming out with all of the sexual abuse coming to the surface, the shadow side of the Catholic Church coming to the surface, the duality of those who have set themselves above everyone else. All of a sudden we find out they are very human just like everyone else. They have the same urges. They have the same desires. The have the same wounding.

J: We have seen that in other areas as well such as the corporations experiencing one financial disaster after the next.

G: That's right. And now you're seeing it in the political system. You're seeing one man and his little group of goons who are deciding against the general wishes of the world to exercise their will.

J: We could also talk about Saddam Hussein and his goons. But I think you're speaking about our President George Bush.

G: Saddam Hussein is no threat to the world. Iraq is a minor state in the Middle East whose only value to the world is the oil resources there that they are not in control of.

J: Well, I'm certainly aware that if the oil reserves weren't there, we wouldn't be there either.

G: That's correct. You're not bombing North Korea.

J: We're afraid of the consequences of that.

G: No, you're not bombing North Korea because they don't have any oil!

J: It isn't because they have nuclear resources and missiles pointed at Seoul?

G: No. You say the reason you're going into Iraq is because of the threat of nuclear resources. Why wouldn't the allies join together to disband the nuclear resources of North Korea? Why bother? They don't have anything we want.

J: It's not out of fear?

G: No.

J: Last night, I saw a pretty convincing report about the missiles pointed at Seoul and other areas. It talked about the potential for millions of people being killed.

G: That threat is minor. China would never allow it to happen. But North Korea doesn't have anything you want. You see, whoever controls the remaining oil resources controls the world of the future.

J: I'm aware the world economy is based on petrochemicals.

G: Not just the world economy, but the food production of the world for an expanding population.

J: Even though you see Saddam as minor, he represents the kind of brutal dictatorship where people who try to oppose him are imprisoned or killed. How should the nations of the world deal with these kinds of dictators?

G: That's not happening just in Iraq. It's happening in many countries around the world. Iraq is convenient. But what you need to understand, dear one, the United States in the past was the one responsible for supporting Saddam's regime when it was convenient for them. Just as they have done elsewhere. Since World War I, the United States has attacked many countries without provocation, interfered with their governments, put puppet governments in power. And of those scores of countries, only a few of those governments have been successful in any way. The rest have all been despots and terrorists the United States put in power.

J: What is the appropriate way for the nations of the world to deal with despots?

G: First of all, each country should be allowed to make its own choices, its own decisions, and its own mistakes. You see, this is where the exclusiveness of individuality is not honored. What you have to understand is that the position the United States and other nations take of "Well, we are democratic and we represent freedom" is a disguise they hide behind because their motivation is not based upon democracy and freedom. Your country is not based upon democracy and freedom. Democracy and freedom suggest for the good of the whole. They suggest the honoring of the individual. In a capitalistic system, you are not honoring the individual. You are succeeding in making the individual give up his or her individuality in order to support a standardized process of production and consumption that creates a deadening of the soul.

Look at your educational processes—they don't support the development and evolution of the individual. They create a collective consciousness, a social numbness that everyone must fit into in order to sustain the production and consumption the system represents, which creates a basic mediocrity and deadening of the soul. The soul must be allowed to express itself and learn through its own progress and process as well as its mistakes without interference from others.

J: I've experienced the same deadening not only in educational institutions, but also business institutions.

G: They come from educational institutions.

J: And the religion I grew up in as well.

G: Of course. All systems are the same in that respect. They create a deadening of the soul. Look at the numbers of people in your country who are numbed out on prescription drugs.

J: Why is that?

G: Because they cannot deal with the deadness they feel inside, so they must numb themselves out.

J: It's their way of coping.

G: Exactly.

J: How and when is all this going to change?

G: That depends upon the individuals who awaken and stand individually and say, "I'm here to create a better system." Not to oppose the old one because that only lends energy to the old one. Instead, you build a better system alongside the existing one. And you make it available for people in their individual process to embrace or not as they choose. You do not impose a new system on them because then you would be just as bad as what already exists. Rather, you offer a possibility for them to see that strikes a chord within them.

As we always say to people when we speak to them, do not take what Gabriel says and make it absolute. Do not turn it into a dogma. Do not say, Gabriel is telling the truth; therefore, I must listen to what Gabriel says. But rather take what Gabriel says and let it trigger the truth within you to express within you what comes alive within you, what inspires you that illuminates within you your own truth that awakens your own soul. Because we are not interested in your taking the information of Gabriel and just repeating it like a parrot. What we are interested in is inspiring the awakening of the individual truth of God within you. We are here to awaken the soul within you, to teach you about that, how to develop that process, how to develop a new system.

J: How can I be a catalyst in this?

G: Well, in what you are doing right now. The fact that you are open to new ideas and to expressing those new ideas to make them available to more people in a language that simplifies it. That way they can understand and they can decide, "Oh, that's a good idea." Or, "That's an interesting idea—I've never thought of that before." So you don't present it as "this is the absolute truth, and you've got to agree with this."

J: So you're saying, don't take this and make it new scripture, new dogma.

G: Exactly, because then it has no livingness, no aliveness. It must grow. It must always become more. So then eventually what Gabriel says becomes obsolete because you have grown beyond it.

J: For the purposes of this book, many people will want to know how Robert Baker's involvement with you came about. Did he choose you? Did you choose him? How did your collaboration happen?

G: Both. You see, in order to be chosen, you must choose. And when you are chosen, you must choose. This is because humankind is given the divine gift of unconditional love called freedom of choice. We come and make ourselves available, but then the being must choose. So on a soul level, he chose to develop through a certain level of growth in this lifetime and to use his soul to serve in a certain way. Because of that evolution of his soul, we were informed this would be an opportunity for us to speak to the general populous. But we had to have his permission—we couldn't just impose upon him. We always have to be asked. We have to be given permission. So we chose him, and he chose us.

J: What do you mean, we were informed this would be an opportunity?

G: What we do is we read soul grids. And we keep in touch with all the soul grids where the general populace and the evolution of the planet is concerned and the individual populace is at certain levels of soul development. There are many levels of soul development. When a soul gets to a certain level of soul development because of the number of incarnations it has had and what it has learned from those incarnations, it is ready then to move to a different level of soul development.

At that level of soul development, they can access certain levels of knowledge and information as a soul in its service because each soul is in service to the divine plan. And each soul is in service to every other soul in the divine plan. One for all and all for one kind of idea. And so the channel chose on a soul level to be of service in relation to informing spiritual evolution and the development of this new awakening in this incarnational cycle. Thus, the doorway of opportunity was opened to us. So we presented ourselves at the doorway of his consciousness to let him know that it was a possibility, and that we were available. Then he had to choose. And boy did he fight us.

J: Fight you?

G: Oh yes. He defied us. He fought us. He tried to pretend it wasn't so.

J: Does he know this?

G: Oh yes, he knows it. Had a hard time dealing with the idea that he could be a channel for an angelic presence because he said, "I know nothing about angels. How could it be than I'm a channel for this?" Usually, we pick people who are untainted by religion and that sort of thing. It's easier because the consciousness is less tampered with, less tainted. So it's easier for us to come through in a clearer manner.

J: What could I be doing that would make this an easier and more effective process?

G: Embrace the process as a little child.

J: Meaning?

G: Embrace the process as if you were starting from the beginning and you are awakening to a world you have not known and you are discovering yourself through it. Christ said to become as a little child allows man to enter the kingdom of heaven. What is the kingdom of heaven? Simply your spiritual connection, your spiritual enlightenment. It is the freedom from the duality of self. Therefore, just notice what the process brings up where the duality of self is concerned, and the duality of self with what's happening in the environment. Through that you will grow and learn and have your being in Godliness of the self that is unfolding in that process.

J: Earlier you referred to the divine plan and the role each of us plays in it. First, what do you mean by the divine plan, and second, how can people determine what is their role in the divine plan?

G: Very simply, the divine plan for physical matter in the earth is to learn to love. That is the divine plan. Now what does it mean to learn to love? Love is a force, a force of God, a force of creation, a force of being. Therefore, learning to love means learning to awaken, realize, accept, express, and experience in the fullest way possible the experience, expression, and potential of your being as an individual. That is the divine plan embodied. That is the force of love embodied. That is the soul awakened. So your purpose in the divine plan is to learn to love.

Now what does love do? Love brings together the fusion of the consciousness of God in physical form. No more duality—instead, there's oneness, unity, wholeness, completeness, merging, connection. But in order to do that, the irony, the paradox is that you must first become individual, because if you do not know yourself as an individual soul, you cannot know another soul. Therefore, you must be willing to reveal the knowledge of who you are and share it with all others freely. You must be willing to uncover the depths of who you are and reveal it, unstintingly, without defense. You must use all of your being to respond to all that life has to offer. You must be willing to stand alone with yourself in order to be unified within yourself. Then, and only then, can you be unified with another. That is the divine plan for the earth. That is the evolutionary cycle you are now coming into.

Now, within that part of the divine plan, it gets more specific according to the individual. Each individual has in his or her being specific talents, abilities, and qualities of self that best communicate the truth and revelation of who that person is as an individual. Those talents, abilities, and qualities of being become the form of expression or tool the person uses to realize that completion of the divine plan, realize that learning how to love.

Many people ask, "What is my purpose, Gabriel?" And we say your purpose is to learn to love. And they say, "Oh, I thought my purpose was to be an actor, or I thought my purpose was to be a CEO of a corporation, or I thought my purpose was to be an accountant." And we say, no, that is the tool you use. That's simply a tool you use. That's why people who seek a career as a form of fulfillment and never find it will always be at a loss and will always feel empty because they are interpreting that the tool provides the purpose. The tool is only providing the access or pathway through which they can bring to life the expression of their being and fill the tool with it. And use the tool as a form of expressing that aspect of what they are learning where love is concerned, and how they are learning to reveal that love and share it with others.

So, if you are a sanitation worker in New York and you are bringing all of your being to it, you are fulfilling the divine plan. If you are a beggar on the street and you are bringing all of your being to it and all of your expression to it and making yourself totally available with that tool, then you are fulfilling the divine plan. If you are writing a book and you are bringing your abilities as a writer to convey the words, the emotions, the feelings, the thoughts, the knowledge, the information, then you are fulfilling your place in the divine plan because through that tool you are expressing your ability to love. You are expressing your ability to show and share who you are. Do you see?

J: I'm struggling to paraphrase it in one or two sentences

G: The divine plan is to learn to love, to learn to embody love by expressing the truth of your being as an individual in all of its knowledge, all of its expression, all of its experience, and all of its form.

J: And what we do in life is only a vehicle for allowing that to happen.

G: That's correct.

J: But most of us allow what we're doing to be the focus.

G: That's correct.

J: And we're kind of missing the point.

G: Exactly, because you're seeking doing to find being, instead of using being to express doing.

J: It's about how we're being when we're doing.

G: That's right. It's what you bring to what you're doing that fills it with the soul of love.

J: Before we finish our discussion, I just wanted to discuss that both Phillip and I have lost our mothers in the last few years. I put it that way, lost …

G: You lost your physical connection to them. They are in the mid-range of the astral plane at the moment. Do you know what the astral plane is?

J: No.

G: The astral plane is the place consciousness goes when it leaves the physical body. It is the place that lies between the physical world and the causal plane, the plane of the soul. The astral body contains the soul body as a container in seven layers or levels of astral matter or what is known as bioplasmic matter. The purpose of the astral plane and its seven levels is for the soul to gradually release itself from physical experience back into the causal plane, the soul plane, which is its home of consciousness. The astral plane is the container of all the collected thoughts and feelings of the physical world that contains and creates physical reality. It's an exact duplicate of physical reality, but in astral matter, bioplasmic matter. If you see it, it looks like a hologram and you can see through it. It's what you call ghosts. [Tape stops and Gabriel completes the explanation in the next interview.]

J: The Bible describes you as a herald of a new age when you announced the birth of Jesus. Are you a herald of this new age?

G: Are we a herald of this new age? Well yes, we are because of our duty. You see, in the last age we announced an idea of spiritual consciousness awakening in the physical by announcing the birth of Christ. And it was brought in as an individual to put the blueprint into the consciousness of humanity, to put the possibility there of what humanity would awaken to in the next age. In this age, our duty now is to impart that message to each Christ Consciousness that awakens to bring it to all humankind. Because people still believe in their religions that Christ the man is going to reappear to rescue them and save them. This is a fallacy. What he was telling you was that it lies within you, that the Christ lies within you.

So now is the time when you must awaken that Christ within you, that Christ Consciousness within you, because Christ Consciousness is soul consciousness. It's simply your realization of yourself as divine, and your connection and your ability to channel that connection to the divine. So we are the herald of that awakening, to teach you how to awaken that, to make you realize it's even a possibility and to get you out of this idea that you are separate from the Christ, that you are separate from God, and that it is something better than you are. Because all that means is that you're little children not willing to take responsibility for that level of intelligence and consciousness. That's all that means.

J: I would guess you've just stated a key mission of this book, to help us awaken the Christ Consciousness or soul consciousness within us.

G: Yes. What we have presented today is an introduction to the development of that.

J: In our next sessions, I want to explore some other questions as well, but it sounds to me as though the thrust of what we're doing in the future will have to do with what you've just stated.

G: Well, that basically is what the evolutionary process of mankind is now. That's what it's all about. Because you see, the divine plan is taking place whether you're conscious of it or not. But how much more beneficial it is to be conscious of it, so you can enjoy it.

J: Wouldn't we do a better job of realizing the divine plan if we're conscious of it?

G: Of course. You see, what they call evil or the devil, they think of as something that's outside or apart from them, so they don't think they have to take responsibility for it. It's man-created. The devil is just ignorance, unconsciousness. The devil is a shadow that lies within the subconscious that rules you and governs you without your knowing it—things you're trying to suppress with which you have never become integrated or never dealt with based upon your unconscious traumas that cause you to react and to defend.

J: One of the reasons I was apprehensive about picking up the book Conversations with God was that I didn't want to be led down the garden path by some evil influence. I'm a little embarrassed now to admit it, but I know a lot of people feel that way about anything new or different.

G: Of course. They're indoctrinated.

J: We've all been.

G: Yes. You're basically a mass consciousness that is held in place by the collective sleep. You are asleep. The word devil if you spell it backwards is lived. The word evil is live.

J: We have about ten minutes, and I wanted to ask you about something that jumped out at me when I was listening to one of your tapes. You pointed out the letters USA were the central letters in the word Jerusalem. I believe you said something about the United States being the light of the world. What does that mean? What were you telling us?

G: It is the place of the awakening of the New Jerusalem. Jerusalem represents the promised land, or the land of the awakening of the new spirit. It's interesting the United States chose the eagle as its symbol of freedom because the eagle, in the ancient cosmology and in the North American Indian cosmology, represents spirit and freedom, spiritual freedom.

Isn't it interesting the United States is the mixing pot of all peoples from all over the world, sort of the synthesis if you will? Isn't it interesting the United States is also the place that began the awakening of the New Age, the culture that started to bring what you call the New Age to life? It started to bring all the cosmologies together— the development of Eastern philosophies in the West, the rage that developed toward yoga, tai chi, and all of that introduced to the West, all of that sort of thing?

J: I want to ask more about that, but I want to be sensitive to Robert's schedule.

G: So we will work closely together. We are most joyous to be in your presence, and so for this time we will close with a blending, a moment. We ask you to just indulge us by closing your eyes and imagine as a child would imagine us, Gabriel, as a pinpoint of blue light in your mind's eye, the frequency upon which we travel to you. And imagine that blue light growing into an elliptic of light that encompasses the height, depth, and breadth of all that you are as we lend our energies of love and light to support you on your journey of a soul. We say so be it. We thank you for allowing us to be in your divine presence at this time. As we take our most joyous leave, we ask always, as you are able to remember, to love one another.

Chapter 2:
Gabriel/God/Creation

J: When you were answering my questions about who you were, you said you referred to yourself as we because you represent many levels of consciousness.

G: We are a communion of consciousness, so we are not separate. We are not an I. An I is only formed in separation. It is only formed as an individual soul. We are not an individual soul. We are not of soul consciousness. Soul consciousness is only required for physical expression. Soul consciousness is the way in which spirit becomes individuated for a particular form of experience in matter. We are beyond the causal plane of the soul. We are a level of consciousness in creation known as the Archangelic Realm of Gabriel.

We act as a medium of connection between the divine and the physical. We deal with the particular realm that teaches of the relationship that brings man into harmony with God as an individual through the awakening of soul. That is our job. That is why we announced the birth of the Christ because we were announcing the birth of the soul in man, his divinity in his physicality. That's our job. We simply carry out orders, if you will. We are simply servants of the divine plan as are others.

J: From whom do you get your orders?

G: We get them from the divine plan. The divine plan is the order of the universe.

J: How do you get them?

G: Through the consciousness of God, what you call God, the universe, divine intelligence. We are given a fragment of that divine intelligence to put into operation, into manifestation. It is an aspect of evolution that we are put in charge of. The Office of Soul Evolution in Physicality is our job. That was just a joke so you can better understand from your own perspective.

J: It must be hard for you because you're dealing with someone with a limited perspective, and you're trying to explain concepts for which there are no words.

G: Your words are very limiting.

J: When you were talking about your role as a messenger, you said, "We act as the interpreter of that portion of the divine plan which is one tiny portion of the divine plan. In your individual experience, you are one tiny infinitesimal part of creation as a whole."

G: That is correct.

J: If we're only one tiny portion of the divine plan, what does the bigger portion look like? And if we're just a tiny portion of creation, what does creation look like? Is that an impossible question? Can we wrap our minds around the answer?

G: Creation is God, or what you call God. You could also call it the universal mind, the universal consciousness. It is made up of all that is and all that is not. It is all that is and was and ever will be and is yet to come. So wrap your brain around that one.

J: In our last conversation I asked you if we could communicate with God. The tape didn't record your complete answer. My question was, if God is all there is, then can we communicate with God? If so, what consciousness are we communicating with? We're not communicating with all there is, are we?

G: Yes, you are. You are only able to take in or fathom one minute bit of that consciousness because everything is stopped down energetically. For instance, our energy is stopped down to bring it into this human body. If we were to bring all of our energy force into this human body, this human body would simply turn into pure light and disintegrate. Therefore we have to stop down all of our energy except perhaps 2 percent. We can bring about 2 percent of our energy into this body. Otherwise, we would blow it up. The same thing with God.

You as a human being live in a body. That body is a self-contained vehicle. The consciousness of God is flowing through it all of the time through the life force called the erotic force. The erotic force is the pure force of spirit or God that creates the desire and excitation for life. That erotic force is undifferentiated until it connects with something called a physical body, a soul body. That physical body contains a life force within it called the sexual force. That sexual force creates a feeling or sensation in the body of pleasure, of being physical. When that sexual force and that erotic force join, you join an individual expression of pleasure in physical matter with an individual expression of God as a soul, a minute part of God as an individual expression of soul.

And so you, as a limited experience of God as a physical experience, if you are in communion with the expression, experience, and celebration of your individual self and connected to the core that is in your being, then you are in communication with God. If you are not in connection with that, then you have separated from your communication with God. And then you form something artificial to create a sense of self called the personality or the ego. The ego then focuses its energy and attention out into the environment of the physical as the source of its sense of self, its well-being, its expression, and its experience of its power of being. And thus it sustains and maintains its sense of isolation, separateness, and aloneness.

J: That's where most of us are.

G: That's where most of you are.

J: Of course, the challenge is to break out of that.

G: That's correct. This is why Christ said: be in the world, but not of it.

J: Easier said than done.

G: Yes. To gain the whole world and lose your soul.

J: Of course, you can know all these things intellectually, but somehow being able to live it is very hard.

G: Well, we will explain to you why. The reason man is so focused on the world around him rather than connected to himself as an autonomous individual known as a soul of God is because he has not, in his parenting experience growing as a child, moved much beyond the infantile state of emotional development. Therefore, he is frozen in an infantile state of narcissism from childhood where he stayed connected to the mother or to the father/mother for his sense of self or sense of well-being—thus the codependency of the parental relationship that you then seek to recreate throughout your adult life. It's simply a child who has never grown up to know himself as an individual, never having gone through the stages of childhood autonomy in a healthy way where the parents were supposed to model for him becoming an individual standing on his own alone and celebrating that connection of individuality within himself.

When that doesn't take place, he gets frozen emotionally at various stages of development. And he never grows beyond that. So he remains narcissistic. When he remains narcissistic, the world now becomes the mother or father that he looks to, to determine his sense of self, his feelings, his connection, whether he's loved or not, whether he's valid or invalid, good enough or not good enough. And then he creates an ego mask that is a false self to compensate for the parts of his authentic self that he disowned, and he projects that ego mask on to the environment seeing everyone as a mom and dad who is there to serve his needs.

Therefore, you live in a world of narcissistic individuals who are focused on conquering their environment where they can never get enough, where their hands and mouths are always open, and they are unable to give of themselves because they don't know who they are. So they are constantly in the process of consuming, as children are in the process of consuming the milk of their mothers and looking to the mother as the source of their well-being. They then consume the resources of the earth to sustain their well-being. And they remain infantile in their emotional development.

For instance, your President George Bush. What he is doing in the world is simply acting out his Oedipus complex with his father. That's all he's doing. I'll go to Iraq, and I'll show you, Daddy. I'll do what you couldn't do. It's the Oedipus complex. It's the child's attempt to kill off the influence of the father over the child's individual nature. That's what all dictators seek to do. They're caught, trapped in the Oedipus complex of childhood.

J: Of course, the challenge is to transcend that as individuals.

G: How you transcend that as individuals is to take responsibility for your own growth and development and go through the stages of emotional autonomy that you failed to go through or were distorted in your childhood.

J: Don't people need help with that? Few of us can do that on our own.

G: They do need help with that. That's why you have more and more practitioners who are learning how to do that, writing books about it, doing television shows about it, teaching about it, and creating centers for that purpose and all of that. The extreme example of the pain and trauma of the emotional body lies in the fact that so much of your population is addicted to prescription drugs to knock out their feelings because they can't handle them. They don't know how to deal with them.

J: When you talked about communicating with God in our first session, you mentioned something I would like to clarify. You said the soul consciousness that lies within us in this lifetime, in this body, is one infinitesimal part of our whole soul, which exists in another realm or dimension.

G: That's correct.

J: You seem to be saying that when we are communicating with God, we are really communicating with our own oversoul consciousness.

G: Yes, your oversoul consciousness is governing your overall connection with the wholeness of you that is fulfilling the wholeness of your purpose in the divine plan as directed by God. So your oversoul is acting as an intermediary between your soul fragment and the unindividuated force of God.

J: When Neale Walsch was communicating with God when writing the Conversations with God books, are you saying he was communicating with his oversoul that was communicating with the God consciousness?

G: Yes. You see you can go beyond that. There are different levels and layers of hierarchy that expand the consciousness of God in its hierarchy. For instance, a cell contains the entire consciousness of God, one cell. It contains the entire consciousness of the erotic, sexual, and love force of God. At the same time it records all of that, that cell expands into individual cells. The earth is a cell of God. It is a physical manifested experience. So you could say that physical manifestation is one level of God's experience. Then, within that experience is the experience of each individual soul fragment. Each of those soul fragments has an oversoul, which is the entire experience of their whole soul, past, present, and future of all their lifetimes. Each soul fragment in a lifetime contains the whole soul of the planet or the planetary monad, the oversoul of the planet. That is the divine plan in evolution through those soul fragments for that lifetime.

Beyond that is the monad of the oversoul of all the oversouls of the planet that contain the entire oversoul evolution for the physical experience of that planet, the entire divine plan for the evolution of matter into its Godliness, in conscious awareness. Then you have the oversoul for the planetary logos. The planetary logos is a solar system that contains the information of all of the planets in interaction with one another for the evolution of that particular solar system where the consciousness of God is concerned, and the divine plan of the evolution for that solar system.

Then you go beyond that to the solar logos, which is the particular sun the mind of God uses to transfer the information of the divine plan into that solar system. So you might say that is the oversoul of conscious evolution of that entire solar system as implanted through the mind of God.

You can go beyond that to intergalactic awareness, and you move into the oversoul monad of the particular galaxy and all of the solar systems within that galaxy and the divine plan for that. And then interconnected intergalactic awareness of galaxies in unification and beyond and beyond and beyond. It gets larger and larger, so to speak.

J: You described oversoul consciousness as containing "all of the soul fragments that make up the whole of the God consciousness that make up the whole of you as a physical being in your evolution through all of your incarnations. All of your physical experience from the beginning to the end because physical experience has a beginning and an end."

G: That's correct—simply an evolutionary process.

J: So our physical experience has a beginning and an end?

G: That's correct.

J: In other words, we began having a physical experience as an entity, and we will stop having a physical experience as an entity at some point?

G: Then you will move into the oversoul. And then you will eventually dispel the soul altogether. You won't need it any more.

J: I think of the soul as sacred. Could you please tell me again, what is the soul, and are we only using it here?

G: The soul is the ability of a physical body to experience a fragment of its divinity in conscious awareness in physical matter used as a conscious process of growth and evolution. The soul is for the purpose of conscious growth of evolution and development for the revelation of the wholeness of its being in physical experience.

J: So it's something we use in physical experience.

G: That's correct. But you also use it in nonphysical experience when you're not in incarnation as it moves back to the astral plane and moves from the astral plane back to the causal plane, which is the soul plane. On the soul plane it reforms its association in conscious awareness with the oversoul and makes decisions about what is the best way to reincarnate to serve the best possible purpose for its evolution in the next fragment.

J: I suppose how often we incarnate depends upon the individual entity.

G: It depends upon the entity. At this time in your evolution, as you are in an evolutionary soul crisis point as you enter into this two-thousand-year cycle of ascension, souls are incarnating more frequently than they have in the past, particularly souls who are at a more advanced state of evolution so that they can participate in the education of the souls who are of lower levels of advancement.

J: So there are a lot of souls incarnating now because they want to help in this period of crisis.

G: That is correct. They are here mainly as educators to raise the consciousness vibration so that man can do that entrainment process with the least amount of pain and suffering.

J: Are Phillip and I part of that group?

G: Of course, otherwise you wouldn't be talking to us. You wouldn't be the least interested in what we have to say if you weren't.

J: When you answered my question about your function, you said, "Our function is quite simply to reveal the truth of the development of the relationship between humanity and God. So as to inform you of your relationship by revealing how to awaken the doorway that allows that to take place, which is the doorway of the soul." I can't quite understand what you're saying there. Could you clarify it for me?

G: OK. God is undifferentiated consciousness. It has no individuality until it takes the shape of a soul. The soul is a fragment of the consciousness of God that is used to express and experience an aspect of God's consciousness that becomes enclosed in a physical body and animates a physical body for the purpose of that experience. The purpose of all physical evolution is for the purpose of learning how to love. The force of love is the force of the soul's expression. The force of the soul's expression in expressing love is expressing the truth of being of that soul's individual fragment for that lifetime. That individual part of God is learning to become experiential.

If you take all the soul fragments of a particular person's oversoul and put them all together, you will create a cohesive whole of that person's experience in physical matter—the person's entire evolutionary process of all his or her lifetimes and bring about the individual's whole experience of God experiencing him/herself in the physical through that particular soul fragment. If you take all the oversouls of all the souls in the physical and put them together, you will have the entire experience of God experiencing himself/herself in the physical.

J: And your function in that is?

G: To bring about the education and revelation of that connection, to awaken that connection. Because you see, when you asked us the question about "how do I talk to God," what we could have said to you was "by awakening your soul," because the soul is the vehicle through which you talk to God. Or God talks to you. Both ways. It's an intercom system.

J: When you say awakening the soul, you may have explained it before, but help me: what do you mean by awakening the soul?

G: Bringing it into conscious awareness, conscious experience, conscious expression, so that you have a connection through your intuition and knowing. You see, the soul is trying to communicate with you all of the time. The soul tries to communicate with you in many ways. It communicates with you through synchronicity, which is the divine order of the universe. It communicates with you through pain, because pain is simply a way of getting your attention, to say you're in your isolation, you're in your separation, you're off the track. The soul communicates with you through guides, guardians, through other souls who teach you about love, who help to reveal a part of yourself. Or a soul that comes in to challenge you to awaken something in yourself. Your soul is in communication with you all the time. But you are not hearing it.

J: What are some simple things we can do to be aware of our soul's communication?

G: Still the body. Still the mind of thoughts, and still the emotional body of separated feelings. This requires a state of meditation. A state of meditation is a state of attention, of stillness, of awareness. You cannot become aware until you are still, until you are quiet inside. When you are in meditation, that is a state in which God can talk to you, in which your soul can talk to you. When you are in a state of prayer, you are talking to God and to your soul.

J: What is a good way to pray?

G: Affirmatively. Understand, you do not beg the universe because you are a part of God; therefore, you affirm the reality you want. You affirm it as if it were so. You affirm it in the moment of being because on a physics level, you are dipping intention into the quantum field of possibility and probability. And based upon how affirmative your intention is and how clear it is will determine what you draw from that quantum field of possibility and probability or from the mind of God.

J: What do you mean by how affirmative it is?

G: That means how positive, straightforward, in the moment, affirming it as if it were so. Most people when they pray beg God. "Please God, give me this. Have mercy on me." They're praying through their shame.

J: That's how we're taught to pray in our churches.

G: Of course. That keeps you subservient to those who keep telling you who God is and how you have no right to the power of God. You have every right to use the power of God. You are God. God is you. You are honoring God by taking responsibility for and responding to the power of God by affirming it.

J: So no one is closer to God than anyone else, and no one has any more power than anyone else.

G: Correct.

J: You warned not to let anything you said become truth for all time, fixed in concrete so to speak, like the word of God being a fixed truth for all time.

G: Yes, because, you see, truth is in evolution always. It is ever revealing itself. The very concept or idea of God, divine intelligence, the great mind, whatever you want to call it, is that it is infinite. It is infinite in its capacity, in its expression, and in its being. What you call God is also evolving because it is infinite. Therefore, the truths that are absolute are not absolute, if you will. They are ever evolving. A belief is absolute. A belief is finite. A belief becomes religious dogma. You believe something and you say, that's it, and there's no more room for flexibility or movement or creation in that. Creation itself is an act of evolution. It is an act that is ever becoming more of itself. Life is infinite.

J: When we think of a heavenly being or a messenger of God such as yourself, we naturally assume that what you say or the source of your knowledge would be infallible. Is there anything you don't know? Do you have access to all knowledge?

G: No. We do not have access to all knowledge. We have access to the realm of knowledge, the realm of consciousness, of which we are in charge of or which we have been given the gift of disseminating. That is a considerable amount of knowledge, but it is not all that is. You see, God is all that is. The universe is all that is. But all that is—is. But that does not mean that it is not also becoming more.

J: Are you also saying that what you know tends to be limited to your mission and job?

G: Pretty much, yes. But don't let that worry you. We won't run out of things to say.

J: I'm not worried at all. I suppose I'm trying to define it so that people can have a better sense of the divine order of things. That would be one way of putting it.

G: The divine order of things is a system, if you will, of consciousness that reveals all that God is in present consciousness. But God in present consciousness is also growing and developing and expanding just as your universe expands. Therefore, everything is infinite in its nature. The order of things is infinite in its nature. In physical form, things appear finite. Physical matter itself in its form is a finite form, in that sense, because in its illusion of reality it has a beginning, a middle, and an end. Or it has a past, present, and a future. But that which animates the form is infinite.

J: You seem to know about any subject I could think of asking. So far, I haven't gotten the impression I could ask anything that you would consider impertinent,

G: Oh no.

J: But I do want to ask you this, and I don't mean it to be impertinent. People who read this material might ask: why wouldn't Gabriel know everything about our history? For example, why wouldn't Gabriel know when Constantine removed references to reincarnation from the Bible? How would you respond to a question like that? [In the discussion that took place on April 27, 2003, Gabriel could not tell me which year Constantine removed those references.]

G: Well, because we have to tap into certain energies. You see, we read energies. It depends upon what energy our frequency is capable of tapping into. Some of the denser energies we are not able to tap into. Some of the higher energies that deal with our own perspective, we can tap into most easily. Things such as dates and times and things like that are not as readily available to us because that is all the concern of the third dimension. That is all locked within the record of the third dimension where the time/space continuum is concerned. That is the fallacy of the finite mind.

J: When I asked if you were a herald of a new age, you agreed you were. I'm wondering if you're currently having similar conversations with others outside of Robert's group.

G: There are others who tap into our realm, yes. Understand that we represent a dimensional realm in time and space, a level of consciousness. Within that level of consciousness, there are many levels. So within that level of consciousness, people can tap into our realm, and they can say, I am channeling Gabriel. So they are in a sense tapping into the realm of Gabriel. The clarity and the availability of the channel will determine how much energy and information they are able to tap into and how clear that information will be. Most channels are rather finite in their ability because most of them are conscious channels or semi-trance channels. That means their own conscious minds are there registering everything to some degree, and thus editing the process based upon what is locked in the belief systems of their own subconscious.

If a channel is able to accomplish the feat of becoming a full-trance channel which is rare—Edgar Cayce was one; the channel, the vehicle we come through (Robert Baker), is another, and there are others as well—if they are able to do that, the information and energy they are able to tap into can be clearer. Clarity is also based upon the vibration of the body we use to come into because we have to raise the vibration of the body when we come in as the body is very dense. If the vehicles themselves are working consciously to raise their own vibrations, in their own processes, then the vehicles become clearer channels, like a computer program that is able to receive a certain channel of energy.

You can only receive the clarity of that energy in consciousness based upon how clear the channel receiving it is. If there is static in the channel, there will be static in the information. If the belief systems of the particular channel interfere with the information, that information will be interpreted as it is coming through, so it can become distorted. Or the channels are able to pick up on the lower frequencies of our realm and tap into some peripheral information and say they are channeling Gabriel. But they may not be channeling the full content. They may not be channeling the clearer essence of the heart of our information because everything operates through signals of vibration and frequency. The clarity and the rate of vibration frequency determine the ability of the vehicle to tap into the informational level or the level of consciousness that is available.

J: I would like to step back for a moment and take a long view of things, especially as it relates to your mission as a herald of this new age. We know of you mostly through scripture. But there isn't much about you in scripture. Can you give us a brief description of your history as a messenger to mankind? When did it start, and with whom? And what were you trying to do?

G: In your time/space continuum way of dating things, we have been around for probably twenty thousand years. And we have come to the consciousness of people in various ways and various times. We have been called various names, with the names, of course, being your own. They are the names you have given us, so we use those names. In the English language, we use the name Gabriel. But always the message has been the same, the same as it was two thousand years ago when the one Jesus the Christ was born, and that is love one another.

We are a messenger of love and truth. In order to convey that message of love and truth, we teach how to reveal the soul, because the soul is the force of love and truth, the love of the truth of being. You see, the love and truth of being is the force, is the glue that holds the universe together. It is the glue that holds matter and the divine together in cohesive form and expression.

Remember, matter on its own without awareness of its divinity experiences the ongoing problem of isolation, the feeling or sensation of separation. Only when it is joined consciously with its creator, the divine, can it realize its freedom from that separation and isolation. That can only be experienced through the force of love, which is the great revealer of the relationship between the physical and the divine, which is the soul. So as the soul awakens, it becomes the arbiter between the divine and the physical. It is the joiner together of the two that makes humanity realize it is not separate from God and God is not separate from humanity.

J: Can you tell us something about your early contacts? Who were you contacting?

G: We have been in contact with various beings throughout the ages who reached the stage of development in their incarnational process where they were available to our frequency. So we have come through in various ways to reveal certain messages. We have come through and given messages in the Egyptian civilization, the Greek civilization, the Roman civilization, as far back as the Sumerian civilization. But none has really been at a state of development collectively where they could hear the message. Even in the last two-thousand-year cycle at the birth of the Christ, how many people have heeded the message "love one another?" You're still in duality and strife. This new age begins the heralding of the realization of the experience of the living Christ, the experience of the awakening of the soul, the experience of the awakening of love.

J: Jesus gave us a prayer. At least it has come down through time to us as the "Our Father." When I asked about prayer last time, you said to affirm what you want as already existing.

G: Yes.

J: Could you offer us a prayer?

G: "Divine love is ever present, all power, all life, truth, and love, over all and all."

J: Thank you.

G: You are most welcome, dear one.

J: When Robert goes into trance and calls on you, where do you come from? Where are you before you come through Robert?

G: In consciousness. You see, we are available on a certain frequency of consciousness. And when the channel calls upon us, he calls on that frequency of consciousness. That frequency of consciousness is now connected to him and us to his frequency. So all he has to do is say our name in his mind and he can allow our energy to come in. Look at it this way: As human beings, as physical beings, you see everything in time and space, as having distance, as having a place. But in reality nothing has a place. Nothing is in time and space. Nothing has distance. Everything is ever present.

J: So everything is everywhere all at once.

G: Exactly. Everything is ever present all at once. We are ever present all at once, as you are ever present as well. But you are not aware of that because you are locked in the illusion of the time/space continuum—that it takes this amount of time or it takes this distance to get from here to there. But consciousness is energy, and energy knows no distance. That's why, for instance, if you are doing healing work, Reiki work, you can do distance treatment, and there's no time or space that creates a space between the energy.

Intention directs energy directly to the place that you intend it. It appears there instantaneously because, in reality, there is no place. In reality, consciousness exists simultaneously in all time and space at once. There is only now. There is only the one moment of reality within everything. Everything finds its existence within that moment of reality. That is the moment of creation. Through the limbic system and through the conscious mind, you focus a limited amount of energy, an idea, a perception, and you divide it into time and space. You slow it down into an illusion that there is distance, time, space—that there is past, present, and future. And you live within that illusion, but in reality that is not so. You are simply confining yourself to one small, very limited dimension of reality so that you can comprehend through something called experience. But we are ever present.

J: Within your level of consciousness, what do you do?

G: We don't do anything. We are. Doing is something that happens in the comprehensive space of the time/space continuum. For instance, you formulate an idea into a thought pattern, and in doing so you slow it down to comprehend it as an idea. If you were at a state of being where you were directly connected to the soul, you would be in a state of absolute knowing. There would be no thoughts. That knowing is a state of being. It's a state of presence, of beingness, of awakeness, of aliveness, of awareness. It is direct. There is nothing to slow it down. There is nothing to create a gap between consciousness and the awareness of it. In your conscious mind you create a gap between consciousness, perception, and awareness. And in that gap you have thoughts and feelings and experience. In our reality, in real time, or non-time, there is no experience. It just is. Everything just is. That is difficult to comprehend from a third dimensional perspective.

J: It's also difficult because I think of us as in a state of becoming because you said that everything was becoming, including God.

G: Yes. But the becoming we speak of is simply your consciousness perceiving in time/ space and remembering what is. So all you're doing is remembering because it already is. Everything already is. Past, present, and future already is. You're not moving toward a future that is yet to be created in that sense. It already is.

J: You said God is infinite and, therefore, is always becoming. How could that be if everything already is?

G: Consciousness is always expanding upon its realization of itself. So the realization is the part that is becoming. In other words, God creates a universe and that universe is what it is. That consciousness of that universe, in its very nature, creates the expansion of more consciousness of consciousness. Nothing is finite. Everything is constantly in movement. Therefore, everything is always expanding and becoming more of itself. So you might say that the becoming aspect of it is consciousness simply realizing its infiniteness, its omnipresence.

J: So consciousness is always discovering more of itself?

G: Well, it's a paradox because everything already is, and yet everything is constantly expanding into what it is.

J: So what is that called, that paradox?

G: There are no words for it other than infinitude, infinity. There is no beginning, and there is no end. You must comprehend the idea first of all that when there is no end, there is also no beginning. So something did not begin and is becoming more. It is. It has no beginning, and it has no end. It is infinite in its nature, in its being. And yet it is constantly expanding, but the expansion isn't in a linear sense. You see, when you think of expansion, you think of it as something that's going from here to there, has a beginning, a middle, and an end, and that the end is expanding, but the beginning is staying where it began. Allow yourself to grasp—which the conscious mind can't do because it's experiential—the idea there is no beginning, that all exists in multidimensional reality. So it is dimensions of consciousness and being interconnecting, interweaving with one another.

For instance, matter is a dimension of consciousness that is interwoven and interconnected with other dimensions of consciousness. Within itself, focused simply on itself, it is a separate or finite field of consciousness. It is its own dimension of consciousness. And it's the only dimension of consciousness that exists in a time/space continuum. Matter exists in a time/space continuum because it's simply an illusion of energy that is slowed to a very dense vibration of comprehension. So it's an extremely low density of comprehension of reality that limits it and makes it appear finite.

J: Talking with you is so fulfilling. What might you suggest that any one of us do to be in touch with the angelic realm in our day-to-day living?

G: Well it would make things a lot easier for you because human beings operate in the illusion of separation. So they go about their lives as if they were separate, as if they were isolated, as if they had no support. So they seek support from one another like children in the wilderness. Being aware of our presence and the presence of others of the angelic and divine realms is to know that the entire universe is in support of your process, is in support of the evolution of you as a soul. So that in itself, keeping that in mind and keeping that in your heart, can allow you to trust the process of living and be available to more livingness.

When you are living in an experience of isolation, believing that you are it, then to some degree depending upon your level of development and your level of consciousness, you are always in a state of surviving life, so to speak, rather than living it. And living it is what it's all about. Surviving it means you are living in a perspective of limitation, in a small box, if you will, trying to fit everything into that box of consciousness, that box of perception that keeps you isolated, keeps you separate. And this is the great conundrum of humanity, their seeking of spirituality, their seeking of God, because they believe that God is something that is outside of themselves.

For the most part, they believe they are separate from that force, less than that force, and therefore, they must somehow earn the right. There is no right to be earned. It is your divine right because you are divine, because you are the expression and experience of all that is. You are the expression of love. You are the expression of God.

Therefore, God is within you at all times. But when you are in that state of isolation, the illusion of separation, you have a difficult time realizing or trusting or acknowledging that connection. It makes things so much easier to flow with the universal force of life when you allow yourself to just entertain the idea of that presence always available to you.

J: So we should hold you in our consciousness.

G: Yes. And not just us, your divinity as a whole, because you see, we are a part of you as you are a part of us because everything is a part of everything else. Nothing is separate. It just has to do with different degrees and levels of awareness. You see, it's not that humanity is evolving—it's that you are remembering. Evolution is simply remembering more of what you are. So it is awakening your awareness of what you already are. So affirm it each day. Begin your day with prayer and meditation to just center yourself in that. Otherwise, you get so caught up in daily life, the exterior world, that you get distracted within your isolation, within that exterior world. You then get caught up in the perception that reality exists in the physical world rather than realizing the physical world is simply a reflection of reality.

J: After my coffee, I hit the ground running and, like many people, I know it is healthy to meditate, to take some quiet time, but I rarely do. What is an effective way of meditating without spending thirty-five or forty minutes? Perhaps holding my divine connection in consciousness and affirming it all day long would be one way.

G: Yes. Make it a walking meditation. Make every moment of your life a moment of awareness of your connection to whatever it is to which you are responding. Begin to see that everything around you is a mirror of the divine, that God exists everywhere, that God is ever present. And it is ever present in every face you meet, in every blade of grass, in the sun and the clouds in the sky, in the trees. You see, that consciousness is ever present everywhere. But what tends to happen with human beings is they tend to take everything for granted so there is little sacredness of what is. So they go on a spiritual search to find God. If they would just relax and realize that God is ever present in everything they see and everything they perceive, then they would be in the presence of God at all times.

The physical world is simply a manifestation of an aspect of the expression of God. And, of course, that is the aspect of expression you are in at the moment because you are incarnate. So enjoy it. Take advantage of it. Let it in. Allow it to affect you. Allow it to penetrate your consciousness, your feelings, your energy, your sense of being.

Allow yourself to experience the connection to all that is because it's all there. Every aspect of God has a reflection somewhere. Every aspect of God has a reflection in the physical in the nature of things. The order of the universe is exemplified in the order of nature, in the balance of all things in interrelationship with everything else, in the individual expression of everything in interrelationship with everything else, and in the equality of that expression as everything honors everything else and holds it sacred.

The only beings on the earth that do not do that are mankind. And that is because mankind has advanced to a point where he has something that other forms of nature haven't developed, and that is freedom of will, freedom of choice. That freedom of choice is there for him to learn about the experience of himself as a God force and to learn through freedom of choice how to take responsibility for that internal God force and direct it consciously. And to learn how to do that through freedom of choice, through trial and error, through something called growth, through something called development, through lessons or challenges. In embracing all of that, you learn through experience the God within you.

J: We are in the middle of our eighth discussion. As I review the transcripts of our past conversations and your lectures, the concepts you are discussing are becoming easier for me to understand. I hope our readers will have the same experience.

G: You see, books, depending on their intention and the clarity of the author and the clarity of the information, create a resonance, an energy, a vibration. Our information carries a certain vibration and therefore, depending upon how it is imparted, will determine what it does within the energetic field of the person perceiving it. We put our force of energy and consciousness into what we say. In doing so, we put it in layers so that as you go back and review it again and again, you will uncover one layer after another, after another. It is our way of encoding it so you don't get overloaded all at once and blow up.

J: That's what I'll suggest the readers do. This isn't something you read through once. It's more like a course of study.

G: Yes.

J: When we began this project, we talked about it being a joint effort. This is your book as far as I am concerned.

G: Oh good—we're writing our first book.

J: [Laughing] It amazes me this would be your first book. You must have inspired many.

G: Well, we did have something to do with the Koran.

J: I read that you dictated the opening lines of the Koran to Mohammed.

G: [Nods]

J: What else did you do with the Koran?

G: Helped to clarify certain points and to inspire the unfoldment of the channel.

J: That's essentially what Mohammed was, a channel?

G: Yes.

J: Is that what most spiritual figures of history are?

G: Yes, they are all channels. Jesus was a channel for the Christ Consciousness. You see, all we are doing at this time is we are coming in and doing the same thing as we did with Jesus. We are setting an imprint into your consciousness of the process of ascension into soul awakening. The awakening of the Christ Consciousness in Jesus the man was the awakening of his soul. That was set as an example to all humankind as an imprint. It created a resonance. People created a religion around it called Christianity. And so he set the imprint for the coming age.

And now we come to give you the step-by-step process and take you through that process for the awakening of the Christ Consciousness in all humanity. People keep waiting around for the Christ to reappear. Some man is going to come along in robes and a beard and rescue us. Tell us what to do. No—it's not going to happen. Wait from now until doomsday, as they say. It's not going to happen. You're it. You are the Christ. The time in evolution has come for the Christ Consciousness, the soul, to awaken in all humankind. This is that time. We are simply here as a messenger to trumpet the news, so to speak.

Chapter 3:
New Spiritual Age/Divine Plan/ Man's Origins and Journey

J: You said we were entering into a new two-thousand-year cycle that involved the development of a new spiritual root race of humankind. What did you mean by a root race?

G: A root race basically governs a cycle of evolution, bringing in a new level of consciousness within that evolution. They are major evolutions of humankind and soul development. There have been several root races of humankind—the Lemurian root race, the Atlantean root race, the Ayrean root race, which was the most recent one in the last two-thousand-year cycle. And now you move from that into the Spiritual root race. The last root race, the Ayrean, was a combination of all the previous root races being brought together or integrated.

In the development of the current root race, you integrate the last traces of all the previous root races to form a new level or new evolution for humankind. The last root race was the celebration in the Age of Pisces of the two fish moving in opposite directions, which is representative of the higher and lower self, or the spiritual and physical in opposition to one another. In that last two-thousand-year cycle, Jesus the Christ came in to set an imprint on this age as a prophesy or as an imprinting into the consciousness of that root race to begin to bring together the marriage of duality, the opposites, the higher and the lower, the spiritual and the physical. He brought in the idea of the birth of a soul, which is the transforming or the integrative force that brings the higher and the lower together, that brings the spiritual and the physical into oneness in the physical plane.

This new age, this Age of Aquarius, with its symbol of the man holding the water pitcher, is the age of the unity or the balancing of all things. So it's the bringing together of duality. In this age, the awakening of the soul takes place in the consciousness of humanity as a whole. In the awakening of the soul, what also takes place is the dispelling of the belief of the illusion of death and the realization of man as spiritual and immortal. Now, it's interesting that already in the beginning of this cycle, scientists have finally broken the code of DNA. In breaking the code, they are discovering how to recreate human life on a cellular level. They will discover, eventually, what the remainder of the forty-four on sites on the DNA are for, which they don't know at this point.

J: Will scientists be getting some spiritual help?

G: Well, there is always spiritual help. You see, if you look at it from a quantum physics point of view, consciousness is raised by the vibration that comes into a space. Quantum physics says that if you put a high vibration into a field as a dominant field of energy or a quantum field, it begins a process of entrainment. That means everything that is of a lower vibration begins to raise itself to the higher vibration. Now, think of higher vibration as higher consciousness. In 1987, the beginning of the Harmonic Convergence as they called it, man began a five-year period in which his consciousness was being raised.

If you remember back in 1987, it was a time when a lot of people were awakening. That's when the New Age, as you call it, really started. All of a sudden there were books everywhere about all these New Age concepts. That was the preparation for this new cycle. At the same time, each cycle is governed by a ray of consciousness—that's the dominant ray that produces a particular level of vibration. The last two-thousand-year cycle, the age of duality, was governed by the sixth ray of consciousness, which is the ray that rules the celebration of the pairs of opposites. And so man evolved through the pairs of opposites and through the karmic wheel.

This new cycle's predominant ray is the seventh ray of consciousness, which is the ray of spirit that transforms all physical structure that is in duality. So it destroys all forms that are in duality to reform them to a unified consciousness or a unified field. The seventh ray creates an entrainment process so that all consciousness in this cycle can raise its vibration to that higher level. Therefore, this new cycle creates an upheaval with everything that is in duality. And so you see duality everywhere around you in the world.

J: When you refer to duality, I sometimes think I understand it, and I sometimes don't.

G: Duality is the opposition of two sides: good and bad, right and wrong, good and evil, positive and negative—opposing sides, anything that is in opposition to itself. Let us look at it from the point of view of feelings. This you will understand as a human. You have within you feelings that you call positive and negative, sadness and joy. Now you have decided that sadness is a negative feeling and joy is positive. So what makes joy a positive feeling and sadness a negative feeling? A decision that was made that certain things are bad and certain things are good. That's what creates duality, that some things are bad or evil and some things are good. That's a definition that was created by humans in their inability to integrate both sides of their being, both sides of their experience.

In the survival brain, this causes human beings to try to get rid of negativity and embrace the positive. But by trying to get rid of negativity, they are creating negativity, because what you resist persists. What you focus on getting rid of, you keep recreating in order to keep fighting it, and the more power you give it. For instance, if you are protesting the war, you will never get rid of war because you are adding energy to it by protesting it. However, if you create peace, you are moving towards peace. So if you are fighting one side of something, you are in duality with it.

J: In our last conversation, you referred to duality in corporations. What did you mean by duality there?

G: Duality that is not for the union or the good of the whole, not for the union and good of the individual, but is polarized in greed, in haves and have-nots. Therefore, the corporate structure creates haves and have-nots. It creates those who are at the top who skim the profits off the top and those at the bottom who expend their energy to create the profits for those who skim the top. There is inequality. In a system of non-duality, there is equality. Understand that equality does not mean herd instinct, does not mean embracing sameness. It means embracing and honoring the individuality of all things in acceptance and love.

You live in a society in Western civilization based upon a profit-making system that breeds duality, breeds haves and have-nots. It breeds competition, breeds defenses to protect what I have at the top and keep those at the bottom oppressed, to keep the herd consciousness in the herd consciousness. The herd is taught that by embracing sameness, or what they share that is the same among one another, that creates a sense of union. It's quite the opposite. It creates more and more separation from their individuality. People are encouraged to adopt sameness and dispel their individuality. When someone is too individual, it is frowned upon.

It starts in the parenting system. And it comes from an age-old tribal system of patriarchy. The family system is a system of patriarchy that has been in evolution since the beginning of tribal times in which the male is the dominant force that takes care of the tribe, hunts the animals, protects the family from the elements, and therefore is worshiped. He is set apart, and everything below him fits into and agrees with what he does or what he says in order to survive. And so your entire system is based upon that tribal system. It hasn't changed. It hasn't evolved. Now you are evolving into a time when that tribal system is falling apart. And in that you have an identity crisis.

J: You said that all of our systems are breaking down. My first instinct was to feel fear because most people in our country have a reasonable amount of prosperity and contentment. The prospect of most of our systems breaking down is pretty scary.

G: Yes, of course. But new systems that are built for the good of the whole will prosper because that is the direction in which consciousness is moving.

J: I worked in corporations for many years attempting to create more motivating work places by empowering employees to be part of the decision-making process. We tried to achieve what you're implying the new systems might create. I think most people are aware there is considerable inequity and little democracy in our business organizations and institutions.

G: Yes. The structure of the corporate system is not created to celebrate the talents, abilities, and contributions of the individual. Rather, it is set up to make the individual fit into what is required by the institution and to support the agenda of the institution to produce the product. Therefore, human energy is dispensable. The product is not.

J: It's easy to relate to what you're saying. Nearly every week, there's a story about some top executive who has exploited his power and position to skim the cream from his corporation. Today, there is a new story concerning the CEO of one of our largest airlines. The union is threatening to throw out its agreement to accept a reduced compensation package after it discovered he had a protected contract that guaranteed his bonus. Another story on a corporate merger relates how a few top executives are positioned to make millions while scores of employees are losing their jobs and benefits.

G: This is the revelation of the duality in everything.

J: You have been talking about the various energetic forces that have been affecting us for some time.

G: Yes, the Shoemaker/Levy comet hitting Jupiter.

J: That, and you have described other phenomenon as well. It sounded like those forces were having profound influences on mankind.

G: Yes they are. They are indeed.

J: I'm assuming they'll help us address these daunting problems as we attempt to move out of a state of duality into unity.

G: Yes. You see, what you are facing in this new age is man moving from a state of infancy in his evolution to a stage of awakening to his adulthood as a divine being. What you are talking about in the birth initiation is the birth of man's knowledge of himself as a spiritual being by awakening the soul. Only when he can do that can he take responsibility for himself as an individual. Only then can he take responsibility for himself in the world, and take responsibility for what he is creating where his world is concerned.

J: So these energetic forces are helping with our spiritual evolution?

G: Yes, they are. Now of course what you do with those influences is entirely up to you. The level of soul development you happen to be at will determine how awake or conscious you are of these energies, and how awakened you can become in order to utilize and direct them consciously. If you are at a very low level of incarnation, a low level of soul development, an infant or a child's soul level, then you will simply be bombarded by these influences and go deeper into your survival consciousness.

But a great deal of the planet has incarnated at a higher soul level. There are more evolved souls at higher soul levels in this age than ever before. These souls are incarnating much faster than they have in previous cycles of incarnation. So you have more highly developed souls in this age preparing for this age than you have had in the past because they are needed now. In the past they wouldn't have been much use because the whole collective of mankind was evolving on a cause and effect evolutionary spiral through trial and error.

J: The population of earth is over six billion and growing. How big is the group of advanced souls you're talking about?

G: Your planet at the moment is divided into thirds. One third are younger souls who will continue to try to sustain and maintain the status quo of separation and isolation. One third are advanced souls who are creating a quantum shift where consciousness is concerned. Another third are leaving the planet. So by the year 2012 upwards into 2020, probably around there, you're going to see more and more souls leaving the planet because of cataclysms, diseases created by you, and wars. Chemical warfare will probably become dominant in the future to some degree, with diseases created because of it as well as from the imbalance of the ecosystem. All these various factors are going to cause about one third to leave the planet. You already have large numbers of people leaving the planet because of AIDS.

J: You're talking about a couple of billion people at a minimum leaving, aren't you?

G: Yes. Also, the World Management Team when they reach their oil crisis has to find a way of getting rid of a lot of the population because they won't be able to feed them as the population expands. To create their New World Order, to control the populace, they will be deciding who stays and who goes. That is why they're creating all their systems of control, why they're taking away your constitutional rights in this country, why they're creating an industrial military complex worldwide when oil reaches a crisis point, when it peaks and begins its decline unless they change their source of energy. The world's food is dependent upon oil because all of the fertilizers and insecticides are hydrocarbon-based. Therefore, the food supply for the world's population is dependent upon oil.

J: What should we do? Is this inevitable?

G: No. Nothing is inevitable. There are more of you than there are of them. It requires that the population as a whole wake up. You have already seen stirrings of this with the reaction to the United States and their coalition that were creating the war on Iraq and how few of the world's leaders wished to join that coalition. Also, you saw the largest number of people worldwide protesting the war antics of the U.S. government and the coalition. That's an indication the population is waking up. But it's still not enough.

J: What more has to be done?

G: People have to realize the power of one. They have to realize that each voice is important, that each individual has a voice and a mind, and they must learn to think for themselves. And they must learn to think in the long term rather than for immediate gratification because most of the population of your country is focused, like their children, on instant gratification—feed me, take care of my needs, make me comfortable. As long as you don't disturb my comfort zone I'll go along with anything that you want. You're the daddy. You know, I don't.

Look at your population and see the disinterest. People are giving away their rights through disinterest. Less than half of your population votes in any major election. That is not an example of people taking seriously their right to speak up and take responsibility for the reality they want.

J: One of the reasons the administration got as much support as it did for the war was that it was able to show the cruelty of Saddam Hussein.

G: It was all smoke and mirrors.

J: I think there's plenty of evidence Saddam was a vicious dictator who killed thousands of his people.

G: Dear one, that is true. But what gives the United States the right to declare itself the one that decides for other countries how they are to be or not to be? The United States has been responsible for terrorist acts in other countries, for instance in South America where thousands of people have been killed. In the Gulf War in Iraq, uranium-tainted shells that were left have caused many of the children in Iraq to be born with life-threatening diseases such as cancers and physical distortions. So the Gulf War was responsible for the deaths of thousands of children since that time. But you don't hear about that.

J: No, I honestly haven't heard that. When I asked you how to deal with these despots, you said, "You should build a better system alongside the system that exists and make it available for people in their individual process to embrace or not as they choose."

G: That's correct.

J: But how do you offer that to people imprisoned by a despotic dictator who allows no freedom of choice at all? And it could have gone on for decades.

G: First of all, you have to wake the people up. You have to make available to them the information of what is really going on rather than what the media, which is controlled by six multinational corporations, is telling them.

J: But that's in America. What would we do in Iraq where people are essentially imprisoned by a dictator?

G: Well, you educate the people if you can. But each country is responsible for its own freedom. Each country is responsible for waking up of its own accord. Understand, dear one, countries are separate because of reasons of karma. And karmic reasons are based upon soul development. Many of which you call the Third World countries that are suffering through despotic dictators and that sort of thing are countries which are evolving at a very young level of soul development where they are just operating though survival. And that is the karmic decree that those soul groups of people gathering together in those specific places have chosen.

You may look at these places and see horrific things, and you may say, well, as Americans we are free, and we represent freedom and independence. Do you? How are you taking care of the people in your own country? How many people in your country are starving? Do you know about them? How are you taking care of the aged? Did you know there are thousands of Gulf War veterans dying at this moment of disease they got from nuclear fallout from uranium-tainted shells they used in the Gulf War? Many are dying and suffering incurable diseases, and the military and the American government are not taking care of them. They can't get medical help. Do you know about that?

J: Yes, I have read quite a bit about that. I have absolutely no argument with you about the huge injustices that exist in this country. And I can see you're bringing in another level of understanding to the question of what is the appropriate behavior of one country towards another when you raise the issue of the karmic development and national identity of people and how careful we need to be about trespassing on that.

G: Exactly.

J: On the other hand, when we're seeing brutal repression, cruelty, and murder, are we to just stand aside and say, well they're just in a different stage of evolution?

G: Dear one, do you not understand, or are you not aware perhaps that since World War I, the United States has made unprovoked attacks on many different countries or states in the world and has usurped their governments? And in many cases, it has replaced those governments with terrorist dictators so it could maintain control of the resources within those countries? The war on drugs in South America has nothing to do with drugs in South America. In fact, Wall Street and your stock market thrive on drug money from those countries. Wall Street profits from the billions of dollars of drug money that passes illegitimately through it every year and through your major banking systems.

J: I acknowledge everything you are saying. I still think that begs the question of when we see torture and cruelty going on in another country, are we simply to respond by just saying they are at a different level of evolutionary development?

G: Yes, to allow them to work out their own problems, and if they ask for assistance, to give it. You see, a better system would be to find a way of feeding all the world's people and taking care of their basic survival needs because it is survival that creates these problems.

J: You mean a better way is spending money on food rather than billions of dollars on arms and war.

G: That's correct. One infinitesimal amount of those billions of dollars could feed the entire population of the world for a year.

J: In our own country, over thirty million children don't have health insurance; therefore, they can't get adequate health care. Our government leaders tell us we can't afford that. But we can afford to spend hundreds of billions on war.

G: That's right. You are building a military industrial complex to control the populace at large. There are hundreds of internment camps throughout the United States that are prepared for the time when a national emergency is declared due to some fallacious creation such as the outbreak of chemical warfare so that the population that dissents can be interred. Just as during World War II with the Japanese who were interred in concentration camps in this country.

J: Who would be put into them first?

G: Probably the blacks, the Hispanics, and any other dissenting minority groups. Whether you realize it or not, there's an ethnic cleansing taking place in your country. What do you see every day in your newspapers and on the six o'clock news about crime? It's always the black man and other minorities.

J: I know most of the people in prison are blacks and other minorities.

G: That's correct. But the biggest crimes are committed by white men. What about your corporate crimes, stealing billions of dollars from the people from their retirement funds and savings? What happens to most of these people? Not much.

J: You've said that systems based on patriarchy are falling apart and that new systems built for the good of the whole will prosper because that's the direction in which consciousness is going.

G: Yes, but you are in the birth process of that.

J: But it sounds as if there is going to be a lot of chaos before that.

G: Oh yes.

J: What would a new system look like that is not based on patriarchy?

G: A new system would look like children who are born and are held sacred by the parental units. And the parents are educated to raise the children in such a way that the child's individual soul is nurtured and supported and its education is based upon the value of the individual rather than the value of the herd consciousness.

J: I would assume new systems would include equal participation by everyone, not primarily males or white males or whoever is currently dominating society.

G: That's correct. The value of all peoples, the value of the individuality of all ethnic groups, the value of the individuality of each individual within those ethnic groups, the value of the individuality of all groups together in the experience of life.

J: You have talked about our civilization essentially collapsing and predicted that one third of the world's population would leave the planet.

G: Yes.

J: My reaction in all honesty is fear. Last Sunday I went to a church service where I may have encountered a little synchronicity. The minister wrote in her Sunday program, "Contemplate the idea that we are dying to our former self and being reborn. It is a death that must occur in order to experience the new, and the new experience is not likely to be achieved without the labor necessary for the rebirth. And that does not feel good, does it? On a universal level we see the same. There is a theory known as the chaos theory in science that states that all systems, no matter the size or simplicity or complexity, must go through a period of falling apart before making a leap to advance to the next stage of evolution." Is that what you're talking about?

G: Exactly. If you look back in time on all civilizations that have advanced to a certain point, they have experienced that chaos, and they have disintegrated. Look at the Roman civilization. Look at the imperialist power of Great Britain in the nineteenth century. And now Western civilization as you know it has reached that point of chaos. But now you are dealing more with the world's civilization because your civilization currently is based upon the Westernization of the world. Therefore, you're dealing with the world economy, the world social system, the world political ideology, the world health climate.

J: What impact are events such as the collision of the comet into Jupiter and other energetic phenomenon going to have on world events over the next ten to twenty years?

G: It has created a movement of energy in consciousness. When it is a major vibration like that, it creates a quantum shift, which creates a ripple effect. That ripple effect is just now [May 2003] being experienced, just now revealing itself in the physical. In raising the vibration of consciousness you create an entrainment process in which everything of a lower vibration begins to be shaken up because it begins to rise to a higher vibration. This is the death and rebirth. This is the destruction of the old forms and the building of the new.

J: In describing the collision of the comet with Jupiter, you said the gaseous surface of the planet was the emotional body of Jupiter.

G: That is correct.

J: What did you mean it is the emotional body of Jupiter, and what's the significance?

G: The emotional body of Jupiter is related to the emotional density of your solar system, that is, how matter experiences itself through its sentient nature, its feeling nature related to the five senses. So it created an upheaval in the emotional body. Everything that is dense in the emotional body, like all separated negative feelings, feelings that are suppressed, that sort of thing, get shaken up and come to the surface. So you have an emotional earthquake basically that produces emotional chaos. You may note that since that time, the intake of prescription drugs to modify feelings has increased enormously in your country alone.

So it has accelerated the emotional body. The purpose of that in the long term is for the healing of the emotional body because the emotional body is the body of the soul, the body through which the soul speaks. When the emotional body is expanded to a higher vibration, it becomes still. It becomes the still waters of the intuition and the knowing of the soul. It becomes the vehicle through which the soul speaks. So the emotional body is the most important body you have right now.

The emotional body of the lower self exists down in the solar plexus and in the navel region. That's where all your primitive emotions, your personality emotions, your ego emotions are located. When that emotional body is transformed and the emotional body is moved up into the heart, it's transformed into the emotional body of the soul. It then operates, as we said, through intuition and knowing. It's the raising up. It is the resurrection of the soul because the entryway of the soul is through the subconscious. The seat of the subconscious is the solar plexus. Therefore, the solar plexus is the womb of the soul, the womb of Mary, the womb of matter through which the soul is born.

J: Are the implications of this greater for the third of the world population that represents the enlightened beings who have come here?

G: That is correct.

J: You also said the moons of Jupiter, especially Io, contain the secret codes of our solar system that are related to the mysteries, the hierarchy of guidance, the codes of the ascendant mastery. And when that explosion took place, it released the informational codes, the spiritual codes, into our solar system.

G: That's correct. After that you began to see a lot of the secrets being revealed in books and that sort of thing.

J: I took a lot of heart from this in that I thought these events were empowering the force for good, the force for the awakening of the soul on earth.

G: It is. It's all good.

J: I guess in my humanity, I'm just concerned about the chaos.

G: Yes, because you see the chaos to you represents the destruction of your comfort zone, of the reality you've known. So you, like every other human being, want to hold onto the reality you know because for the infant inside the limbic brain, change represents death. Human beings don't like change. They fight change. They fight to remain small. They fight to remain within the limitations of the small framework of their comfort zone. That's why the nervous system becomes an editing system that edits out all except one, one billionth of reality that's taking place this moment where you are. Your nervous system is editing out everything that it has decided is not reality based upon how your nervous system is programmed to perceive reality. This is the veil of illusion, the veil of the third dimension.

J: I'm certainly aware we tend to resist change. But what I'm concerned about is the death and destruction that comes with some of this change. That's pretty scary.

G: Yes. Well, death and destruction have been going on your planet for eons.

J: I know, but that doesn't make me feel any better.

G: Of course. And you seem not to have learned from it.

J: Not very much, have we?

G: You see, this is not something that's happening to you. It's something you have created. Over time, you have created a resonance of destruction. Now you are experiencing the ultimate point of chaos of that commitment.

J: How should we respond if we start to experience the chaos?

G: Accept your feelings. Allow the feelings that come up to flow through you. That is part of the healing. The fear, the feelings that are suppressed, are the very reason the chaos exists because if you're fighting a feeling, you create the circumstances to continue to fight the feeling. Feelings are very ephemeral. They're constantly changing if you allow them to by accepting them as they come. If you fight them, suppress them, avoid them, they stay. But they stay as the experience of pain because of the resistance. The feeling is trying to move, but it can't because of the resistance. The more resistance there is, the more pain there is, and the longer the feeling takes to move. Emotion is the movement, the emoting of a feeling. Emotional experience is how the feeling moves. If it moves through resistance, it produces pain. If it moves through acceptance, it moves and it is gone.

J: I keep coming back to the comet colliding with Jupiter because you said some pretty dramatic things about it. I want to quote you again. You said, "The explosion of the comet into the body of Jupiter represented, on an etheric level, the birth of the divine child, the Christ Consciousness in your solar system."

G: That's correct.

J: That sounds pretty momentous.

G: Yes, it is. It was the birth of this millennium, the birth of this time, which is the birth of the soul, which is the birth of the Christ Consciousness, the birth of mankind awakening through initiation into the knowledge and experience and expression of himself as a spiritual being of God.

J: But isn't that what Jesus brought to us?

G: Yes. Jesus brought it as an example, as one man's example, to show the way, to show the method through his example and, therefore, set an emotional imprint into the planet through his example and through his teachings. So he created, he lived through, all the stages of initiation as a man to create a prophecy for the new age that all mankind would live through. The return of the Christ, the return of the Messiah that everyone is waiting for, is nothing more or less than the awakening of the soul in each person, each individual. Did he not say, "The works that I have done ye shall do, and greater than I have done?"

J: You have said before that this is the Second Coming.

G: That is correct.

J: How is the Second Coming connected to the collision of the comet with Jupiter?

G: The collision of the comet with Jupiter is what opens the doorway, the consciousness of that. In other words, it raises the vibration for man to now begin that awakening. It initiated a new level of evolutionary consciousness in your solar system.

J: You said the secret codes in Io were related to the mysteries, the hierarchy of guidance, and the codes of the Ascendant Mastery.

G: Yes. It's all the same thing. The Ascendant Mastery is responsible for governing and taking care of the codes of the mysteries of the universe. Those mysteries involve the evolution of both the etheric (nonphysical) universe and the physical universe. They are the codes of mastery that involve the soul's evolution from one level of development to another until its ultimate mastery of physical reality and then its ultimate mastery of its own plane. And, ultimately, the dissolution of the causal plane and the soul altogether because it is no longer needed, and the merging of all that with all consciousness, with the consciousness of God.

The first stage of those mysteries has already been revealed through the fact the planet in this new millennium is beginning its next evolutionary cycle through the experience of initiation. The initiations the Christ illustrated in his life were the example of revealing the beginning of the mysteries. The first mystery, the first great mystery, is the connection to the soul, the awakening of the soul. And that is what you are going through now. As you go through these steps of initiation, that mystery is revealing itself in your experience as you evolve—for many, unconsciously; for some, consciously; for some, in greater awareness than others. But it is being revealed, nonetheless. It's like anything else. How do you know reality unless you are conscious it is taking place?

If you live in the reality of the past and you are imposing that past onto the present, then you are never experiencing reality as it is. Therefore, the first step is to be able to see reality as it is, which is an absolute requirement of the awakening of the soul. You must first clear all your personal history—emotionally, mentally, and how it impacts you physically. That is the first major step. That involves the birth and the baptism even unto the transfiguration.

Christ spent most of his learning life in the first two initiations, the birth and the baptism. It wasn't until he was an adult that he was able to realize the transfiguration. Then shortly after that, the rest of the initiations followed. But most of his concentration was on the birth and the baptism, the baptism being the purification, the release from all personal history, emotionally, mentally, and physically, in order to set you free to respond to the moment of now.

J: Birth as the first stage of the initiation process means …?

G: The birth of the knowledge of himself as a spiritual being.

J: I'm asking this next question from the perspective of the people of the United States. As I reviewed our last discussion, you seem somewhat critical of the United States in terms of how it has conducted itself in world affairs over the last century or so. Yet many people here would argue that the United States has helped liberate Europe twice in the last century, even rebuilt our conquered enemies and returned their land to them. And we defended nations such as South Korea, helped protect the world from Soviet domination, and intervened in Yugoslavia and Africa to stop ethnic cleansing. So many of us who are U.S. citizens believe we have done a lot of good things. How would you respond to that?

G: We would say, first of all, that we are not criticizing the United States. We are simply stating facts about what is taking place. There is no judgment about right or wrong, good or bad. It's simply stating facts. As far as the other things you spoke of, you believe those from the point of view of what you have been told and taught based upon how history is interpreted in your country. You are seeing it from the perspective of a country that sees itself in a certain way and declares itself the liberator of freedom for democracy. In some ways it is, and in some ways it is not. You see, the position you use to justify the actions will determine the intentions and will determine how people will see that intention based upon how you send out the propaganda.

For instance, isn't it interesting that no one has launched an investigation to any degree [as of April 2003] whatsoever into the happenings of 9/11. Now why do you suppose that is? Why has it become a dead issue? Why is it, for instance, that the United States has now taken over Iraq, and now the issue of finding nuclear weapons has been nearly forgotten? It's no longer in the newspapers, and no one has found any because none exist. But the memory of the people is only as long as the sound bytes that keep it focusing its attention. Reality is based upon what you believe it to be. What you believe it to be is manipulated by what you are told to believe. You are told one point of view. Part of it is true. Part of it is not. It is manipulated by those who want you to pursue their agenda and to justify their position.

Great Britain was able to justify building an imperial nation by saying it was bringing freedom to all of these poor ignorant peoples in these Third World countries. In truth, it was building an imperialist power throughout the world, and it was destroying the civilizations of those countries and putting its own system into place. Now who says it was right and its system was superior to the system that was there? You see, it's all a matter of how you're interpreting things. And it's all a matter of what you believe based upon what you've been told rather than doing your own independent investigation into all sides.

J: I want to explore at some future point the 9/11 attack and the world organizations you have referred to because we need to spend considerable time on that. But I want to relate what you just said to something we've discussed before. You observed the letters USA were the central letters in the word Jerusalem, and I believe you referred to the United States as the light of the world.

G: The New Jerusalem.

J: We didn't develop that very far. Would you explain what you mean by that, and what you see as the role of the United States in this coming age we've just entered?

G: The United States is a new world, a new country. Its original intention was to be a synthesis of all the people of the world who have lived under oppression and have come here to find spiritual freedom and expression of their individual being. It was supposed to have been a collective of that democratic idea of freedom of speech, freedom of religion, freedom of individual social construct, so that every person and every group can live together in harmony and peace. That was the original intention. Therefore, that creates a collective consciousness that brings together a synthesis of all peoples around the globe to begin to be able to synthesize all the belief systems into a new world of spiritual development. A new world that takes bits and pieces of everything and creates a synthesized whole to lead the world into a new level of unity, oneness, communion, and freedom, spiritual freedom.

But that has been distorted. That does not means it is not still going on. It is. But when you raise the consciousness within a system, all things that are out of sync with that new vibration will begin a process of entrainment. So those things that are in opposition will have to come to the forefront and go through their struggle in order to become part of that synthesis. And that is what you are experiencing now. You're experiencing the entrainment of that separation of duality. You're in the throes of discovering and learning how to govern that unified principle.

J: I've been reading about the population trends in our country. Apparently, what we refer to as minorities as a percentage of the population will become the majority by 2050. And the implications of that, it seems to me, feed into the original intentions of the United States.

G: Yes, exactly. You see, if you look at it from a different perspective, if you look at it from a higher perspective, if you look at it from the perspective of the North American Indians, they spoke of their prophecy of the return of the rainbow tribes. The return of the rainbow tribes is also referred to in the Jewish religion as the coming together of the twelve tribes of Israel and the discovery of the New Jerusalem. Both of those references are related to the coming together of the twelve star systems, which produces the ascension of your planet because your planet is originally made up of twelve star systems. This is the first planet ever that has decided to create a process of evolutionary ascension by bringing together twelve star systems in one unit.

J: We discussed that it would be valuable to create some context or big picture of man's journey here on earth, man's origins. It sounds to me like you're doing that now. Could you restate what you have said in a clear way?

G: Each of what you call stars now in your immediate solar system and galaxy, what are now stars, originally were planets. Each of those planets went through a stage of evolution—as Earth is going through now—from a primitive phase through an advanced phase. Each of those planets eventually came to a point of ascension, which is where it went into light. That is why it is now a star.

Each of those planets became stars as the populations of those planets ascended individually. In other words, the Sirians ascended as Sirians, the Orions ascended as Orions, the Pleiadians ascended as Pleiadians independently. Then the intergalactic community—we'll call it that—decided, "Let's create an experiment in this new solar system where twelve of our star systems that have recently ascended get together, and let us create a (physical) body that we can all descend into with all of the qualities of all of our star systems. And we will create an ascension process that creates a unification of twelve star systems, and we will bring those together." And so that unification of the twelve is the ascension process on your planet. This is also why you have different ethnic backgrounds and traits. Those are some of the ethnic traits of some of the star systems that have bred into the one body the star systems chose to inhabit, the human body.

J: Is there any special reason why it was twelve?

G: Yes, because twelve is the number of completion. Twelve is the number of wholeness. It is the number of ascension into spiritual unity. The twelve star systems are encoded into the physical body of each human being through the endocrine glands and the twelve power mind centers of the body. As the power mind centers awaken and the endocrine glands awaken, it will awaken the information of the star seeds within each person. So each person now, because of the interbreeding over the millennia, is now interbreeding all of the star systems, and all of their genetic material into the body of each individual. So eventually you can have the awakening of the entire ascension of all twelve star systems in each human being, although some beings are predominantly in their origins from an original star system.

J: So the ascension of the human race would produce the ascension of all twelve star systems.

G: That is right.

J: And that was their goal and what they intended to happen?

G: Exactly.

J: Why?

G: So they could have a communal ascension, which had never been done before. Each of the star systems chosen has a specific archetype that relates to the divine plan. So it's a way in which God, God that's all there is, is able to bring together the twelve main archetypes of its being into physical form in the ascension experience.

J: Why those twelve star systems?

G: Where your earth system and your evolutionary process through soul development are concerned, those twelve star systems are the best possible archetypes to choose for this experiment. It is to bring together twelve archetypes of the divine plan that are related to this particular solar system and the part of the divine plan it represents.

J: Is it just an experiment, or is there some larger good or purpose associated with it?

G: Well, its larger purpose is to integrate twelve archetypes of the divine plan. But it's an experiment in the sense that it's never been done before.

J: It's never been done in other galaxies or any way?

G: Not in this way, no.

J: Is there another way of explaining what was to be achieved by combining the twelve archetypes? So the archetypes are combined. So what?

G: Well, it allows you to experience twelve aspects of the divinity of the force of love, to learn through those twelve aspects and to bring a communal experience.

J: How did it all get started?

G: It got started by the seeding of the twelve star systems through the star gate of Sirius. Sirius is the star gate into this solar system.

J: What is a star gate?

G: It's a dimensional opening in time and space. All the star systems came through the Sirian system and created a common vision, a common plan, a united nations, if you will. Isn't it interesting that you have created something you call the United Nations on your planet, which is a physical manifestation of an attempt to realize the integration of those star systems? And in making it an experiment that is experiential, the divine gave this solar system freedom of will so that all star systems would have their own freedom of will to sustain and maintain their own progress and process of development into this intergalactic wholeness.

J: When did this start?

G: Millions and millions of years ago.

J: How did it begin to manifest in terms of life forms?

G: It manifested in life forms as human beings, homo sapiens.

J: How long ago was that?

G: Millions of years ago. There have been civilizations that have come and gone millions of years ago of which you only have inklings. For instance, the Lemurian civilization, the Atlantean civilization. These different civilizations were different attempts to come to a certain stage of advancement where all the star systems were concerned, but they failed. But they carried on and evolved beyond that into the next level, developing an evolutionary advance of the root race based upon the previous root race they had formed. There has been a Lemurian root race, an Atlantean root race, an Ayrian root race, the most recent two-thousand-year cycle. And now you are entering the Spiritual root race, which brings about the evolutionary cycle of ascension.

J: One of the great speculations about Atlantis was its location. Where was Atlantis?

G: At one point the continents of Africa, North America, and South America were interconnected. And that was Atlantis. You can see the remains of that in the south (Atlantic) seas. In an area they call North Carolina there are remains, as well as in the area called the Bermuda triangle.

J: What kinds of remains?

G: Under the sea is part of the civilization of Atlantis—parts of the stones of the buildings remain.

J: Edgar Cayce prophesied there would be evidence of Atlantis as the sea floor rose off of the Bahamian island of Bimini. Many years ago, Life magazine published photos of what looked like a stone road under the shallow sea.

G: Yes.

J: I've always wondered— if these civilizations were so advanced, why did they build using big, heavy stones? I should think advanced civilizations would have had lighter and more sophisticated metals and building materials.

G: No. You're talking about physical technology. They weren't concerned about physical technology. If you look at the great pyramids of Egypt, the physical technology of the great pyramids can't be duplicated by your technological advancements today. The way in which the stones have been refined and fitted together, and the sacred geometrics and the alignments they create in the heavens, are something present scientists are only able to detect with their most sophisticated equipment. And they are connected along major lei lines of the earth. So they had advancements to which you have not advanced.

For instance, the pyramids were created through the power of levitation. They were created because the Atlanteans who remained on the earth after Atlantis sank, those who didn't go back to their original planet, migrated to the area now called Egypt. They were the ones who taught the Egyptian priests about the ways of Atlantis and the powers of building and of moving matter through the power of the mind.

J: You said Atlantis had sunk. I thought you said Atlantis used to be the combined landmass of the continents, which later separated.

G: No. There was a landmass that connected North America, Africa, and South America. That landmass was an interconnector. It was its own individual landmass. And that was destroyed, which is what created the disconnection of the continents. Since then, over thousands of years the continents have drifted further apart as well. So the size of Atlantis was not the distance you now have between the continents, and the landmass wasn't that great.

J: What caused Atlantis to be destroyed?

G: The misuse of energy.

J: Edgar Cayce referred to large lasers that were misused and caused the destruction.

G: Yes. That was the mastery of atomic energy, which is what you have come to now once again. Atlantis is rising. The consciousness of Atlantis is rising, not the landmass. The consciousness of Atlantis is the consciousness of duality. And now you are in the throes of balancing that consciousness of Atlantis. You are also balancing the remains of the Ayrian, the last two thousand years of development, which was the development of the mind to its highest level of being, and the remains of the Lemurian race, the healing and the development of the emotional body. All of those synthesized will bring about the development of the next root race, the spiritual man, which will synthesize the physical, the mental, and the emotional into the higher perspective of the soul's awakening.

J: Is the help we're getting from all the new energy influences a new phenomenon on earth?

G: They are not a new phenomenon, no. But they are specific phenomena to this time. In other words, the energies that are coming in at this time are specific to the purpose of evolution of this root race.

J: Could we mess this up and have the same fate as Atlantis?

G: Yes, because you have freedom of will. You see, freedom of will causes you to learn to guard the sacredness and the power of divinity because you learn through choice the importance, the value, and the integrity of the divine plan. By misusing it, you use it as a destructive force. By using it in alignment with the divine plan, you learn to use it as a creative force. You have been developing over the last two thousand years through the sixth ray of consciousness, which is the worship of the pairs of opposites. And so you have been learning through duality. Now you come into a time during the Age of Aquarius where those pairs of opposites come together. But they don't come together without a fight. First, you see them in the light of their opposition in order to bring them together. You have to see both sides clearly to be able to see which choices, in your freedom, will serve you best.

J: Before we move from the history of man, another question has always puzzled me. We seem to have fossil remains that go back millions of years, and we have evidence of geological events that go back hundreds of millions of years. Why isn't there stronger evidence of advanced civilizations that were much more recent than some of the fossils we're finding?

G: There is. But just as man has not been able to unlock the secrets beneath the paw of the Sphinx because he has not yet reached a vibration that can comprehend the consciousness that is there, so it is that as man develops, things are revealed according to his ability to conceive of them. Here's an example of how the nervous system is able to edit out reality based upon what it's been trained to see: When the Spanish first came to the shores of South America, as they moved across the waters coming to shore, the natives saw them as walking or floating upon the water. Therefore, the natives bowed down and worshipped them as gods. They couldn't see the ships because they'd never seen a ship. Their nervous systems had no point of reference for it. It wasn't until later when they got used to the reality that they began to see the ships. In the beginning they did not see them.

J: Can you give me an example of a ship that we're not seeing?

G: Most of you don't see there are intergalactic visitors in your atmosphere all of the time. Some of you see them. Most of you don't. There are some beings, alien beings, that have taken the form of a physical body that, if you were able to see on their frequency, you would be able to see their alien form. If, for instance, you were to look at your friend in the room with you, and you were able to see through his physical form, you would be able to see in his hologram his original alien form. And he would be able to see yours. There are ETs among you. You are all ETs.

J: In terms of the physical evidence we're not seeing in our archeological digs, is there something there representing a ship we can't see?

G: Well, an example would be Egypt. Archeologists don't see the advancement of the civilization of Egypt. They still believe the pyramids were built by slaves. Yet, no matter the number of slaves, there is no possible way they would have been able to bring the stones up an incline to put them near the top of the pyramids, particularly at that time because of the way the landmasses were. They have changed a great deal over many thousands of years. They are finding that the pyramids are much older than they thought, but they still don't know how old they are. They're finding the Sphinx is much older than they thought because they see from the erosion of it that the erosion was caused by water, which means the area at one time was flooded with water—it wasn't desert at all.

J: How old are the pyramids?

G: Some of the pyramids are ten thousand years old. Some go back as much as fifteen thousand and twenty thousand years.

J: Would you state again how the stones were moved?

G: Through levitation. Through mind power.

J: When I was in Peru, I saw walls made of stones the size of rooms.

G: Same thing, with them fitted so closely together you couldn't get a piece of paper between them.

J: Was the wisdom from the Atlantean civilization?

G: Some of it was Atlantean. Some of it was Lemurian. For instance, archeologists recently discovered the city of Lemuria at the bottom of Lake Titicaca in Peru, the highest and deepest lake at that altitude in the world. It's part of the ancient civilization of Lemuria. Lake Titicaca was a Lemurian gateway. So they are discovering things all of the time as they are needed. These are parts of the mysteries that are being revealed.

J: So the mysteries are being revealed with some purpose and intent.

G: That is right. Because man can only discover based upon his ability to comprehend.

J: When I asked you to explain what was to be gained by combining the archetypes of the twelve star systems, you answered, "It allows you to experience twelve aspects of the divinity of the force of love and to learn through those twelve aspects to bring a communal experience." I interrupted you, and I didn't feel you had completed your thought about what was to be gained by bringing together the twelve star systems as an experiment.

[Gabriel's answer outlines the entire ascension process, which is quite complex. I suggest you read it several times and don't worry if you still don't understand it.]

G: The twelve aspects are related to the twelve power centers of the body. The twelve power centers of the body are each connected to one of the endocrine glands. Each of those power centers has an individual aspect of the order of the universe. Each of those aspects of the order of the universe represents one of those archetypes of the twelve star systems. Those twelve archetypes are related to how you integrate the seven levels of initiation that awaken soul consciousness, that awaken you to the force of love. Those seven initiations are related to the seven main chakras of the physical body, which are seven levels of consciousness that bring about in physical reality the awakening of the soul light or the soul consciousness—the ego and the soul coming together.

Those seven archetypes of physical consciousness in the seven chakras, representing seven levels of consciousness, are related to the twelve levels of the light body. The twelve levels of the light body relate to the twelve levels of spiritual development beyond the physical, but they relate directly to the star systems, and they relate directly to the seven chakras. The seven chakras take care of the physical aspect.

Then you have seven spiritual or soul chakras that we call the seven gateways of the heart. Those seven gateways are seven levels of consciousness of the soul that bring about the integration into the seven levels of physical consciousness in the seven chakras. When those are awakened and the etheric bridge is built between those seven chakras and those seven gateways, that begins to awaken the endocrine system to reveal the archetypes or the encodements that allow the use of the information of the archetypes of the twelve star systems to bring the planet into ascension in this age.

All of those systems interrelating and awakening simultaneously at various degrees and levels brings about the infusion of the star systems into consciousness physically in the physical world and awakens each person to his or her individual path and contribution to that ascension process and how that all comes together through twelve systems.

J: I can see why we need two thousand years for this.

G: Yes. There's a great deal to be done. For instance, the Book of Revelations in the Christian mythology. When it speaks about the seven seals, what it is speaking about in the breaking of the seven seals is the breaking of the seven etheric seals on the seven chakras, the seven levels of physical consciousness. When it speaks of the seven angels of the seven seals with the seven trumpets, it is speaking of the seven gateways of the heart that connect to the seven physical chakras. The experience of Revelations is a pathway, or it is a step-by-step design to reveal to man the revelation of his awakening to soul consciousness in this age, the Age of Aquarius. It is the personal account of one man's awakening, the man who wrote it down, and he gives the levels step by step. They are encoded in symbols, and when the time is right, those symbols will be revealed.

J: Who wrote the Book of Revelations?

G: The man called John.

J: So is it attributed correctly?

G: More or less. Yes.

J: Assuming we know who John was.

G: Yes. He was a disciple of the Christ. The Book of Revelations is the process of the revelation of the Christ Consciousness. That is through the seven initiations that are integrated into the seven seals of the seven chakras and that awaken the twelve star systems. And it speaks in there of the end of the world. It speaks of Armageddon. Armageddon is what you are going through now. It is the end of history. The end of history is the end of the 26,000-year cycle. That cycle ends in the year 2012. At that time you move out of awareness of past, present, and future linear time and you begin to move into multidimensional awareness on a more conscious level. It ends the experience of evolving through the time/space continuum, through the process of cause and effect, the process of karmic development. And it awakens a time when you move into evolution through conscious soul awareness. It's when the Christ Consciousness is born in the physical on a conscious level.

J: How are things going to be different? Is this something the average person is going to be aware of?

G: To some degree, yes. It all depends on what you do now with your choices. You are at that point right now in your choices as physical beings that determines whether you create a cataclysm on your planet and nuclear destruction or whether you create a new and golden age. This is the point of that decision. And that has been recorded in many cosmologies, including the Egyptian cosmology, the Mayan, and the Incas. It's the end of a 26,000-year cycle, the end of history.

J: What governs that cycle? Is there a cosmic event?

G: The cosmic event is this shift of consciousness that has to do with the awakening of higher consciousness into the energies of the physical plane, your physical solar system.

J: Twenty-six thousand years ago did we shift into a …

G: A new cycle. Yes, you shifted into a different cycle of evolution.

J: Did it have anything to do with the Atlantean or Lemurian civilizations?

G: Yes, it did. What is important at this time is to understand that you are coming to that midpoint. You are coming to the point of the soul crisis, or the dark night of the soul. That is the point where the angel on the threshold meets the angel of presence. The angel on the threshold is the ego lower self. The angel of presence is the soul light. It's where the two meet in awareness, and the soul now imbues the personality with its light and consciousness and takes over the direction of it. But in order to do that, the conflict of duality between the two must be dealt with. That is the Armageddon. The Armageddon is within. And that's what is taking place on your planet right now. That is why you see all the duality around you.

J: If this is the Armageddon, what can or should we all do? The dark forces of duality are controlling the world in such a way that the outcome from all of this could be pretty ominous.

G: What can you all do? Take responsibility for your own reality. Shift yourself out of duality within yourself. Come into the empowerment of your own soul consciousness, and let your light shine in Christ awareness. That then begins a cycle of change, of quantum shift. It produces a ripple effect. That's why we always focus on reminding you of the power of one. You do not have to change the world. You have to change yourself.

As people take responsibility for changing themselves, developing awareness within themselves, they create a collective awareness that shifts the collective consciousness. At some point you create a collective vibration that begins to overpower the lower vibration, creating a quantum shift, a quantum change. It's the hundredth monkey theory. You're probably familiar with it. Are you?

J: OK. What is it?

G: The hundredth monkey theory is a theory of quantum physics. It was developed when scientists discovered on a small island off of China …

J: About monkeys washing the food?

G: Yes. And once one monkey did it and then another and then another, by the time one hundred monkeys did it, the entire kingdom of monkeys throughout the planet instantaneously began to wash their food. That is quantum theory.

J: That reminds me of what was said in the Conversations with God books when it talked about reaching critical mass, which it said required only a small percentage of the population to effect change.

G: Yes. Yes. It's what is spoken of in the Book of Revelations when it speaks of the 144,000--that 144,000 will enter the kingdom of heaven. What they are talking about is the quantum physics theory, the critical mass theory.

J: Some Christians think it means that 144,000 of their holiest will get into heaven.

G: Yes, exactly. They believe only 144,000 will get in. It's interesting, if you divide 144 by twelve what do you get?

J: I don't know. What do you get? Is this a test?

G: Yes. Divide it and see.

J: Twelve.

G: Yes. Interesting isn't it?

J: OK—what's it supposed to tell me?

G: Well, there are twelve star systems. And twelve is the number of transcendence, and it is the number of wholeness. When the twelve star systems awaken in their consciousness, when those archetypes awaken, you will have that quantum shift. It is in the encodement of those numbers. It is also interesting that you have in there the number forty-four. There are forty-four co dens in the connecting sites in the on sites in the DNA molecule that are not connected. This is what the scientists say is the junk DNA. They don't understand it—it's the spiritual DNA.

J: When you say we have to change ourselves first, are you simply saying that when we encounter differences, we should respond with love rather than with hostility?

G: Well, yes, but you cannot do that unless you respond with love instead of hostility in yourself to yourself. Therefore, first you must be at peace with you. You must be at harmony with the you within because you certainly can't be in harmony with the world unless you're in harmony with yourself. Charity begins at home. So, it's important that you integrate you first, that you do your internal process to be at peace with you and awaken the soul in you. Then you can love one another. You can only love one another as you love yourself. If you cannot love yourself, you cannot love one another because you're only having one relationship, and that's a relationship with yourself. And you train others to relate to you by how you relate to yourself.

If you are in duality rather than full acceptance of yourself, how can you possibly be in full acceptance of others? If you're not able to integrate the wholeness of your individuality and respect and honor it and experience the integrity of it, how can you ever possibly expect to do that with the individuality of everyone else? You can't. Therefore, the blueprint begins with you. This was the example of the Christ.

J: I suppose I should know how to do that. Did you have something specific in mind?

G: Yes, you need to deal with all of your past history. Deal with all the traumas and conflicts within you. Deal with everything within yourself that divides you from loving yourself and accepting yourself unconditionally and completely. And you should be able to separate, reveal, and share every part of your being without reservation and without judgment. How many parts of yourself are you able to share? How many parts of yourself are you able to accept? What are the parts of yourself that you hide, that you are ashamed about, that you cannot accept? What feelings within yourself do you find difficult to embrace and accept and respond to? These are all divided parts of yourself, all parts of yourself you've disowned or suppressed or judged or shamed. Do you see? All of that needs to be owned. All of that needs to be brought into integration. All of that needs to be healed.

J: Can we do that alone? Or is that something we have to work with the Robert Bakers of the world to achieve?

G: Well, some people can do it alone, but it's a longer process. It's better to take advantage of people who already have a process that you can utilize, who have tools they can teach you so that you have a tool kit. If you don't have a tool kit, how do you do it? You feel around in the dark until you stumble upon something.

J: I can hardly think of anything more important than to learn how to help myself and others with their process.

G: Exactly. And once you have the tools, and you're able to help yourself with these tools, then you can help others with them as well and pass those tools on. That's what creates that quantum reality, building the resonance.

J: In creating the synthesis of the twelve star systems, you said the divine gave our solar system free will. I assumed God gave everyone freedom of will in all systems. Is that not so?

G: Not all places have freedom of will because not all places need it. Where freedom of will is needed is in a system growing through experience. So not all systems need freedom of will. Some systems are beyond that need. Some systems are no longer living and experiencing through separation, which is what allows you to evolve through experience.

You see, you have to understand that the physical world, as you know it, is an extremely primitive aspect of reality in its evolution. Physical reality is a very dense, low vibrational aspect of reality. Not that it is not valuable. It is of equal value to all other aspects of reality, but it is a primitive stage of evolution. There's a point where you move beyond the physical. Now that's hard to conceive of as a physical being. But you might ask us, what do you mean, Gabriel? How could I possibly find any sense of value in life not attached to the physical? Well, that's the illusion of the physical—the idea that physical reality is the only life form that exists, and without it, there's nothing. In reality, physical reality is one minute aspect of reality as a whole.

J: I thought we were a unique experiment—one that has some import. Now you're saying we're a very primitive form of ...

G: Well, you are, but it still has import. You see, physical reality has evolved through individual species via individual star systems evolving in physical reality by themselves. Through that, each of them has developed a very specific archetype or aspect of evolution. Each part is a part of the consciousness of God evolving physically at that primitive point of evolution called experience. Taking twelve of those systems of experiential evolution and putting them together all in one was a new experience, a new experiment.

It's God saying, let me see how I can take twelve physical levels of evolution of experiential parts of myself and put them all together and see how they all interact and come together by putting them through the same process of evolution. How can all those parts of me commune with and contribute to one another so that in this way I begin to realize more of my wholeness interacting with itself?

J: You said that each one of the star systems that had seeded us had already experienced ascension of the soul.

G: Yes, each experienced that individually.

J: That sounds to me like they were no longer primitive, that they had moved on to a higher level of evolution.

G: Yes. They have. They've gone to the etheric. But then they've decided to incarnate again in physical form for the purpose of contributing what they have to offer through a process of evolution of all twelve together. To do that, they must lose the memory of what they've evolved into and again go through the process of discovery and uncovering. However, this time the twelve are all together to see how they interact and contribute to each other to create a whole within that.

J: As you were describing us as primitive, I couldn't help wondering—why did I choose such a primitive place?

G: Because that's the stage of evolution of your soul development. You chose as a being from a star system that had evolved into ascension. You chose and were chosen to be a part of this grand experiment. Therefore, you said, "Yes, I'll go through that process of evolution if I can do it with eleven other star systems. Think about what I can learn about unity on that level, on a physical level of experience. Nobody has ever done it on a level of physical experience before. They've all done it individually, but they've never done it as a collective."

J: So all of us here made the same decision.

G: That's right. You all decided to evolve again all together through the same process of evolution, but it's not the same process of evolution because it now combines twelve archetypes of evolution to create a unity of twelve archetypes into oneness.

J: You've said our world is now divided into three groups of souls: those who are younger souls who want to keep the status quo, those who want to make a quantum shift in consciousness, and those who are leaving the planet altogether. That seems to be an odd mix of attitudes for people who have chosen to come here.

G: Why is it an odd mix?

J: If they've chosen to come here, why would one third want to leave?

G: Why would one third want to leave? Because they feel they can be of more benefit in the etheric in this evolutionary process. Also, many of them will reincarnate again after a number of years when the one third has evolved the planet to a certain state. And they will be evolving off planet. So they will be working off planet to help out. And they will decide to incarnate again at a certain state of evolution where they will best be served or they can best serve in physical form. Once again, it is the concept of the belief that says, why would they want to leave? Isn't this the most valuable place to be? Shouldn't they be here? What good are they if they leave?

J: What about the younger souls who want to thwart the quantum leap in consciousness and preserve the status quo?

G: They are serving a purpose. They are illustrating to you parts of yourself that still need to be integrated, that are still in duality, that you have not unified the whole consciousness of in your collective intention. So those souls are evolving also. They act as a reminder to illustrate and reflect back to you parts of yourself you have evolved through.

J: All of that makes sense to me. What puzzles me is—why are we running the risk of destroying everything with a potential Armageddon?

G: Because you have freedom of choice. Duality helps to teach you the value of things. It helps to teach you the value of life.

J: But if we blow it all up, there goes the experiment, doesn't it?

G: Well, then, you'll start over.

J: Oh, brother—that sounds like a real drag.

G: Of course it does. Because part of you is only interested in getting to the end result. You're not interested in the process.

J: We're supposed to be enjoying the process, right?

G: That's correct. But you see, you believe: "I have to get it all done right now. I have to get it done and get it perfect. And I can't make a mistake. I don't want to get it wrong. If I get it wrong, I've failed." Instead you should realize that all that's important is the process.

J: Yes, I want everyone to get what you're teaching this week, right away.

G: So there's your challenge. So that's what needs to be healed in you. You see, this process we are doing with you is not just for the purpose of writing a book to help others—it's also for you to evolve your process.

J: I know, you've said that. Much more than I know, I guess.

G: Yes.

J: To change the subject somewhat, religious scholars have attempted to identify the date of the birth of Jesus by trying to figure out what constellation of stars might have looked like a giant bright star. What was the Star of Bethlehem?

G: It was a configuration of planets that were aligned at the particular time that created this star in the heavens. Just as in 1997 there was a configuration of planets that created a six-point star in the heavens that initiated the first stage of initiation on the planet in the new age. It was the Star of Bethlehem January 23, 1997. At that time there was a configuration in the sky that created another Star of Bethlehem. It created a six-point star in a planetary alignment that initiated the birth of the soul or the Christ in matter where all of humanity was concerned. It began the process of planetary initiation.

J: With Jesus, it was in one man. This time it is within all mankind.

G: That is correct.

J: Robert has been talking about this trip to Burma this coming fall [November 2003].

G: Yes.

J: He alluded to yet another star of Bethlehem.

G: Yes, it is a different planetary alignment from the ones that occurred in 1997 and at the birth of Jesus. This particular planetary alignment has not occurred for more than four thousand years and is even more powerful. In 1987, you had a phenomenon called the Harmonic Convergence. This new alignment brings about a phenomenon called the Harmonic Concordance, which is the initiation of ascension into the physical. It brings about the time of the alignment and the awakening between the unconscious and the conscious. It brings the time of the opening of the doorway of the soul in the heart into the lower self. The reason we've chosen Burma is that energetically with its vortexes and its temples, Burma represents the awakening of the unconscious. Therefore, the unconscious can be tapped into in that particular energetic alignment. The time they are doing the journey is when that planetary alignment will take place that brings about the awakening of the soul.

J: So the Star of David that appeared when Christ was born and in 1997 was a different planetary configuration from the one appearing this fall.

G: Yes.

J: The Bible refers to a bright star in the east that the Wise Men followed to visit the Christ child. So was it referring to a bright star or an alignment of stars?

G: The particular alignment created a brightness in the sky. There were certain planets at that time aligned in a certain way with the sun and moon that were particularly evident in the sky, just as when the channel and his group went in 1997 and witnessed that configuration. It appeared as a bright star in the sky because the brightest of the planets at the time, which was Jupiter, was extremely bright in the sky. So it looked like a star.

J: What is the significance of a configuration of stars forming a Star of David?

G: That shape, the two triangles, one imposed over the other, is the physical Merkabah. The Merkabah is the energetic configuration or light body shape that contains physical form. So the activation of the Merkabah awakens the physical Merkabah of the earth plane, and it joins together the spiritual and the physical. You have around you two triangles of light and energy that form the Merkabah. They're pyramids of light intersecting one another. One brings down the force of spirit and aligns it with the force of the physical. Both of them are spinning around you. When they are spinning at a certain degree, it enables them to come together and awaken the force of spirit through the soul in the physical body, in physical consciousness. When that's not happening, they are inanimate or reasonably inanimate; therefore the lower sheaths are able to maintain their separation. When the Merkabah is activated, it creates the ascension process.

J: You've said the seventh ray governs this two-thousand-year cycle.

G: Yes. The seventh ray is the spiritual ray, sometimes called the ceremonial order of magic or the order of ritual.

J: From where do these rays emanate?

G: They emanate from the central sun of your solar system.

J: From our sun?

G: Yes, from your central sun. Your central sun is like the heart chakra of divine mind. It is the planet through which the consciousness of the divine plan enters this solar system. It contains the solar logos, which is the divine plan for the evolution of this particular solar system as it has been unfolding for many billions of years in your time/space continuum. You're now in the last phase of the evolution of this solar system, its ascension, the Earth phase of development.

J: So there has been a Mercury phase, a Venus phase, a Mars phase, etc.?

G: That is correct.

J: Were there sentient beings on these planets in the past?

G: Yes. Yes, there were.

J: So there were life-forms that we would recognize?

G: Yes.

J: And they evolved, and then what?

G: Went to the etheric.

J: So they've all gone through the ascension process.

G: Just as stars, what you see as stars, one time were planets. For instance, the star systems that make up this planetary system, the Sirians, the Arcturians, the Andromedans, the Pliadians, at one time were all physical beings as you know them, not in the same form as you. But they were in various forms of physical density. Once they evolved individually into ascension as individual planets and then moved into light as stars, they chose this experiment. And twelve of them chose to come together through the portal of Sirius and create an experiment of twelve star systems becoming one.

J: If all the planets in our solar system have gone through the ascension process, why didn't they go into light? Why aren't they stars now?

G: Because they've decided to remain in their influence in a particular way related to the density of this planet. This planet is denser than most other planets, and, therefore, it has experienced a longer evolutionary process. Its vibrational progression and the experiential process of that evolution have been longer than some previous planets. This is necessary to enable the twelve star systems to realize the evolution of ascension on this planet for this time.

J: Because it would be a longer process?

G: That's right.

Chapter 4:

Ascendant Masters/Evolution/ Awakening of the Soul

J: You've said stars are planets that have gone through the ascension process.

G: Yes, they are now in the etheric process.

J: I assume that has happened countless times.

G: Yes.

J: So the process of repeating the ascension process, I gather, is God's way of experiencing himself?

G: Yes. It is the divine plan in operation. In a larger sense, God is doing the same thing you are, constantly evolving, constantly becoming more of the realization of itself. Creation, God, the universe is infinite. It has no beginning, and it has no end.

J: And so that process of ascension is going to be the process we follow into eternity?

G: Up to a certain point where physical matter is concerned. After you have ascended physical matter, then you move into a new dimension of the divine plan that deals simply with the causal plane, the soul plane, which is consciousness still dealing with itself through the experience, expectation, and expression of individuality, but without matter, without physical form. Then at a point, you move beyond the causal plane, soul consciousness, where the soul is no longer needed. That is when you move out of individuation entirely and you move into the communal oneness of being.

J: Is that your level of consciousness?

G: No. That is returning to the God force completely. There is no more individuation. The parts of God become as one with God. They are no longer separated through the concept of individuality or separation. But that is a concept that cannot be even grasped except in an intellectual sense by physical reality (mankind). Physical reality has not yet even realized individuality.

J: What do you mean?

G: Man has substituted separation and duality for individuality.

J: You mean we don't see that we're part of each other?

G: Exactly. And you don't see the value of the individual fragmentation of each and every expression of the parts of God. You separate yourselves from each other and defend yourselves in that separation from each other. Therefore, you live your life isolated within yourselves to a greater or lesser degree depending upon your personal development.

J: I remember reading in one of the Conversations with God books where Jesus said, "Love one another as you would yourself ..." and God finished the sentence, "because it is yourself."

G: Yes. We would also say, love one another as you would yourself. You can only love another as you are able to love yourself. What you cannot accept and embrace within yourself, you will not be able to accept and embrace in another. So, if you are not able to accept and embrace all parts of yourself, how are you going to accept and embrace all parts of the individual whole?

J: We have talked about the therapy people such as Robert and Ron Baker are conducting that help us accept all aspects of ourselves.

G: Exactly. That is your journey.

J: I believe it would be helpful if we could give people as clearly as possible a sense of what the ascension process looks like. In a previous conversation, you said the ascendant mastery was responsible for containing, governing, and taking care of the codes of the universe. You talked about the master plan of the twelve star systems coming together in the experience of ascendancy on earth. I thought a good place to start would be to talk about the ascendant masters. Are they guiding this process?

G: Yes, they are. It is like a council that has a plan. Equate it with your United Nations. You have within that (divine plan) a process that is called the divine plan for a solar system consisting of stages of evolution into oneness. The ascendant mastery is responsible for putting into operation on an etheric level, within the soul consciousness, the operation of that divine plan in its evolutionary process. It is responsible for influencing the movement of that divine plan where the evolution of matter and man are concerned. It governs physical evolution, but also soul evolution and the way that eventually fits into returning to the heart of oneness or the heart of God—completing the journey, so to speak, for each solar system, for each galaxy, for each universe. For there are many universes within the wholeness of the universe, many galaxies, many stars, many solar systems, many planets.

A particular ascendant mastery governs what is called the solar logos for this immediate solar system. Think of the sun that governs this solar system—that brings the light, the energy, and the life force into the solar system—as the heart chakra of the God force that contains the divine plan for the solar system. The ascendant mastery takes that divine plan and breaks it down and applies it to the soul plane, which is how that plan will evolve through individual experience, through the pieces and parts of God evolving together in physical incarnation. Those soul notes then take on physical form and evolve through many, many incarnations and cycles of evolution until they get to the final stage of physical evolution, which is the stage of this two-thousand-year cycle.

This two-thousand-year cycle is the ascension evolution that every solar system and every planet in matter goes through at one point or another in its evolution. You're at that more advanced point in your evolution now where you begin to no longer evolve through cause and effect, no longer through karmic development, no longer through trial and error, because they represent the evolution through duality, through separation.

Now you make a transition to the next phase. You have evolved as separate beings. Now you come into the evolutionary cycle where you begin consciously to realize the connection to your divinity. Therefore, the first stage of this cycle requires coming into the knowledge of your wholeness within yourself as an individual. It requires that you individuate guided by your soul consciousness and your oversoul consciousness. That process that is taking place on the planet Earth is guided by the ascendant mastery guiding the planetary logos, which is the soul plan of evolution for this planet and for this two-thousand-year cycle of soul evolution.

As you enter this two-thousand-year cycle, you stop operating through cause and effect and you begin to operate through resonant causation. You begin to resonate with the essence of your being as you contact your individuality. As you begin to operate through resonant causation, you bring into consciousness and into the physical experience the radiatory light of the soul. The God consciousness of which the soul represents a fragment begins to radiate forth from the core of the being of each physical individual. As that takes place, that radiation of light goes through several stages of development. As you enter this evolutionary cycle, physical growth no longer takes place through duality. Physical growth now takes place through conscious evolution as a spiritual being, which means you come into a cycle of spiritual initiation.

This spiritual initiation is the process of mastering the physical vehicle, preparing it and raising its vibration to a vibratory rate where the physical body and the soul body can awaken as one within each other—where the etheric body joins and communes consciously with the physical body, where the vibratory rate of the physical body matches the vibratory rate of the soul. This is the Christ Consciousness. The Christ Consciousness is soul consciousness. The one Jesus the Christ who initiated the imprint of these initiations two thousand years ago into the earth plane was the example. He was the master who illustrated through the life of a man called Jesus the conscious development of these seven stages of soul evolution, the seven initiations: the birth, the baptism, the transfiguration, the renunciation, the crucifixion, the resurrection, and the ascension. And so he left the imprint in the consciousness of the earth plane and humanity.

J: You have referred many times to Jesus leaving an imprint. Was that an energetic phenomenon?

G: Yes. He left the imprint energetically in the consciousness of mankind and also in the illustration of the step-by-step process of how to do it in how he lived and evolved his own life as a physical being. So he left the instructions. If you read the information in the Christian mythology called the Bible, you will see the step-by-step instructions of that initiation process in the evolution of his life.

J: So the Bible would have to have been divinely inspired in order for that message to be preserved for mankind?

G: Of course.

J: It's just that the Bible has been challenged on so many levels because of the translations and so on.

G: Well, there are a lot of distortions in it, and there are a lot of distortions in how people interpret it. For instance, as recorded by one man who wrote down his own individual experience of that process, the Book of Revelations is a forecast for the plan of how that initiation process awakens in the physical body. How it awakens the seven chakra system, how it awakens the seven gateways of the heart. It's all in the Book of Revelations, step by step how to do it. In the last thirteen years, we've been giving the information through the channel for breaking the code.

J: That sounds pretty profound to me. This would be as momentous as anything in spiritual history.

G: Yes. Well, it is. It is the time of the return of the Christ. And that return of the Christ is not a man coming to rescue you. That man came and left the imprint. That was his gift. That was the divine exemplification of his gift to humankind. He left a plan, left a blueprint. But you see, most people in their consciousness are still children waiting for Daddy to rescue them. They say, "I'm waiting for the Christ to rise me up. I'm waiting for Jesus." They are waiting for Jesus, the man, to come back. Did not Jesus, the man, say many times in the scriptures, "Do not worship me, but worship my Father who is in heaven"?

J: Since this is such an extraordinary time and such an important experience, I would think Robert must stand out as being as significant as any prophet mentioned in the Bible. Is he another Moses?

G: Well, yes, in that sense. All good teachers are.

J: Well, it's kind of nice to know I was hugged by Moses yesterday.

G: All good teachers who dedicate their lives to service are examples of the Christ Consciousness. They are attempting to embody that process and be teachers of that process. But it's not about idolizing them or worshiping them—it's about taking the information and using it in the best possible way that you can for your own evolution, to see the gift and to use it. Because every man has that within him, but it depends upon how much of it wakens, and how conscious and aware the person is.

The channel happens to be a soul who has reached a rather high evolution in his soul development. Therefore, he is at a stage of evolution in this lifetime where he is able to bring through the information, to understand it and teach it. So that is his life path. But, as with all life paths, when you are chosen, you must also choose. So it is a constant process of choosing, and in that choosing is how you redeem your own self, your own process. So the teacher is the student, and the student is the teacher. Jesus, the Christ, was not without his struggles as he evolved consciously from stage to stage in his evolution.

Remember, he spent thirty years as a student. He spent three years teaching.

J: He was an ascendant master, was he not?

G: Yes, he ascended in his lifetime in the physical. He became a master.

J: He wasn't an ascended master who was governing the evolutionary process who came down to earth? He wasn't one of the ascended masters before he came?

G: The Christ Consciousness is the ascendant master. Jesus embraced the teachings of that ascendant master and became a master. He mastered that process of fully awakening the divine within the physical. When the soul is awakened in the physical body, the divine is awakened in the physical. And that is what he accomplished. He became an awakened soul, and, therefore, he mastered physical reality.

J: Earlier I read to you the statement you made that the ascendant masters were responsible for maintaining, governing, and taking care of the mysteries of the universe.

G: Yes.

J: And you said that ascendant masters had come to the earth as Buddha and ...

G: And as Jesus the Christ.

J: I guess I understood that to mean that entities that already were ascendant masters came to earth at critical stages in earth's evolution.

G: What you are confusing is the personality of Jesus, the man, with the ascendant master of the Christ. Jesus was a man who evolved through the consciousness of the ascendant master, the Christ. So he became a channel for the Christ Consciousness. And through that he evolved into self-mastery.

J: Was that true of others such as Buddha?

G: Yes.

J: I think of Buddha, Krishna, Jesus, and Mohammed as being the great spiritual figures of scripture. Were they all ascended masters?

G: They became masters in the process of being taught through the ascended mastery. In other words, they were channels for a master.

J: So they followed the same process as Jesus.

G: Yes. You see, the man Jesus, if he had not connected to the Christ Consciousness, would never have become a master. But because of his level of soul development, he was at a point of vibration where he could connect to and be guided by the ascended master, the Christ.

Therefore, he became the embodiment of that ascended master. So the process of his life through the levels of initiation was the preparation of his physical body for the full claiming of the knowledge of the master who moved through him or spoke through him or he embodied, that he channeled through him.

J: And as you said, it was the same experience of Buddha, Krishna, and Mohammed.

G: Yes, in different ways.

J: You have spoken about the role Buddha played and the role Jesus played. Is there a simple way to describe how the coming of each one of the ascended masters was part of the process that helped the spiritual evolution of man?

G: Yes. Buddha represented the height of development of the mental evolution of humanity at that time to prepare him for opening the passageway to receive spirit. The Christ, in the next stage of development, prepared the physical vehicle for the awakening of the soul that the individual could contact and exemplify.

J: Did it have to be the mental first?

G: Yes, because it is the higher mental body, the crown chakra, that must be opened in order for spirit to penetrate and guide the consciousness awakening in the soul. Then the Christ brought about the awakening of the soul body to bring spirit into individual consciousness. And he did that through the awakening of the love force, the love force being the soul force, the force of spiritual individuation realized.

J: I noticed you only mentioned Buddha and Jesus in this process. Were there others who were important?

G: There are others who are important, but not that important from the point of view of the physical plane. They operate more in the etheric plane, and they take care of different facets of the evolutionary development of the solar system based upon that plane. In other words, they handle energetic grids. They initiate vortexes of learning and energy. They initiate astrological information from the other planets that have evolved into the etheric, and they plan the way in which the information awakens periods of evolution that are necessary, different planetary influences, that sort of thing. So a lot of that is done in the etheric. The reason we concentrate on the Buddha and the Christ, particularly the Christ, is because it's the most recent one, because the Christ is representative of the preparation for this age, the age you are in now.

J: There are millions of people who worship Krishna and Mohammed.

G: It's all the same information.

J: Well, their followers would feel they are as important as Jesus.

G: Krishna is an ancient teaching of mastery that prepared a certain portion of the world to raise the overall dominant consciousness of that time. The value of Krishna is that it combined the archetypes of the natural world and helped man to understand the power of the natural world exemplifying through its archetypes the principles of spirit. That's why where the teachings of Krishna are concerned, you have the many different Indian gods that are all representative of different aspects of the natural world as spiritual facets or phases of spiritual development. That was the value of the Krishna then. It no longer has the same value because man has evolved beyond his need to worship the archetypes of the physical world in order to understand his spiritual being.

Now the worship has gone to an internal place. The Christ takes it within, connects it directly to the core of being, the spiritual consciousness within. This age takes you from the external focus of the world to the internal focus so you begin to understand how reality is created. You begin to understand that reality is created in the nonphysical realms by the direction of energy through the intentions of the mind and the emotions.

What are the watchwords of the day? Everybody is talking about energy. His energy is good or bad. Talking about moving with energy, healing with energy, positive thinking, learning how to direct the mind through the power of thought. That is an indication of moving inward to the source, as are all the new thought movements in the last century—the Church of the Science of Mind, Christian Science, Unity, all these different churches that have to do with the evolutionary process of thought. You see, that's the moving inward to the mental, the realization of the mental's part in creation.

The newest realization awakening now is of the way the emotional body creates reality because, after all, it is essential to feel in order to contact the soul. When you understand all the energetics that make up life in your physical body, when you understand the function of the emotional body in its soul form, then you will have command of the forces of the universe, the forces of creation. And then, as Jesus the Christ did, you will direct those forces through the divine plan related to the individual part played in that divine plan by your soul consciousness.

J: One of the big conflicts in our world is between Islam and Christianity. Islam is connected to Mohammed. You haven't mentioned him. What was Mohammed's role as an ascendant master?

G: To unify a certain portion of the world and to bring about the concept of inner and outer as a part of the same thing. So while Krishna before him taught people about the spirit that lives in the archetypes of nature and the worship of those gods as archetypes, Mohammed began the process of bringing the understanding of the inner and the outer and how they affect one another. He also began to bring about the understanding of the need for the purification of the physical form and raising its vibration for the exemplification of the God force or the expression of the God force.

J: Isn't that what Jesus did?

G: Not in the same way, but as a beginning. Each master who has taught through the ages has taught according to the overall level of evolution of the dominant consciousness of humanity at that particular time. Remember also that each two-thousand-year cycle is governed by an astrological symbol. Therefore, that astrological symbol is a way in which the etheric masters are using the astrological influence to hold into place a certain evolutionary force. In the last two thousand years, you had the Piscean Age. That's why you have so many symbols of fish in your Christian Bible and in the teachings of Christ.

The Piscean Age is represented by two fish swimming in opposite directions. These represent the lower and the higher self that are in opposition to one another, that are evolving through duality. So the higher and the lower selves in the last two-thousand-year cycle have been evolving in duality. Now you have evolved to a state where in this age the two can join together in the Age of Aquarius, which is represented by the water bearer, balancing the emotional body to bring about unity. The Aquarian Age is the age of unity, with the water bearer carrying the two buckets of water in balance. The balance of the emotional body will bring about the awakening of the soul, which is the experiential aspect of spirit or God that now awakens in the Aquarian Age.

J: There's such an unfortunate conflict between some of the followers of Mohammed and some followers of Christianity and Judaism.

G: There is no conflict. The conflict lies in the way in which the people have distorted the ideology into duality. At their root, they all say the same thing, and they've all been saying it for thousands of years: Love one another. Love one another. Buddha said it. Krishna said it. Mohammed said it. Christ said it. We are saying it. Love one another as you love yourself. You can only love one another as you are able to love yourself. Until you are able to love yourself, you cannot love one another. As long as you are separated from yourself, you will be separated from one another. There's nothing out there. The only relationship you're having is one with yourself. There is only one God.

J: Is this spiritual ascendancy going to happen with all souls during this two-thousand-year period?

G: Yes, all souls, eventually. You are just in the embryonic stage.

J: What's going to happen at the end of the period? Will we go into light?

G: That depends on you. It depends on whether you are able to embody soul consciousness in the physical. If you can embody it in the physical, then you can choose whether you want to continue in the physical or not. You will have the choice. You will be able to leave the physical or come back to the physical. You will be able to create a body at will or discard that body at will.

J: Each individual soul?

G: Yes.

J: What about the collective experience on earth?

G: It depends upon the evolution of the consciousness and how the souls use this cycle, whether they are able to raise their vibration to a point where they no longer need a physical container for their soul's experience. Then they will go into light.

J: That seems pretty challenging for that to take place in just two thousand years. Would another age follow this one?

G: That depends on you. You see, the speed of your evolution depends on how you use your freedom of choice. The imprint, the plan, is there. How you access and guide yourself through that plan consciously determines the speed at which you evolve. Remember, you are evolving in a belief in time/space. In reality, it has already happened.

J: In the eternal moment of now?

G: Yes, in reality it already has taken place. Past, present, and future are all one. There is no difference. There is no separation. They exist as dimensions in consciousness in time and space. So, in reality, you have already evolved, but in physical three dimensional experience, you have not. You see, it's not as if you're discovering anything. You're simply remembering. You are God remembering yourself in physical form. You are regaining your memory of what you already know. You are awakening your memory as you gradually evolve your ability to remember.

J: In one of your lectures you made this statement about our current times: "It is the time when the divine will, the spiritual energy of creation, takes over and creates a process on your planet that is known as the ascension process." Could you explain what you mean by "it's the time when the divine takes over"?

G: In every evolutionary process where the ascension of matter is concerned, there comes a point in the evolution of that process where that particular planetary configuration reaches a point of development or evolution where they (a planet's inhabitants) are ready for the stage called ascension.

Once they are ready for the stage called ascension, then they are ready to receive the divine plan consciously. Up to that point they've been operating through the divine plan unconsciously. In other words, they've been operating through trial and error. They've been growing and evolving through cause and effect and through karma. Karma means action and reaction. In other words, you make a choice. It produces a consequence. There is a reaction. You take in that reaction. You respond or react to that reaction, and you make choices accordingly. That is a process of growing through trial and error. It's more experiential. And this is a necessary process for physical matter to evolve under its own experience.

Eventually it gets to a certain point of evolutionary sophistication where it is ready to handle more consciousness. Therefore, it is ready to begin to consciously perceive aspects of the divine plan. It is ready to evolve into soul consciousness. That means it is ready to bring the soul light into consciousness so that it can start to access aspects of the divine plan. It is ready to begin to realize the meaning, purpose, and value of life related to an overall arc or plan that is governed by the whole, governed by the order of the universe, or governed by God.

Unless humanity has reached a point where it is capable of that, it is not yet capable of using the power. So it must first learn to evolve to a certain state in its lower self where the vibration of the lower self is now capable of consciously handling the vibration of the soul. That is when the planet begins to learn about the love force, what love is. Until the planet learns what the love force is and connects that love force to the sexual force—which is simply related to the movement, evolution, and reproduction of physical matter—until it has reached that point of physical evolution where it's ready to learn to love, it cannot awaken the soul. It's necessary to open the heart and awaken the soul, awaken the force of love, before man is in a space or place where he is capable of using the power of divine will, the power of the divine plan.

The power of the divine plan develops when he can access the power of the divine mind and then direct it through the erotic force consciously because that is the power of creation itself. Until he has developed a conscience of the soul, developed a conscience of responsibility for the reality he is creating by learning how to love—that means learning the purpose, meaning, and value of life—he is not ready for the power of the divine plan. He is not ready to consciously direct the power of the divine will as a God creator force.

As he comes into this the ascension stage of evolution, he comes to a point where he is ready to learn those things. He is ready to transform the lower self. He is ready to awaken the Christ or soul consciousness by learning how to love. Once he has learned how to love, he then has developed the conscience he needs to know how to use power in a creative way for the good of the evolution of the species through the divine plan. He is ready to use the power of manifestation and to take responsibility for it and not misuse it—that is, not use it to control, destroy, or misdirect life. Instead he must use it to honor all life, to hold in sacredness all life, and to infuse life with more life, to introduce life to its concept of omniscience, omnipresence, and infinite being.

That point is now coming to awakening, which is just the tip of the iceberg, so to speak. Man has now reached a state in his evolution, a crisis point, a soul crisis, a dark night of the soul, in his final struggle with duality to end the system of duality. The duality is the split or the schism between matter and spirit. What produces the joining of those forces of matter and spirit, physical and spirit, is the awakening of the soul, the awakening of the love force.

Man is now ready for that awakening—and thus the awakening will now begin. Now the planet will begin the Christing process through the process called initiation. He will be born. He will experience the birth initiation. He has already experienced the first levels of it. He will experience the purification process, the baptism. He is now in that baptism process.

He will experience the transfiguration, which is the time when the lower self and higher self are introduced to one another and the soul takes over and transforms the lower self. He has reached the top of a mountain and the lower self has bowed down to the soul, and the soul now governs the personality. Then he can come back down off the mountain through the renunciation, which is when he renounces the lower will completely and surrenders fully to soul consciousness in a place of purpose and service to the world. This is when the Christ began his service after the transfiguration. The renunciation, "Thy will not mine be done."

Then comes the crucifixion when matter surrenders to spirit and spirit surrenders to matter. That is the place when the divine plan is revealed to the soul and the soul takes its place in the divine plan for service to humanity. Then the resurrection takes place, and the soul is born fully in its light. It completely takes over the physical being, and then he is ready for the ascension.

The ascension transcends matter as an individual experience of separation, isolation, and duality. He then becomes the Christed one. He becomes the living, breathing light of the soul consciousness guided by spirit, God force, in every moment of his life. He then has the power of God in his hands to transform all mankind.

J: All of these initiations have been activated?

G: They have all been activated. This is the purpose of the sacred journeys the channel and his partner have been taking around the planet, going to various sacred sites at times we have selected so he could take advantage of certain planetary configurations that bring in a particular stage of initiation at a particular sacred site whose alignment is geared at the particular time to the planetary configuration.

J: I would guess the initiations affect people differently depending on their level of consciousness.

G: Of course.

J: There are only a relative handful of people who are conscious of it.

G: All are affected, but they are affected by varying degrees of density. If they are affected in such a way where they are unconscious, then for many of them it just seems as though they are being victimized by something. If they are operating consciously, they can use the energies to be able to direct their path in a spiritual direction for their spiritual evolution. And then there are those where the heat is too hot in the kitchen, so to speak. So they'll be doing it off planet. They'll be leaving the planet by the millions.

J: So it will be important to try to engage those who choose to understand what is unfolding here in the process consciously. That's the challenge.

G: That's the challenge because, you see, the masses as a whole are not all at the level of soul evolution that approximately one third of the planet is at. But all you need is that one third to create a quantum shift.

J: Actually, we don't need that many, do we?

G: No, there's resonant causation, or the hundredth monkey. Once you create a collective mass, a collective consciousness, to some degree it begins a ripple effect. This, for instance, is the reason we send the channel and his friend on these journeys to sacred sites, because in doing so, they can create a ripple effect. This is true because they plan a worldwide meditation around it, and they alert people all over the world to tune in at that particular time when they are meditating for the world. That mass consciousness joins together while they are in a particular sacred site.

Now, why the particular sacred site? Such a site accelerates the degree or refinement of the vibration and connects with certain lei lines of the planet. It sends the energy out when the consciousness of the planet in various parts of the world is focused on that site with them. That is the focus of intention. That is the quantum effect. That is like the particle called the quark. Wherever you focus the intention, the energy moves.

J: With regard to the ascension process, I would like to learn more about the energetic forces that are coming in to facilitate the whole process. Isn't that part of what is going on when you say it is the time when the divine will takes over?

G: Yes.

J: Let's take it a step at a time as we explore the effect of the various energetic forces so that we can keep the discussion as clear as possible. In one of your lectures, you talk about the archetypal mind of each of the twelve star systems that seeded us and their influences on our development. You state that each of the twelve astrological signs is the seed of a star code that has been unlocking in our system through the planets in our solar system helping us with their energetic and consciousness influence. That strikes me as being a powerful ongoing source of different kinds of energy.

G: Yes, most definitely. You see, as the planets move and change their configuration within the solar system, it produces certain alignments. Those alignments produce certain influences from the various star systems as they come into alignment with one another. For people born under a certain sign, that sign can be related to a particular star system, either their star system or a star system with which they are aligned in some way that they need to awaken or learn about as part of their evolution.

Let's say you're a Scorpio, and in your lifetime Cancers have a tremendous influence on you. Cancer is related to another star system. Why would you have the influence of so many people in your life related to the sign of Cancer? The influence is there because of the configuration when you were born that your soul chose because those were the influences you needed in order to balance the growth process—the way the growth process of your life operates through the influences of that particular star system in relationship to your own. So, in a lifetime it may be that you need to interrelate more with the archetype, the traits, of that star system to learn more or awaken more of it within your own behaviors. Remember, each person was born under a star system originally. Over the millennia, you have interbred with other star systems and produced a whole twelve endocrine system, if you will, that holds the encoding of all the star systems.

In order for each person to ascend and for the whole planet to ascend, all the star systems have to be fully awakened in all the persons who are within each of those star systems. Therefore, all the Librans have to awaken, all the Sirians, etc. All the information of the archetypes has to awaken in each and every individual to experience the fullness of that ascension. So that is why through various incarnations you will have influences and awakenings from other star systems that will accelerate the process of wakening the codes of that star system within you in preparation for the time when you are ready for the integration of all the information of all the archetypes. Does that make sense?

J: Yes, it does. So all of these influences are now contributing to the age in which we now find ourselves?

G: Yes. And Aquarius is the dominant symbol of the age. It is related to the star system of the ascendant mastery that is more or less in charge of what you might refer to as the council, the council that is instituting the plan. Therefore in this age, the star system related to Aquarius is the one that is predominantly guiding the work with all the other star systems where the ascendant mastery is concerned to bring this ascension process into a successful awakening, fruition, and integration.

J: This council—what is that?

G: Each of the star systems is related to the government of the ascendant mastery. An ascendant master, who is the most advanced being chosen from each star system as a representative, is one of the masters in the governing body of the twelve star systems of the ascendant mastery. So you have a representative from each star system, sort of like your United Nations. Each ascendant master is related to a particular star system in the governing body that is responsible for the institution of the solar monad.

The solar monad is the entire plan for the solar system. It is related to the sun. Think of the sun as the central spiritual sun, as the encodement of the divine plan in your solar system—how (the divine plan) is poured into your solar system, how it awakens the codes within the different planets and their alignment with one another in varying degrees at various times, and how it is downloaded from the sun into the solar monad. That plan for the solar system is then configured through the various star systems. The ascendant mastery uses the various planets and the various star systems as beacons or magnetic points of energy where information is encoded to be released at certain times when they align with one another and with the planet Earth.

Therefore, during certain astrological cycles, various encodements of the solar monad—the divine plan in its evolutionary plan—are downloaded through the planets and encoded into the planet Earth. Through two-thousand-year cycles, a different code of evolution is released into the earth plane, into the planetary monad. The planetary monad is the band of energy, the band of DNA, surrounding the planet Earth that holds the memory of the Akashic record of the evolution of all the cycles of the Earth and all of the living organisms of the Earth. It is the oversoul of the Earth's evolutionary plan.

As a new cycle is downloaded from the solar monad into the planetary monad, it then becomes triggered in the band of DNA and is released from the Akashic record as a particular planet evolution for the next two-thousand-year cycle. And then it begins the influence energetically and consciousness-wise of that cycle in the physical beings that are inhabiting the planet for their evolution.

J: Wow! To be able to describe something as complex as that as clearly as you did. It's wonderful.

G: Well, that's how it works. It's both simple and extremely complex. So the ascendant mastery is in charge of their part in that divine plan to see that it is configured correctly and instituted according to their watchful eyes as to how well humanity is working with it. They will create influences to shift and change various events to bring humanity to a certain point where they will ready themselves for the next part of the evolutionary cycle. They create shifts in the DNA band, which creates shifts in the mutational process of physical reality on the earth, including the consciousness and evolution of human beings. So that is how the ascendant mastery is in charge of instituting the divine plan.

J: So they direct the evolution of everything on earth.

G: That is correct. They direct the evolution of each two-thousand-year cycle. They have the overall plan where the process and progress of evolution as a whole needs to start and where and how it needs to finish. Then, working with each evolutionary cycle, they make as much happen as they can. But understand also that the divine has given all of humanity freedom of will so that the evolution of self, self-development, can be consciously chosen so that mankind can learn through experience. As you come to the point of evolution that you have now, where you're now prepared to deal with more divine power on a conscious level, evolution will no longer operate so much through cause and effect as a survival process.

You're now shifting into quantum physics. You're shifting into the idea of maintaining a quantum field of energy and operating through resonant causation rather than cause and effect. Resonant causation is when humanity evolves through knowing and is able to maintain and sustain a certain vibration and frequency overall to shift evolution consciously rather than through unconscious choice.

J: So our experience will be created through resonant causation.

G: Yes. And that's what you're shifting into at the moment. You are in the conflict between cause and effect, duality and resonant causation, spirit.

J: To create critical mass, to begin to add some momentum to the shift …

G: You have been doing that, particularly since 1987 in the Harmonic Convergence.

J: My next question was going to be about the Harmonic Convergence.

G: Yes. The Harmonic Convergence was a five-year period that started in 1987 in which the consciousness of the earth was blocked from the development of the consciousness of humanity. So humanity was developing and raising its consciousness independent of the earth so that it [humanity's consciousness] couldn't influence the movements of the earth. This gave humanity a chance to achieve a quantum catch-up in consciousness, because at that point in their choices, humanity was at a stage where they were in the process of destroying the planet.

J: Was the confrontation between the Soviet Union and the United States a part of that?

G: Yes.

J: Was that when communism began to disintegrate?

G: That's when the Berlin Wall was brought down and all that sort of thing. It was a time when you became more aware of spiritual development, of tremendous awakening, a time that heralded what they called a new age. You started seeing New Age materials, books coming out on channeling, self-help, and all that. That started it all. That was a five-year period of acceleration of consciousness. After that period, the consciousness of earth and humanity reconnected.

J: Did we achieve a quantum jump in consciousness?

G: Yes. You created a quantum shift. Then you began a seven-year cycle after that, 1992-98, a cycle of awakening. Each year had a specific purpose in that seven-year period that then brought you to a three-year cycle of purification. That three-year cycle of purification ended last year [2002]. During the three-year cycle, a tremendous releasing of kundalini energy occurred from the core of the earth. That began a purification process creating tremendous shifts in weather patterns and a cleansing within the emotional body of human beings, who started to become much more emotionally aware. As they did, the medical community accelerated the use of drugs trying to balance those emotions and shut them back down.

The year 2002 began a new seven-year cycle for the preparation of the healing of duality. It brings about a process of healing the lower self and the revealing of the soul, the joining of the lower self and the higher self, the soul and the physical, the soul and the personality.

J: When you say the healing of duality …

G: Ending duality—creating reality through opposite poles, through wrong and right, good and bad. Being able to embrace all experience without judgment, without separating it into right and wrong, good and bad. Right and wrong, good and bad, negative and positive, are something you create. It's not something God has created. The last two-thousand-year cycle on the planet, the Age of Pisces, was the age of duality. It was a two-thousand-year cycle during which man learned through the separation between his lower and his higher self through the pairs of opposites. He developed through trial and error, through the extremes of duality, between the emotional and the mental, between the physical and spirit. The two fish, the Piscean symbol, swimming in opposite directions, as we have explained many

100

times, are representative of the separation between the lower and the higher self.

In the last two-thousand-year cycle, the Christ was born to begin the healing of the emotional body to show people how to love. His message was love one another. Loving one another can only be possible through the awakening of the heart, only through the awakening of feelings until you can experience the feeling of communion in the heart of humanity, as only then are you then ready to release duality.

J: In discussing the energetic forces that are influencing our evolution at this time, you have referred to a 26,000-year cycle of the revolution of our solar system around a central sun in the Pleiadian System. What is that about?

G: The 26,000-year cycle ends in 2012. It is a galactic cycle connected to the Mayan calendar. The end of the 26,000-year cycle is the end of history as you have known it. Some people interpret it as the end of the world just as they interpret the Book of Revelations as the end of the world. It is the end of humanity's evolution through cause and effect. It is the time in which humanity shifts more fully into resonant causation. It's when you shift more readily into conscious connection with soul awareness, soul consciousness, and more awareness of being connected to a spirit that unifies all creation, connected to the cosmic forces of oneness. It is the end of consciousness as you have known it. So it's the end of a cycle. It's a beginning of a new world, a new cycle that brings about a new root race of human kind, the development of the spiritual being.

J: So that is another way that the divine is taking over and creating this ascension process.

G: That is correct.

J: You stated in one of your lectures that in 1994, a vortex opened where Sirius began to send feminine energies needed to help balance a world system of patriarchy.

G: That is correct. Sirius is the gateway to your solar system. It is the gateway from other star systems and other solar systems. Sirius acts as a vortex, a gateway in time and space. The Sirian system is the gateway through which all twelve star systems traveled into this dimension when your planet was originally seeded. It is the gateway of the divine feminine, which means it is the gateway of the soul. The Sirian system is also the system that has trained many ascendant masters. It is sort of a gateway or an initiation through which many of the ascendant masters have passed.

The ascendant master, the Christ, was educated in the Sirian system and passed through the Sirian gateway before he became an ascendant master. You see, the ascendant master Christ is not the man Jesus the Christ. Jesus the Christ embodied the mastery of Christ. That means he embodied, he became, a master through the Christ Consciousness, through the teachings of the ascendant mastery of the Christ. Do you see?

The Christ Consciousness is the awareness and it is the job, so to speak, of the Christ to awaken the awareness of the soul. The Christ Consciousness is the ascendant master who awakens the awareness of the soul in physical matter. Therefore, it awakens the connecting point between spirit and matter, the physical. So he is the one, so to speak, who trains you, carries the information energy to awaken that within you. Jesus the Christ was the physical embodiment of the Christ Consciousness and became Jesus, the Christ, man of the soul. So he embodied the teachings of mastery of the Christ Consciousness.

Jesus the Christ taught about the awakening of the heart, which is where the soul awakens. He taught about the divine feminine because until you awaken the emotional body, you cannot awaken the soul. The emotional is the feminine. He worked with the ascendant mastery from the Sirian system, which is the vortex that opens the solar system to the divine plan.

J: You said that Jesus taught about the divine feminine and linked that to the awakening of the heart and the soul. These wars the United States is engaged in, I would guess, reflect the patriarchal system.

G: They are the extremes of duality acting out of the physical objectification of the world. They are simply mirroring what is going on inside, the wounded child inside of each and every one of you. What happens in the collective is mirrored in the microcosm. As long as there is duality within between the mental and the emotional, between matter and spirit, between the inner child and the adult, between the divine feminine and the divine masculine, until soul and spirit are joined together in the physical, you will see the duality acted out in the world. What you are seeing right now is the battle between the patriarchy of the masculine as it has been interpreted for power and control in its distortion. You're seeing the ultimate acting out of its distortion and its denial of the divine feminine.

J: Are we in a period of healing of that?

G: That's what you're going through right now. You're going through the healing.

J: We don't know how it will end up.

G: That's entirely up to you.

J: If we're going through a healing, wouldn't all these energies aid in the healing process?

G: You are going through the healing process. You are being given all the energies needed to be able to create the balance. You will create the balance according to your choice. You will either create it through pain and suffering, or you will create it through divine grace and inspiration. The more of you who choose divine grace, inspiration, and acceptance rather than resistance, the easier it will be. That is where freedom of choice comes into it. It's man who creates pain, not God. Man creates pain through duality. Duality is created through holding onto the past. The wounded child within is the child who holds onto the past, all the past emotional memories of trauma in its experience that created its defense patterns, and it then has to defend itself against the world.

J: I would like to continue discussing the energies contributing to the ascension process. The next event was one we have discussed before, the July 1994 collision of the Shoemaker/Levy comet with Jupiter. That was a major cosmic event.

G: Yes, it was. As the Shoemaker/Levy comet collided with Jupiter, it released in the gaseous atmosphere of Jupiter an explosion of Jupiter's emotional body. It represented the birth of the cosmic Christ, the birth of the soul body in the solar system, the birth of the Christ Consciousness in the solar system. The birth of the Christ Consciousness in the solar system was created through the release of the mystery codes in the moon of Io, one of the moons of Jupiter. The codes of self-mastery, the mystery codes of the universe, were held there that began a process of releasing information to prepare humanity for the initiation process.

The initiation process then came about as scheduled at the beginning of the New Age in 1997 and began to affect the earth. It took that long for the information and energy to travel through the cosmos, through the various alignments, and to begin to be made manifest in the earth energetically and consciousness wise.

J: You said the birth of this new Age of Aquarius was January 23, 1997. And you said it was heralded by the appearance of the configuration of the Star of David, a six-planet configuration, which was the same configuration that appeared when Jesus was born.

G: Yes. It was a particular planetary alignment that creates a Star of David in the heavens and initiated the birth initiation on the planet. And the same configuration also occurred at the time of the birth of the man Jesus Christ.

J: Now, governing all of this is the seventh spiritual ray of consciousness?

G: It governs this age. The sixth ray governed the last two-thousand-year cycle. The sixth ray is the worship of the pairs of opposites, of duality. The seventh ray is the ray of spirit, and has the responsibility to reform all physical structure through spiritual consciousness or through the balance of the divine plan, what this two-thousand-year cycle is about overall.

The seventh ray is also joined with the second ray of love wisdom. The second ray governs the awakening of the planetary soul. It's the ray that governs soul consciousness and enables you to experience and utilize more consciously the wisdom of the divine plan and put it into operation in the physical. Therefore, you have the soul ray and you have the spirit ray governing the overall awakening of the divine plan for the earth.

J: Have we pretty well covered the energetic forces at work here?

G: Yes, pretty much. Except for the astral force, the astral world, the collective consciousness that is held emotionally and mentally in the astral realm. That also is being gradually disintegrated at this time for the revelation of the planetary soul. Because the astral body of the earth, just like the astral body of each human being, contains the soul body. And just as after physical death, there is a gradual disintegration of the seven sheaths of the astral body to release the soul into the causal plane from the physical world, so now in the physical body, you are doing that same thing as you go through the initiation process. You are gradually releasing the astral sheaths to release and make ready and available the light of the soul in your physical bodies. It is the astral body that contains the soul body, the causal body. And it is the astral body that hides its light and its power as well as the availability of its consciousness. It acts as a kind of cocoon or protective device until man is ready to release his collective consciousness of the density of matter.

J: That is an amazing combination of energies coming together to assist in the ascension process. We seem to be getting a lot of help. It would take a lot to screw it up, I would think.

G: Oh, you could manage.

J: That's what I'm afraid of. [Laughing]

G: You have before. You've gone through many cycles where you've just kept repeating yourself. But it doesn't matter because time is only relevant to the physical world. You see, there's no judge saying you've got to get it right.

J: You've said this before. It's still hard for me to absorb the idea that it doesn't matter, that it's all about process, not the end result.

G: Yes, we know. It's difficult for you to comprehend because desire, attachment, and attraction keep you result oriented, keep you yearning after results. They do not allow you to embrace the process of reality, to be in the now, to experience reality. You are always in a description of reality. You are always yearning after something that doesn't exist. Very seldom are you embracing and able to realize, see, and experience the value of what exists. You're always yearning. Look at your planet. You're consuming all your resources yearning for more. Can't get enough. It's never good enough.

J: I guess that's the way it's supposed to be, isn't it? That's how we seem to define progress.

G: That's how you've chosen to evolve up to this point. Now you have the opportunity to change that. But to do that you have to become more involved in your own life. You have to take charge of your own life, be the master of your own life.

J: You have said we've been through this process many times, and, hopefully, we'll have a different outcome this time. I'd like to read an excerpt from one of your lectures because it takes us back to the beginning: "For thousands of years on your planet, you were all aspirants of ascension. You came in simply to connect to substance where form was concerned. So the origins of your being were substance and form. But much of it was undifferentiated by sentient awareness and by different levels of interpretation that consciousness allows. In other words, your planet began as a mineral kingdom, then developed a plant kingdom, an animal kingdom, and then, finally, a human kingdom."

J: Are you saying that our first appearance on earth was as minerals and then we evolved into sophisticated forms from plant to animal to human?

G: If you look at the physical body, you will find that it contains all aspects of all the other kingdoms. It contains the mineral kingdom, the plant kingdom, all of the kingdoms in nature, and so, yes—you are a combination in your evolution. Now, that doesn't mean that you evolved according to the Darwinian theory or that you evolved simply from a cell or an amoeba. What it means is that when you chose to bring about what you call a human experience, you used all of the elements of evolution that were in place to create that experience.

Because the star systems had to decide upon an overall form (body) that would best survive where the structure of the kingdom (earth) was concerned. So it used all the elements to create a common form that all could evolve through. And they included all those kingdoms so you could be a part of the nature of God that produced this kingdom called matter in the first place. They included the memory of it within the cells of your DNA so you would have a connection to all things. Therefore, you have the memory of all creation and the connection back to the smallest cell encoded within you so that you would then honor those parts of yourself. You would honor all the kingdoms in balance with one another, which over time you failed to do because you got a little too big for your britches, as they say.

J: Has the form that we originally occupied evolved over time?

G: Yes it has evolved physically, emotionally, and mentally.

J: Was it like a guided evolution?

G: Yes.

J: Was it guided from more primitive forms such as the apes and so on?

G: You are not derived from apes. Apes are an animal form within themselves. They are a part of the evolution of the animal kingdom to a high form of development, but they are not human. The human form is individual in itself. It has evolved as an individual form. The human kingdom is an individual kingdom just as the animal kingdom is an individual kingdom. The plant kingdom is an individual kingdom. But you contain all of the elements of all of those kingdoms within the given form.

J: In the beginning, from where did we emerge?

G: You emerged from the twelve star systems. The twelve star systems agreed upon and created a common form through which they could all evolve together. This is why you have the various races as races are left over from some of the analogous parts of the different star systems. Originally when you evolved, you did so through a common human form, but you have some of the differences of the particular star systems within the forms. So the Chinese are predominantly a certain combination of star systems as are the black population. All of them have mixtures of various traits of various star systems. There were a certain number of ethnic groups so to speak—the white man, the black man, all of that. And now they're all coming together. They are intermarrying and interbreeding. And that is for the purpose of bringing all the star systems together.

J: So different races have existed from the very beginning.

G: Yes.

J: Obviously, they were able to interbreed.

G: Well, you see, this is why the common form was chosen out of all of the kingdoms of nature, so they could create a common breed, so to speak, within the different star systems where they could intermingle and reproduce. So they had all the common elements of nature that would allow them to interbreed and reproduce with one another.

J: In the beginning were there twelve different versions of man?

G: No, there were not. There were combinations of star systems that were bred into basic races. There were six original races. Each of those races was a combination of two star systems that had interbred.

J: How did they come to earth?

G: The original gateway through which they came was Tibet, which is the first chakra of the planet from which they came into form. They came from the etheric into form.

J: So it wasn't Africa.

G: No, Tibet.

J: They went from the etheric into matter?

G: That is correct.

J: How did it happen? Did they just appear?

G: They transformed into a common form. You see, it's much like shape-shifting or creating a hologram. You don't understand it because you think everything needs to be bred through the physical world. Different star systems had very high technologies. When they ascended into the etheric, they all came from very high technical know-how. Even today they can come into your dimension and appear in physical form. It's a hologram of consciousness. All physical form, all matter, is a hologram of consciousness.

In reality, physical form is just a bunch of molecules rubbing together in empty space. In order to perceive it as dense, you have to lower the vibration considerably so that light can reflect off of it. If you were to raise the vibration to a certain rate, your form would literally disintegrate into light. This is the ascension process. Gradually, the physical body will raise its vibration to a point where you don't need a body any more. You can come and go as you please with or without a body, create a body of any grade and frequency that you want and use it as you please. This is what they were able to do. Right now they can make their light ships appear. This is why people sometimes see space ships. Then all of a sudden they disappear. All they have to do is change the frequency, and it is no longer perceptible to your sight, to your reality. Just as some sounds are imperceptible to you.

J: When those six different racial types appeared in Tibet …

G: They migrated to various points on earth. That doesn't mean that they walked from Tibet to Africa or to what you would now call Southeast Asia. What it means is the vortex that allowed them to lower their frequency to the frequency of the earth to produce a physical form was available in Tibet. So they came in through the vortex into form. They were then able to travel in their light ships to various parts of the planet and begin their various civilizations.

J: Were they primitive civilizations?

G: No, they were not primitive civilizations.

J: Well, what about all these fossils we keep finding of what is described as early man?

G: Yes, they are fossils of man, but they are fossils of man who evolved to a certain point. You see, the earth has had many eras of destruction and recreation, many times when the entire history of the planet has been lost and, in a sense, started over again. So they have evolved from what you would see as primitive forms compared to what you relate to now. There have been times on earth when it was inhabited by forms far more advanced than you.

J: And then what happened? Did they destroy themselves and go back to a primitive state?

G: Some of them destroyed themselves. Some of them left and went back to their original stars, their original planets.

J: And so the fossils we're finding of so-called primitive man …

G: Are based upon the most recent evolutionary cycle. Man has been through many periods, many cycles, many risings and fallings of civilizations, many endings and beginnings.

J: In the past have we been through a near duplicate of what we're going through now, going through the ascension process?

G: Yes, you went through it in the Lemurian Age and in the Atlantean Age.

J: Did we have all of the energetic help that we're getting this time?

G: No, you did not. You hadn't evolved to a point where you were capable of dealing with it.

J: So we're really in a new ballgame.

G: Yes, you are.

J: And what would we call this new ballgame?

G: You are evolving into the ascension of the spiritual man.

J: And we haven't had the ascension of the spiritual man in any of the past incarnations?

G: No. You have evolved in many ways to a high level of technology. You have evolved to a high level of spiritual understanding in many ways. You have evolved to a high level of ability, and then have come to a point where you have misused it. So now as you evolve through this cycle, the ascendant mastery is directing it a little differently having learned from their past mistakes. You see, it is trial and error for them as well.

J: What a surprise. That would never have occurred to me.

G: Everything is evolving continuously, dear one. Everything is evolving continuously.

J: Speaking of evolution and our spiritual growth, you have told us that we come here in each incarnation with a mission,

G: Yes.

J: It seems so easy to get trapped in so much destructive behavior or circumstances that seem to limit our incarnational experience. I guess I'm puzzled as to why it is so easy to fall into these traps that seem to limit our ability to achieve our mission and to grow.

G: As human beings in your experiential process of growth you've been given freedom of choice. Now, you can look at it from the perspective that you get trapped in your defenses and you don't learn, and then you carry it on from lifetime to lifetime. But, you see, you're looking at it from the perspective of the limitation of time. Therefore, you're saying—well, why don't we get on with it and get it done?

There's the judgment of time that says "I should really achieve this and get it done and do it right" rather than realizing you have infinite opportunity where life is concerned to incarnate as much as you want, to progress and develop at whatever level you need to through your own experience of growth, through your own choices, because that is how you learn. So if you make enough mistakes in a lifetime and you carry that through many lifetimes with the same patterns, eventually, the pattern from lifetime to lifetime becomes more pronounced and more extreme and more obvious. And as it becomes more extreme and more obvious, it produces more disease or suffering or pain. Eventually the organism wakes up and goes, oh, pain isn't the way to do it. Pain is not the way I choose to do it. Let me do it by embracing reality. So, you see, gradually over time, over incarnational history, you learn to take responsibility. You learn to be aware of your choices rather than live in ignorance of them. But, you see, that's a level of soul development.

We divide soul development into three categories. We call it development through the Hall of Ignorance, development through the Hall of Learning, and development through the Hall of Wisdom. Most human beings in the earliest stages of their incarnational development, in earlier soul levels of development, learn through the Hall of Ignorance, through cause and effect, through action and reaction, through the process of duality. Then there comes at a certain point in their development as souls after they have had enough incarnational experience and enough growth where they start to wake up, and they move into the Hall of Learning. The learning process then becomes more of a chosen process. Choice is something for which they take more responsibility. They learn to respond more rather than react through their incarnational process. So you awaken one lifetime and you go, as you are doing, oh, I don't have to create reality through being a victim. I don't have to create through resistance. There's another option—I can create as a conscious creator. Let me try that. Then I enter the Hall of Learning.

As I enter the Hall of Learning, I start to clear the vehicle and I start to realize that there's something more. It's a point at which the conscious mind in an incarnation says that there must be more than just the physical. And that's where in its incarnational process it begins to develop an interest in its spiritual development. As it does so, it enters the Hall of Learning. It then begins to prepare the road through the purification process, readying the body to awaken the soul consciously. When the soul starts to become awakened, then you move into the Hall of Wisdom. As you move into the Hall of Wisdom, you move into the path of beginning to consciously realize the soul's vision and carry it out.

The Hall of Learning is the process by which you awaken the soul. You start to awaken to yourself as a spiritual being. That's the learning process that transits you from the world of desire and objectification to searching for the meaning behind the form, that which makes up physical reality. And you start to understand. This is the path that you're on in this incarnation. This is what you are embracing with us. This is what you are embracing with the channel in your sessions. As you're starting to enter the Hall of Learning and go,

"Oh, there must be more behind the form. Life is not just the form. There is a spiritual me. I want to contact that."

J: Is this the process that most humans will follow during this new two-thousand-year age?

G: Yes. During this two-thousand-year cycle you will go through the ascension. That means the soul becomes fully awakened and the bridge between your spiritual self and your physical self will be achieved. This is done by awakening the soul because the soul is the individuated personification of deity that lives within the physical and makes it possible to experience God as a physical being.

J: It seems a little unrealistic to me that in just two thousand years, mankind will go from a level of ignorance to a level of wisdom.

G: Yes. Of course that is entirely dependent upon their choice. They still have freedom of choice within that, but that's the plan. You see the divine plan is influenced in the etheric by the ascendant master that implements it. Still, human beings always have the freedom of choice as to what they want to do with the energies. The ascendant mastery brings in certain frequencies of energy for the raising of consciousness. As that energy begins to influence the DNA band of the planet and gets interpreted into the organisms themselves, the organisms still have freedom of choice as to how they want to respond to the higher frequencies. So you always have a choice as to how you want to respond.

What you do with it will determine the outcome. How conscious you are and become will determine the outcome. Of course, the process of quantum physics that you are moving into at this time in your evolution is very helpful in bringing that about because quantum physics requires a certain number of persons to develop at a certain level of consciousness to create an instantaneous shift of resonance, an instantaneous shift of consciousness. And you have been experiencing some of those shifts over the last twenty years or so. The progress of the planet is doubling about every ten years.

J: As far as spiritual evolution is concerned?

G: As far as evolution period is concerned. What you have accomplished in the last twenty years, for instance, is more than you have accomplished in the last five thousand.

J: In terms of technical know-how and material things, yes.

G: The physical is always a mirror. So the technological interconnection of the planet is mirroring what is happening on the inside. There is a telepathic interconnection that is awakening on the planet between souls and is then mirrored in the technological functioning of the physical world. Everything in the physical world simply mirrors the relationship that is going on behind the form.

J: My perspective is limited, I suppose, because I can't begin to understand the impact of all the energetic influences.

G: Yes. You're only just beginning to understand the idea that it's taking place. You must understand, dear one, that this time is a quantum shift in consciousness. You have now shifted from the sixth ray, the governing ray of the idealization of the pairs of opposites, to a new planetary ray, the seventh ray, which is the divine ray. In this cycle, the seventh ray begins to shift all consciousness from a spiritual perspective. So the predominant energy of this ray is for bringing you out of duality and into unity. That's a whole new concept. And so those of you who are incarnated at this time, you are the pioneers of this.

In past evolutionary cycles you may have had a few here and there that embraced consciously a spiritual path of development and became masters at it. They became masters for the purpose of imparting that information as a blueprint in the consciousness of certain aspects of the planet, certain groups or numbers of people. That has increased exponentially to a point where now, in this age, because of quantum physics and the quantum shift possibilities, you now have the possibility that millions of people can realize themselves consciously in a process of self-mastery. Now the initiation process of spiritual initiates is available to the planet should they want to embrace it because you have come to a certain progress, level of vibration, where it is possible for more people to embrace the concepts.

And as the soul consciousness awakens, the idea of world service, the idea that every soul is a part of every other soul and that you are there to serve one another, not just yourselves in separation, will become a viable alternative and is becoming a viable alternative. As you just begin to glimmer the awakening of soul consciousness, people are being directed and being guided and feeling that interconnection of synchronicity that the order of the universe operates through to connect them with their soul groups to begin to see these possibilities. So you are at the tip of the iceberg.

J: You said the spiritual initiations have all been activated and that if we were working with them consciously that we could use the energies to direct our path in a spiritual way for our conscious spiritual evolution. What do you mean, if we used them consciously we could use them to direct our path?

G: First of all, the purpose of the initiations is to bring about the conscious awareness in the physical experience of your soul's presence—to awaken the soul in your physical body so that you are consciously aware of its directives, of its path, its purpose, its meaning, and its growth as a consciously chosen experience through the guidance of the soul, through the intuition and knowing of the soul. What that requires is that the ego or the lower self be stilled. It requires that the lower three bodies, or as we call them, the lower three sheaths of the physical, the emotional and the mental, become still. So there is not so much chatter and clatter. So that the stillness can bring you into the awareness of now where the soul exists, where it lives, it has its being. So that you are not caught up in the desire body with all of your attachments and attractions and all of your focus on the outside world, on the form so that you cannot see the substance or the life behind the form.

The life behind the form is the soul that animates and guides and directs the physical reality from a consciously chosen perspective, a perspective that has to do with being in direct contact with the divine will. The soul is connected to spirit. The soul is the differentiated, individuated experience of spirit. Without the soul there is no conscious connection or awareness between the physical experience and the spiritual experience. They are divided. They are separated. They become pairs of opposites. So then you are constantly through the ego will fighting against the guidance of the spiritual will, and there is never clarity. There is always confusion. There is always the bounce between pain and pleasure.

So when the soul is allowed to awaken, it acts as the median or spokesman, if you will, for the personality and spirit coming together as one. And it acts as the guiding force through an individual experience of the I Am because spirit itself is undifferentiated. Spirit itself is not individual. Spirit itself is not individuated into a form. It is just consciousness. It is pure consciousness that includes everything that is infinitely inclusive of all form and non-form because there are many dimensions of reality that exist in non-form. Form is only one tiny infinitesimal experience of reality itself as a whole.

Physical form is simply one very dense separate experience of reality, of consciousness. But spirit itself is all consciousness combined, undifferentiated, all inclusive, infinite. In order for a spirit to experience itself in an individual experience, it creates a soul. That's the causal plane of existence. The causal plane of existence is called that simply because it allows spirit to experience the cause of its reality, the meaning of its reality, and the actual experiential process or progress of its reality through a differentiated form, which is one fragment of the wholeness of its being. And all the different fragments of that being called spirit in form make up a whole soul that encapsulates one evolutionary experience of matter called the planet Earth, let's say. At one time Mercury, at one time Saturn, at one time Jupiter, was going through this process as well. Now they exist in etheric form because they have transcended, they have ascended in physical matter as far as individuated form is concerned. And now they exist in consciousness in the etheric.

J: They exist in consciousness?

G: That's right. For instance, what you call astrological influence is actually each planet in your solar system contributing its experience to the evolution of your experience because you are the last planet to evolve in your solar system. Therefore, if you were born under the sign of Libra or the sign of Sagittarius, that means you have a very direct connection to that particular sign. So that sign influences your learning and progress, your soul's path and your soul's growth during that incarnational experience. So that is how the different planets communicate etherically with you.

J: In order to direct our path in a spiritual way, it seemed at the beginning of your answer you were suggesting that we meditate.

G: Yes, meditation is a method whereby you can begin to still the physical, the emotional, and the mental. So it's a methodology, a tool. Concentrative meditation allows you to focus your attention. Contemplative meditation allows you to then take that focus and begin to connect it to the soul guidance and to contemplate the reality behind form. So meditation is a tool to get you into a state of being that you are still enough to be able to awaken the soul consciousness in the consciousness of the physical experience. When you are able to do that, life becomes an experience of meditation itself because then you are in the stillness, the awareness, the concentration, and the contemplation of now, which is where the soul exists. But, you see, it's an ongoing experience and you understand that any tool you use and its success depends upon the commitment of the subject.

J: Of course, that's always going to be true.

G: The commitment and the ability of the subject is always going to be based upon the subject's level of understanding and comprehension, which are going to be based upon the level of soul development and growth at which the subject is at. So, for instance, an infant soul is not going to be the least bit interested. Infant souls aren't even going to pick up the book as it would be Greek to them.

J: As you said in the past, our responsibility is only how well we send a message, not how it is received.

G: That is correct. I know what I've given you. I don't know what you've received, and it's none of my business. Because, you see, it operates at a certain resonance and that resonance is going to attract soul levels and soul groups that can benefit from it. That's why you have so many different procedures, theories, religions, philosophies, and that sort of thing. They're all necessary and they're all beneficial because they all allow awakening on some level to some group of people somewhere, depending on their level of soul advancement and development. So it's all good in that sense.

J: So they all speak to people in their infinite diversity.

G: Exactly. Understand that it is God speaking to God. It's not really like you are growing because everything already is. All you are doing is experiencing and experimenting with an aspect of being to remember what you already know.

J: What is the value of going through an experience of remembering what I already know? Why would I leave a state of knowing and come to a state of unknowing?

G: So that you could experience, so you could know, one aspect of yourself as God. You see, if you were undifferentiated, there would be no experience of yourself. There is only the I Am. There is only the whole. So in that sense, physical matter is serving God, and God is serving physical matter. We don't even like to use the word God because it has been so bastardized over time by the way in which humans have used it. So we prefer to use the term universal mind or divine mind, the all-inclusive divine mind. You are serving divine mind by incarnating as an individuated entity of spirit called the soul. So you are serving a progressive experience of spirit being able to experience itself. And spirit is serving you by infusing you with that aspect of the life force to be able to do that.

For it's an interesting conundrum because spirit is coming home to the realization of itself at the same time as you are coming home to the realization of spirit as a whole. Spirit gets to experience its wholeness through its fragmentation, and you get to experience the fragmentation to lead toward wholeness. So you are doing the same thing. Do you see? Spirit is remembering itself through individual fragments of experiential learning and remembering itself that way through all its different facets of its being. And you are getting to experience, through incarnational process and levels of soul development, the gradual integration of the wholeness of the one divine mind. So you are moving towards undifferentiated consciousness and spirit is moving toward differentiated consciousness to realize its wholeness. An interesting paradox, wouldn't you say?

J: That reminds me of when God, in the Conversations with God books, says you can know your magnificence in spirit, but to truly understand it you need to experience it, and you can only experience it in individuated form.

G: That is correct.

J: Is that why we do it because the only way we can know our magnificence is to experience it?

G: In that sense, yes. You know that if somebody says something to you, you understand it is not the same as if you experience it. It's not the same as if it drops into the body and you feel it.

J: I suppose it's like the difference between being told that chocolate tastes good and actually tasting it.

G: Exactly. So God or divine mind gets to experience all parts of itself through the actual experience in form. And it's the difference between, as you say, talking about chocolate and experiencing it, tasting it, eating it. You see, that's why, as a soul, you were created as a sentient being, a feeling being. Feeling is the desire elemental. It is the way in which spirit has taken the erotic force that it is, which is its divine will, and its will for life, and infused it into a form through sentiency or feeling. So it puts the desire elemental into form and objectifies it.

Now the only problem with that is that man has lost the connection to spirit consciously. Therefore, he has concentrated only in the lower self, on the objectification of desire. He has taken that erotic force and objectified it through desire by focusing it on the form (the physical world) as the source of life and being. And that's what creates in the physical the duality within the self because you've lost the connection to the divine will, the erotic force guiding the excitation for life. The excitation for life has been shut off and substituted as just desire focused on attachment and attraction in the environment.

J: Because that's all there is as far as we can see. There's nothing else.

G: Exactly. And so, the connection with the self has been lost because the soul is absent in consciousness. Once the soul is present in consciousness, the true sentiency of the wholeness of the individual of being is experienced within. The reality of the physical world is informed from within. Then you have the experience of the God self as the creator informing, creating, and manifesting the physical experience. And then you have the ability to shift the shape of things at will because you have control of the erotic force and you are directing it through the will of the divine plan through the individuated purpose and the fulfillment of that purpose in the soul.

But if you are operating only through the desire elemental, through attraction and attachment in the physical, then you are constantly looking to the physical to give you the meaning and the value and the fulfillment that cannot be found there. You are asking form, the illusion, to produce and give to you the life behind it while focusing on the outer form and being unable to see what is behind the form that informs it. The soul informs it. So you have to be in contact with the soul to inform the physical.

Therefore, the reverse has to take place. You have to move inward with the desire elemental and transform it into the connection to the divine will. Once it's transformed into the connection with the divine will, the desire elemental becomes the wholeness for all desire for life related to all the parts of the individual incarnated fragment that is incarnated in this lifetime and the connection of that individuated fragment to all the soul fragments of which it is a part in the earth plane.

J: So the only way to get there is through the ascension process.

G: That is correct.

J: And that is what will happen to all individuals during the next two thousand years.

G: That is correct.

J: Unless we destroy ourselves.

G: That is correct. You see, one way or another you'll do it because it's the process of God's own evolution. It's divine mind evolving into itself. So you'll do it on plane or off plane. You'll do it in the physical or off the physical plane. It doesn't matter. It only matters to matter.

J: I'm trying to accept that it doesn't matter if it happens in the physical or not. My whole experience is physical, of course, so that is a little hard to accept. Though I certainly believe our reality transcends the physical. I guess that means I'm growing with your help.

G: Yes, you will not be so trapped in the desire elemental and, therefore, in the artificial experience of growing and learning through duality, through the pairs of opposites. And the pairs of opposites are simply the difference between pleasure and pain and the degrees of it. Because in the experience of divine will, when the desire elemental is transformed and taken inward in the experience of divine will, there is no pleasure or pain. There is only love, joy, and peacefulness of being. But you have to make that transition. And your planet right now is at that midpoint in the initiation process of making that transition because you're at the fourth level of the initiation stages. There are seven levels altogether to be initiated. Now, once they're all initiated, that doesn't mean you've accomplished it. It means that all the stages have been initiated, which means you are now capable of using the energies and consciousness to bring it about.

J: In one of our conversations, you said that all of the planets in our solar system have had sentient life on them in the past and that all the planets except earth had already gone through the ascension process. I asked if we would be able to see evidence of life through any of the unmanned space probes we were making. You answered: "If you are at a level of consciousness where you would be able to see it." And the tape stopped. Then when it picked up, you were saying, "All of the time there are star ships in the sky and your atmosphere and you don't see them." So I assume you made some comments about our ability to see evidence of earlier civilizations on planets …

G: Or the presence of star ships just within your atmosphere. You see, in order for something to be seen, you must have a comprehension of its possibility. That means you must be at a level of vibration in consciousness that you can open the doorway. If your body consciousness remains at a level of density where it remains impenetrable, then it's not possible to open those doorways in consciousness. It is not possible to perceive what is there. Through its programming, the nervous system is constantly editing out reality. At this moment you are experiencing one one-billionth of the reality available to you in this room at this second because of your attachment to how you see reality in physical density. Therefore, your attachments, your attractions, and your desires program what you believe is reality, and your thoughts confirm it.

The example of how reality is relative to the perceiver is contained in the story we have told you about the South American natives who couldn't see the Spanish ships. They had no frame of reference for a ship. They had never seen one. Therefore, the nervous system couldn't register it.

It's the same thing with you. For instance, there are other planets in your solar system. But because you have not been able to detect them through your telescopes, you don't experience their influence. When you began to detect the planets that you have now through your telescopes, you began to experience their influence. There are two new planets that have entered your solar system. That means they have entered your consciousness. Your scientists have detected them over the last eight years. One of those planets is the planet that governs Libra. Libra has shared a planet with another sign because it didn't have its own planet. Now it has its own planet. Now that is has been detected, the people born under the sign of Libra have begun to experience its influence.

J: The planet for Libra has entered the solar system?

G: It has always been in the solar system. But you have not been able to detect it because you didn't have the means.

J: It didn't influence the Libra sign even though it was there?

G: No, because consciousness has to be available. You see, consciousness has to have awareness. For instance, why for thousands of years have you had no awareness of God within you? For thousands upon thousands of years, your religions have all talked about God as though God was something outside of you, somewhere in the heavens. They refer to something apart from you. So you have perceived God through the duality that you have created in your reality, yourself as separate.

Now why is God separate? God is separate because you are separate. You've created separation; therefore, God couldn't possibly be a part of you, but rather something the ego is always seeking through its desire body. Now as you come into this age, you begin to awaken body consciousness as the vibration raises in the body. And now the possibility arises that you can detect and awaken God consciousness within yourself. You can begin to realize yourself as God, as God beings.

How do you do that? You do that by awakening the soul, because the soul is the bridge that differentiates undifferentiated spirit from matter. The soul is the differentiated experience of spirit that connects to matter and expresses the individuality of God as an individual entity of God's being and consciousness and wholeness and oneness.

Now that has become a possibility because of the evolutionary point you have reached. Your consciousness has reached a high enough point where the body is now going to resonate at a frequency where it is able to detect the awareness of God within. That is what is happening in this two-thousand-year cycle.

At this particular time, why are the higher chakras vibrating and moving their energy down into the lower chakras? To raise the vibration of the lower chakras so that the lower chakras are capable of detecting in their consciousness the connection to soul awareness, to God awareness. Because the lower chakras, or the lower vibrations, keep the physical reality in place and keep you separated in that physical reality from your God awareness. So as long as the first chakra vibrates at its own frequency of density, you remain very much pulled into the earth and grounded into the gravitational field and feel the impact and pull of gravity. You feel very connected to earth consciousness, very connected to density, and you feel a secure and safe connection to that. That is a reality that overwhelms any other reality because you remain in that level of consciousness.

As you come into contact with your second chakra consciousness, your emotional body, you become more and more emotionally aware, more sensitive to feelings. Its vibration is slightly higher than the vibration of physical matter, which is governed by the first chakra. Physical matter (first chakra) vibrates at a very low density, a very low vibration. Second chakra, emotional, is the beginning of the etheric experience. It moves out of the physical into the etheric. So the etheric experience is first detected in physical matter through the feeling (second chakra).

The next etheric experience, through the development of the lower mental, is called thought. That is governed through the third chakra. Through thought you create beliefs about yourself in relationship to physical density and feelings. And you divide that into thoughts to create, maintain, and sustain the desire body attached to objects in reality.

When those lower chakras are separated from the other chakras, that's all you experience. You experience thoughts and feelings as well as a physical body. You experience that through desire related to the lower will. The desire body is the body of the lower will. It is the struggle for the survival of a limited, dense reality through physical matter that is experienced through duality of feelings—divided into good feelings and bad feelings, into pain and pleasure—because the mental body is dividing them through its belief systems in separation, good and bad, right and wrong, good and evil. And then those thoughts and those feelings govern the experience of physical matter, including how the body responds; how it moves, acts, expresses, and experiences, and how it evolves through the limitation of separation.

As the higher chakras move their energy into the lower chakras, they raise their vibration to where the body becomes the temple of the soul (first chakra), the emotions become the expression of the soul through intuition (second chakra), and the mental body becomes the knowing of the soul through the direct inspiration and revelation of the divine plan (third chakra). So that's what you're in the process of incorporating in raising that vibration of body consciousness.

J: You said our ability to perceive form on the other planets had to do with whether or not we had a level of consciousness to be able to see it. We have had a lot of cameras scanning the surface of Mars. But, I assume, they won't be able to perceive the life-forms that are there.

G: Well, the camera is physical. It is an electromagnetic experience. It doesn't have sentient awareness or body consciousness, so a camera can only record the electromagnetic field of physical density. Therefore, it can photograph the surface of Mars as it is seen physically, but it won't be able to detect anything else.

As your body develops awareness, you can see what is on Mars or Jupiter or Saturn. But it's not what is on Saturn in the density of physical matter because there are no physical beings on Saturn or Mars, not in the density of form that you are used to seeing through your eyes, through the electromagnetic density of the body. You have to raise the electromagnetic density in order to see what is there. As you raise your electromagnetic density, you become a channel to see or to hear or to sense or to feel as you develop your clairsentient, clairaudient, and telepathic abilities. Those are forms of seeing that move beyond physical awareness, physical density.

J: What might we see if we raised our vibrations?

G: Then you would be able to see the form that is there on a different level of density.

J: Like what? What's there?

G: You would be able to see the beings that exist there in the etheric. The planets are inhabited etherically.

J: Do they have structures and things, or doesn't that have any meaning?

G: Oh yes. They all have structures, certainly.

J: So we would be able to see signs of civilization.

G: Yes, signs of civilization that exist on a different vibrational frequency.

J: I don't know if this is synchronicity, but last night after writing the question about cameras on Mars, I came across a television program that was examining some formations on Mars that appeared to be man-made. Some looked like pyramids. One resembled the Sphinx. The program was speculating that it might relate in some way to the pyramids and the Sphinx in Egypt. Is there anything to that?

G: Yes, it's the remains of a civilization that existed in physical density at one time. So it's like the ancient ruins of Mars, if you will.

J: They were speculating there might be some direct connection between it and Egypt.

G: There is.

J: What would that be?

G: There are direct connections between all of the planets and the various sacred sites upon the planet Earth because many beings from those planets have been in contact at various times with the Earth and have been a part of its civilizations. They have helped to instruct and to bring about the evolution of certain civilizations through their influence and instruction.

J: This program stated that it was very difficult to get photographs out of NASA. Some senators threatened the agency. They complained that NASA was stonewalling and insinuated the agency was trying to hide something. Any comment on that?

G: Yes. You see, certain beings on your planet have contact with other dimensions or what you call ETs. After all, you are all ETs in your origins. So they have the ability to interconnect with some of those dimensions of time and space. And they are working with certain elements related to the control that is taking place right now. They have support from certain beings, what you might call your darker forces, the unenlightened beings. And the reason they have those interconnections is because, just as they are trying to control the Earth, they are trying to create some kind of cooperation with those beings so that those beings don't take over control from them. Therefore, they've worked out an agreement. Just like countries work out agreements, different intergalactic beings work out agreements.

Remember that at this time as you're healing duality, you're becoming aware of the dualities that exist in all dimensions at all levels. Understand that what happens in the physical is the last place that it happens. Physical reality is a mirror reflection of what is happening on other levels of consciousness and being and awareness. Because you've evolved through light and dark, through good and bad, you've evolved through duality. You still have a belief in the forces of duality, the forces of good and evil. So there are still "unenlightened" beings, if you will, from other dimensions of intergalactic awareness that are quite happy to go along with imprisonment, control, and domination and all that sort of thing, sort of like what your Star Wars films depict. Those are not entirely fictitious.

There is an intergalactic council of light, and there is an intergalactic council of the darker forces. This is the way you have grown and evolved in your intergalactic awareness and in your sentient physical awareness. When you have come to a point where you no longer need to evolve in that way, you will dispel the darkness of that consciousness by bringing it into the light, which is what you are in the process of doing now.

J: Will it be a peaceful transition or through war?

G: That's up to you.

J: You have made it very clear that opposing these darker forces wasn't the way to go. Creating an alternative model was.

G: That's right. Raising your consciousness to a new vibration because the law of physics dominates the law of manifestation. The law of physics says the higher vibration that is dominant creates a quantum shift. It creates an entrainment process that begins to instantaneously cause an effect that shifts consciousness. Remember all manifestation is the result of consciousness.

J: I think I just got that.

G: You cannot raise consciousness because consciousness is not something that happens independent of the body. The body is the temple of consciousness. It is the receiving set of consciousness, the TV set or the radio, the satellite dish, if you will. You see, your satellite dishes out there, your mobile phones and all that, your Internet with instantaneous connections in the physical, they are all mirroring what is happening in the nonphysical where the raising of consciousness is concerned. They are mirroring the interconnection of all things. All the physical does is mirror what is going on elsewhere, what is going on behind the form. Therefore, you have to have body awareness, body consciousness, first in order to have higher consciousness. Higher consciousness is not about leaving the body, which is what you have done for so many centuries. That's why you're separate from God. The ancient mystics who have attempted to contact God or higher consciousness have always condemned the body. They have mutilated the body, beaten the body. Just look at your Catholic religion, for instance. They decry the body as the body of sin.

So you have to raise body consciousness. That means you have to awaken the body. Until you can awaken the body, until you can make the body aware, you have not plugged the body in. As long as the body is armored, as long as the body is dense, as long as those two spirals of energy cannot interconnect in the body, as long as you have layers of density and armoring in the muscle tissues of the body that prevent the flow, you don't have those transistors connected to the radio, and you're not going to be able to connect the different wavelengths of consciousness that the radio brings through.

It's the same with the human body, which is a field of different frequencies and different vibrations. You have seven main vibrations of consciousness in the body, the seven chakras. Those seven chakras develop from the time you are in the womb until you reach adulthood, which bring about the main levels of consciousness. The first three, particularly, bring about the three levels of consciousness related to manifestation in the physical world. If the development of those chakras, the body's awareness, the vibrations, is distorted because of trauma and problems in childhood, and you develop the density of defense, the armoring and the ego mask, then those chakras, those levels of consciousness, don't function autonomously. The transistors aren't connected—they are distorted.

J: So we have to get rid of the armoring and get the energy moving.

G: That's correct. Otherwise the body remains in a very limited dense form with a very limited view of reality for which your psychological defenses then fight. The body fights for limitation of life. It is constantly in its defense and in its armoring, limiting the life that is moving through the body, limiting the amount of comprehension and perception that the body is able to experience by the programming of the nervous system and the five physical senses. The five physical senses and the nervous system are editing out all other reality, limiting it to the density of all of the attachments and attractions that the ego self is imprisoned of which the objects in the physical world are concerned. That's all you can see, and you remain in separation.

As you develop body consciousness, consciousness moves down deeper into the body. If the body is armored, it cannot penetrate into the body, and, therefore, it cannot expand the body's awareness. Consciousness must deepen in order to expand, not rise up in order to expand. If you raise it up, you are disconnecting it from the radio receiver. Then you have to leave the body— which is why you have the process of death because leaving the body is the only way you can get out of your way to connect to the other levels of consciousness that are separated from the body because the body's frequency is too dense to have the awareness of the soul in matter. So you have to leave matter (the body) to have soul awareness. And then even when you leave the physical body through death and you disconnect the astral body, the soul body is still trapped within all the desire attachments of thoughts and feelings through the astral body.

The soul is still enclosed, and you have to go through the seven levels of the astral realm to free it so the soul can finally have its awareness awakened in the causal plane.

Now you're bringing the causal (soul) plane down into awareness. To do that, you have to dissolve all the desire attachments and attractions in the astral body. You are breaking through the etheric web that separates all the levels of consciousness in the astral body and burning away the astral sheaths. This is the burning away of the attachments and the attractions of the desire body that keeps the astral body attached to the physical as the source of reality. It is what is referred to in the Book of Revelations when it talks about the breaking of the seven seals.

It's talking about the breaking of the seven seals on the seven chakras, the etheric webs that keep the density of the astral body enclosing the soul and don't allow it to penetrate through into the consciousness of bodily awareness. The Book of Revelations is the map of evolution for this age as written by the apostle John. He described the evolution of Christ Consciousness as he applied the seven levels of initiation to his own experience. He has written it in such a way that it is symbolically encoded so that those symbols could be awakened when man's resonance was ready to see the meaning behind the symbol. It speaks, for instance, of the awakening or the sounding of the seven trumpets. Those seven trumpets are the trumpets of the chakras. Each chakra is a trumpet. It is a cone. When each chakra is awakened, you have the awareness of the consciousness available on that level of vibration. It speaks of the seven angels, who are the seven levels of soul awareness, the seven levels of soul consciousness that awaken the seven doorways, the seven gateways of the heart.

J: You have made it very clear that getting rid of the armoring is an essential part of the process. In the therapy Phillip and I have had with Robert, we seem to be mostly doing breathing exercises, which I know are important.

G: You must first learn to breathe. It must become a habitual part of every moment of your life. Until you learn to breathe, nothing else is possible. Breathing is the most important doorway to access where the energy is blocked. Unless you can breathe into the temple, into the torso, you cannot activate what is there. Then the addition of sound begins to vibrate. And as it begins to vibrate it begins to move the energy. Then the addition of physical movement in particular areas begins to loosen up the armoring and move it. And then the sound and the breath move it out. Without the sound and the breath, it won't move. That's why you can do physical exercise in a gym and nothing moves. You can move energy inside the body, but you can't move it out of the body.

J: Why?

G: Because there's no sound or breath involved. And the sound and breath must be connected to emotional awareness because everything is encoded in the armoring though emotion. The reason there is armoring in the first place is because feelings were concealed and trapped. So the emotional connection must be made. Just making sound, just breathing, just moving, won't do it. You have to make the emotional connection to move it out of the body because that's what traps the energy inside.

J: So we should be breathing deeply all day, every day.

G: Yes. Breathing deeply as a matter of habit. It must become your habitual nature. If you are not, then you are not going to be able to be available and opened and awakened on a daily basis, on a regular basis. It will then be incremental. It will then be only occasionally. What prevents people from doing it is as soon as they start breathing a lot is that they start to feel. And they're not used to feeling, they're used to being numbed out. As you breathe, you develop more awareness. You can't handle the awareness. The awareness that is seeking to awaken and the feelings that are seeking to move produce anxiety. And the ego goes, "We don't want to feel. Stop the feelings. Feelings are bad. We don't want to be out of control. I would rather be controlled and dead then be alive, aware, and feeling."

J: I guess we have to engage our will too, because we really want to do this. We want to grow.

G: Then you have to engage your will of consistent and constant choice. It has to become a discipline. This is why mystics and yogis spend their lives just doing spiritual practices. But the time for that is gone. The planet must awaken; therefore, the practice of breathing must become part of your daily life.

J: At the beginning of this process we said we were to teach people how to awaken the soul consciousness or Christ Consciousness within each of us. Are the breathing exercises at the heart of the process?

G: They are at the heart of that process because until you can clear the vehicle that holds the soul in consciousness awareness, it doesn't matter how much the soul attempts to awaken. It will be blocked by the unconsciousness of the vehicle receiving it. So the physical body must be free flowing without blockage and without the density and pollution of lower vibrations. Your body is the temple of worship, the temple of your being, the temple of God. Therefore, it must be maintained at a vibrational level of awareness and presence of being that allows you to evoke the conscious awareness of what is passing through it.

The only thing that prevents you from accessing the soul right now in total awareness is that your physical body has become so dense and blocked to the flow of the life force that it is barely living. It is living off the amount of energy that is just able to seep through it minimally. It's like the minimal food it takes to keep a starving child alive. You are using approximately 15 percent of your lung capacity, the life force that is the source of God breathed into your being every day. It is the pure life force of creation. And you ignore it. You split off from it. You shut it down. Breathe deeply constantly. It should be your religious discipline. It should be your mantra of life. Breath is life. And life is divine.

J: You have said that we are our own redeemers. Our redemption comes from what we do.

G: That is right. It comes from awakening the consciousness of the body. The breath, movement, and sound are for the purpose of awakening the consciousness of the body. If the body is asleep, there is no vehicle to receive the consciousness. Therefore, the breath, movement, and sound awaken the consciousness of the body. They are the tools of process for taking charge of making the body conscious. Quite the contrary to what your religions have taught you, which is ignoring the body. The body is the church. The body is the temple. The temples, the churches that you have created in the large structures outside of yourself that are ruled and dictated by heads of those structures are not the temple that you need.

The temple you need is the temple you have ignored, and that is your physical body. You must awaken that. That is the purpose of those tools—they are to awaken you to more aliveness within yourself, more comprehension, more awareness within the vehicle of comprehension, the television set upon which your play your frequencies, your physical body. Therefore, it is the most important aspect of your expression and experience of being.

Chapter 5:
USA/Democracy/Geopolitics/ September 11, 2001

J: In one of our earlier sessions, I asked about the size of the group of souls you said were incarnating now in large numbers, the ones who have come to help in this new age. You said that at the moment, the planet is divided into thirds. One third are younger souls who will try to sustain the status quo through separation. One third reflects a higher consciousness who will consciously be creating this new age, and one third will be leaving the planet. We seem to be a very divided country politically right now. Can you identify which political groups in our country reflect the younger souls who will try to sustain the status quo versus the ones who have come to try to shift consciousness?

G: Yes. You see, the ones who as you see it are in the so-called liberal camp are simply souls who are at a little higher level of soul advancement. But they are still not souls who are at a high enough level that they're really going to change anything because they're still addicted to duality and party politics. Until you understand that politics has nothing to do with government, you will continue to be run by politicians and politics.

Politics is simply propaganda. It has nothing to do with government. Various politicians have very little to do with government. It doesn't matter whether they are Democrats or Republicans—they are all in the same soup. Why do you think there is so little dissension among the Democrats with what is taking place in your government at the moment [2003]? They are just sort of going along with everything. Well, they protect their positions and the large retirement they will have at the end of their careers. So it is all motivated by greed.

Politics has to do with image, position, and deception. You have a country that is based upon government for the people, by the people. Until the people individually begin to take an interest in their own government, very little will change as far as politics and parties are concerned because one is just the lesser evil of the other. It's not Bush who has created all these problems. His problems were started in the Clinton administration. And the Clinton problems were started in the previous administration. They just shift the chess pieces around a bit and make promises they don't keep.

J: So the souls that are coming to create a quantum shift aren't going to show up as political activists.

G: They will also show up in political parties if people start to wake up and realize things have to change and that they have to take their government back. That means each person must develop an interest in what is happening, not just go along with what he or she is told. OK, Daddy, you just keep going along with what you are doing. Keep me comfortable.

J: What could enlightened souls be doing more of that they are not doing?

G: Wake up to what is really happening and the choices that are being made within your political system. Stop them (those in control) by getting in touch with the people you have elected and who have been put into the position of power and saying, "No, I don't agree with this. This is what I want." You have to get involved.

J: Raising the individual voice.

G: That is correct.

J: Of course, individual voices are heard more strongly when they become a collective voice.

G: That's right. But how do they become a collective voice? The individual tells his neighbor, and the neighbor tells his neighbor and that is how you begin to create a quantum wave. For instance, if the collective consciousness of the United States, simply the United States, were to all turn off their televisions and boycott the television stations, which are run by the conglomerates, that would be one huge step in taking back the power of your country, your consciousness, and your freedom.

J: What else could we do?

G: Stop consuming everything you are told to consume and becoming consumer dependent, and start looking at what is necessary for a quality rather than a quantity of life.

J: We're consuming our planet, aren't we?

G: Yes, you are. You've consumed half the resources of your planet in the last hundred years. The United States consumes more than half of the world's energy, and you have less that 5 percent of the world's population.

J: You said the original intention of the United States was to "lead the world into a new level of unity, oneness, communion and freedom, spiritual freedom." Then you said, "But that has been distorted. That does not mean it is not still going on. It is." How has our original intention been distorted?

G: Well, if you look around you can see isolation and separation, the division of peoples. You can see it through the division of races and the problems with race relations even though they are subtler than they were a hundred years ago or even fifty years ago. They're starting to come into synthesis, but there is still duality in your country where taking care of all people is concerned, having concern for all people existing at different levels of economic and social stature. That is division. That's not individuality. It's divisions of deservability.

All people deserve to have all of their basic needs met. If you are taking on the responsibility as a government to represent the people as a whole, then part of your responsibility is to make sure the needs of all the people are met in equality. All people deserve the same respect, the same integrity, the same supply. Not a division of haves and have-nots. Not an economic system where 10 percent of the population controls most of the wealth.

J: We have discussed what I see as a major difference in the political philosophies of our two major political parties. As I see it, they seem to be split between those who want private business and market forces to address most of our country's problems (Republicans) versus those who want the government to play a larger role (Democrats). You seemed to take issue with that view.

G: You see, you have a political, industrial, military system. It is a system where the political system is dominated by militarism. That is why you have such a huge military budget. Therefore, those who you call Democrats no longer have the individual voice they had. To maintain their positions in government and in power, they must synthesize their views so that they are not in too much opposition to the predominant force that is in control. Basically, the political system is controlled by the economic military industrial machine. You can no longer fool yourself by believing that a governing system controls the policies of your country or the policies of the world. That is not so. They are subject to the people who provide the money. Basically, the Federal Reserve controls the system of government of the United States, which is really a system of twelve banking families.

The reason you have the close association between Tony Blair and George Bush is because the center of the Federal Reserve is the Bank of London. Therefore, America is still a colony in that respect, still controlled by the British. But the British are also controlled by the Federal Reserve as well, as are most of the political systems of the world. But according to the U.S. Constitution, the Federal Reserve itself is illegal. It is illegal to have private banking institutions running the monetary system of the federal government. According to the Constitution, the system is supposed to be run by the Congress and the Senate. All monetary decisions are supposed to be made by the U.S. Treasury.

But back in 1913, a bill was passed that turned the U.S. Treasury over to the Federal Reserve, to these private banking institutions. Ever since then the country has been run by the economic industrial complex of rich bankers and corporate conglomerates. Your political system is determined by the monies that come from those conglomerates. Now your media is controlled by about six major conglomerates.

J: In terms of what you were saying about the original intention for the founding of the United States, was the United States, in essence, to be the prototype of the coming together of the twelve star systems?

G: Yes. On a spiritual level, in the ideal, it is a prototype for the communion of the soul. And it is a prototype for leading into the ascension process in this stage of evolution, this new millennium. But that has been distorted by the people who have been the rulers. Now, you must understand the various secret organizations that are basically in control of creating this New World Order. Basically, the American government has been put in place by the Freemasons. All you have to do is look at your dollar bill. Look how Washington D.C. is laid out according to the pentagram of the Masons. Look at the Pentagon. Look at the fact that all the main buildings are interrelated as to the number of blocks according to the sacred numbers of the Masons. The head of the Masonry in the United States in Washington DC is exactly thirteen blocks from the White House, the sacred number of the Masons, etc., etc., etc. The plan for a New World Order has been going on for hundreds of years. Now that's one side.

On the other side is the spiritual evolution that is embraced by more advanced souls who are embracing the good of the whole rather than controlling the whole. So you have those two opposing forces, the forces of duality. As we have said, for the last two thousand years you have been evolving through the Piscean Age, the age of duality.

J: The Masons are a product of that duality.

G: That is correct in the way in which it has been distorted. All of these ancient systems, the ancient mystery schools, all your religions, started out as an ideal. But people, through their freedom of will, through their fear, and through their embracing of isolation, produced the duality within those systems, distorted the original intentions of those systems. The Masons in its original creation was a system of self-mastery. It was not a system used for duality and control and the production of a New World Order.

J: Where did the Masons originate?

G: They originated in Egypt, but they go back to earlier systems that grew out of the Sumerians and the Assyrians.

J: How is the ascension process being distorted by these powerful global economic interests, which you have called the New World Order (NWO) or the World Management Team (WMT)?

G: The ascension process is a process of unity. The process of the NWO is a process of separation and duality. Therefore, the more separation and duality there is, the more you have to work through in order to create the unity. You have entered into a two-thousand-year cycle that is the cycle of unity. It is the beginning of the evolution of the process. The reason we give the information about what is happening behind the scenes with the WMT or the NWO is because people need to be aware so they know what choices are being made behind their backs. They can then make conscious choices to take back their power. We do not give the information to frighten people, although it does frighten people. It disturbs their comfort zone and their illusions about what is happening.

You see, your world depends upon sustaining illusions. All you have to do is look at Madison Avenue. Everything sold to you is through illusion, though a promise of what the product is going to do that has nothing whatsoever to do with the product itself. So you are sustaining illusion all the time. It's an illusion of children that want daddy to take care of them. They don't want to be bothered, and they don't want to know.

J: Whenever I suggest that there may be global powers controlling the economic and political systems of the world, people usually laugh and dismiss it as a joke.

G: All those conspiracy people are at it again.

J: Exactly. I'm not looking for a detailed history, but could you tell us a little about the origins of these secret organizations?

G: They go back to secret societies, secret orders. They were originally mystery schools that got distorted such as the Illuminati, the Left Eye and Right Eye of Horus, where the Egyptians are concerned. The Freemasons are an ancient mystery school who are responsible, for the most part, along with the Illuminati for the present maintenance of the NWO in the United States in Washington, DC. Where the Masons are concerned, the pentagram is the ancient symbol of magical powers that have to do with black or dark magic manipulating the astral world. The NWO has been manipulating the astral consciousness of humanity through the news media, which is almost entirely controlled by a few major corporations.

J: Most of us have the impression that these corporate entities and industry groups are populated by a passing parade of people who get their academic degrees, start their careers at some level of the organization, and work their way up.

G: If you were to examine the news media and all the major figures, the news anchors, the producers, the ones in power, you would find that every one of them is either a member of the Masons, the Trilateral Commission, or another secret society like the Skull and Bones at Yale. They are all initiated into these orders, then given their positions and sworn to abide by the covenant of these orders. Now, many of the people in the lower aspects of these orders have no clue what is going on. All they're doing is their jobs, and they are made to do their jobs. If they alter what is expected of them in any way, they are reminded that they could lose their jobs. Only those at the very top are aware of the deepest secrets of the secret society and its ultimate plan.

Every one of Bush's cabinet is a member of the Freemasons or the Trilateral Commission. All of them are also connected with major corporations such as Halliburton, Enron, etc. The entire government is run and ruled by the corporate structure, the international bankers and the military. Bush is but a figurehead, a puppet. The Bush family goes back to Ramses II. They were a part of the Illuminati, part of the Horus mystery schools. The grandfather of George W. Bush was an officer in a bank that contributed to the buildup of the Nazi party before World War II. The bank was disbanded by the government because of it.

J: How big is the controlling group?

G: The ones at the top measure a few hundred. Only twelve families control the entire banking structure of the world.

J: Does it matter which party or person is elected president of the United States?

G: It makes no difference. There is very little difference between Democrats and Republicans. Republicans are just more obvious about it. They are all bought and sold by money, by corporate and banking interests. Politics is about money. It has nothing to do with government.

J: So when I hear a candidate saying something that inspires me in a way that John Kennedy did, it's just an illusion?

G: Well, no, it's not just an illusion, but they probably would not get the corporate support they need to be elected, unless the people pay attention. There are more of you than there are of them. If the people pay attention, they could back a candidate and take back the government that was created for you in your supposed Declaration of Independence, which has now been usurped by the decisions and choices the various presidents have made in the past. And, where Bush is concerned, it has been usurped further with the construction of the Patriot's Act and the Homeland Security Bill. Have you ever looked at the Patriot's Act? Have you ever read the Homeland Security Bill?

J: No, I've just read comments about them. Most Americans seem pretty complacent about them.

G: We suggest you read the bill itself to find out what is being done to your government, to your country and to your people.

J: The only thing that seems to be getting the attention of the American people are the daily reports of American soldiers being killed in Iraq. It's starting to dawn on them that we might have gotten involved in a quagmire that may be a lot more costly and painful than we were told by our government to expect.

G: Yes. Wake up and smell the coffee, as they say.

J: But, it's a challenge. I don't pretend to know how to get people to wake up.

G: It's the power of one. And then telling another and then another and then another. Then each person taking action, you see? Because for the most part, people believe they don't make a difference. How do you think those people got into power? Because they decided they made a difference.

J: Well, some of them were allied with the corporate interests you've just described.

G: Of course. But you see, you have to be the powers that be. You have to become interested in how your life is being governed and what decisions are being made about it. Not like a bunch of helpless children that just give your power away and say, Daddy, take care of me.

J: Well, the Internet has certainly been buzzing and it seems to be a tool that ...

G: The Internet is a wonderful tool for instantaneous international communication if you use it to your advantage. Another powerful influence that keeps the masses quiet, numbed out and in a somnambulant state is television. It is the greatest single mind control device on the planet. They are beginning to put certain frequency devices into television sets now. When you turn the set on, it immediately begins to activate certain brain wave patterns that put you into a state of receptivity. They can then send subliminal messages through commercials or through the programs that you watch. It's the new method of warfare, subliminal warfare, mind control.

J: Do the New World Order and World Management Team have a spiritual purpose?

G: Everything is spiritual. Everything is there to show you your commitment. Everything is there to evolve your freedom of choice, for you to look at your commitment and decide whether that commitment serves the reality you want to create. You see, when you have extremes such as are taking place now, you are in a soul crisis. You're in a time of the dark night of the soul, which is an indication that there is a tremendous evolution going on because it has reached a point of critical mass, which means a tremendous shift is taking place.

Remember that the last two-thousand-year cycle was governed by the sixth ray of consciousness, which rules the idealization of duality, the promotion of all your ideologies. Your separate ideologies were promoted and brought about during that two-thousand-year cycle to their highest point of evolution and separation from one another.

Now you enter into the Aquarian Age. The seventh ray has now moved in. The sixth ray has moved out. So now you have the tail end of all the extremes of duality left over from the last age to now balance with the purpose of this age, which is the restructuring of all reality through unity because the seventh ray governs formation and structure through spiritual divine purpose. It is the ray that governs the divine plan. Therefore, it can be a very destructive force because anything that is not in alignment with its high vibration begins to fall apart.

J: What effect is the seventh ray having on these power centers of the New World Order?

G: It will bring them all into the light of consciousness so that everything will be revealed, so you will see exactly what is going on. And in that process they (those in control) will fight, deny, and seek more control. More and more people are becoming aware of what is taking place, what's really going on. So the resonance is beginning to awaken. The ripple effect of quantum physics, the quantum shift, is beginning to take place. It has been taking place for many years. That's why the progress of your planet on a physical level has doubled every ten years. That's quantum physics. That's quantum effect.

J: When you say that the forces of dualism are being revealed in their extremes now, I immediately think of the Iraq war. The motivations for it are under greater scrutiny as are the corporations that are getting the huge contracts. And they failed to find any weapons of mass destruction, etc. The war seems to be turning into a vehicle for revealing the deceits and illusions you have been talking about.

G: That's correct. The emperor is wearing no clothes. It will start to be revealed gradually. They will deny it. They will try to find every way around it, but it will be revealed because as the vibration rises, everything must come to the light. It can do that either through destruction or creation.

J: You have referred before to destruction. What are you referring to?

G: Referring to all the destruction that is taking place on the planet: the wars, the imposition of the will of the United States upon the rest of the world as it tries to become an imperialist power as Great Britain was in the nineteenth century.

J: I sense that as people begin to see that the evidence to support a war was nonexistent, any future attempt on the part of Britain or the United States to perpetrate another war will get a lot more scrutiny and challenge than it did the last time.

G: Yes, hopefully it will. There has never been any supported evidence to justify the war in Afghanistan. But, you see, people forget. You have to keep their attention. The consciousness of your people is used to sound bytes, and they are so easily manipulated by what the media tells them. And when the media stops showing it, they forget, conveniently. And then their attention is drawn by the next sound byte. They're like a bunch of sheep being led to the slaughter.

The entire experience of 9/11 was a sound byte. It was a deliberate creation to get the public to agree to begin a war, basically an oil war to control the remaining reserves of oil in the world that still have not yet peaked. Nine-eleven was a problem, action, solution scenario that has been used for thousands of years by governments, back to the ancient Romans, the ancient Greeks, back to the Syrians for that matter.

J: You have alluded to this several times in the past. And I don't have a clear understanding of what you're saying. You seem to be stating that 9/11 was ...

G: Created by your own government.

J: What do you mean it was created by our own government? Who created it? Are you saying it wasn't executed by terrorist groups from the Middle East?

G: No. No. Osama bin Laden. As a matter of fact, the bin Laden family are major investors with the Bush family in the same corporations. The bin Laden family were original investors in the Arbusto oil company that was started by George Bush Jr. many years ago. They're also investors in the Halliburton Corporation, which was headed by Dick Cheney, George Bush's current vice president. Who is receiving the big contracts of restoration in Iraq right now? Halliburton.

J: When you say that 9/11 was created by our own government, what do you mean?

G: We mean that the planes were controlled by your government. If you examine the passenger logs of the planes that crashed into the World Trade Center, you will find that none of the passengers named was on board the planes in the original passenger logs. The military has the ability to control a plane from the ground by remote control if they wish. Why do you think the military did not respond to the fact that two commercial aircraft were heading towards the south of Manhattan, off their course? They didn't put any fighters into the air to intercept them when they have the capability of doing it within minutes and under normal circumstances would have?

How do you account for the way the World Trade Towers fell? They fell straight down, an impossibility for the type of explosion that took place. The tops would have toppled. They would have fallen over, and they would have created a tremendous amount of destruction. The only kind of explosion that can cause buildings to disintegrate and fall upon themselves so as not to damage too much around them had to be set by demolition experts who are used to destroying buildings in cities so that they fall straight down and don't damage anything around them. That means there had to be explosions set throughout the buildings

J: But how do you keep a thing like that a secret?

G: How is it possible? Have you seen any investigation? Has the investigation of the World Trade Towers gone on since that happened [2003]? It has been stopped by the Bush government. No investigation has taken place. At the time of the explosion, in upstate New York where they measure seismic responses, they measured a seismic response that was the equivalent of an earthquake of 5.6. That means there had to have been an explosion underground.

There has been nothing exposed to the public about the fact that after they removed all the debris, they found tons of melted metal at the bottom, a huge pool of melted metal. That could only happen if a bomb was set at the base of the towers. At the time of the explosion, there was a demolition expert who stated that this had to have been done by a demolition expert who knew how to fell buildings. There had to have been bombs set in that manner throughout the building. Two days later he recanted his statement because he was on his way to Washington to get a huge contract for his company from the government.

J: Was this reported anywhere?

G: Yes. It was not reported in the main media, but if you look at the alternative media you can find it. What is reported in the main media is carefully controlled.

J: This is all really unthinkable. Why would our own government do such a thing?

G: Nine-eleven was a problem, reaction, solution. A problem, reaction, solution (create a problem, get a desired reaction, create a solution) is as ancient as the governments of Greece and Rome. It works like this. You have something to which you want the people to agree. You know that if you approach them, they will never accept it. Such as, we need to go to war in Afghanistan to control the oil pipeline to get the Russian oil to the Indian Ocean to get it to the world market, particularly the Asian market because that is the growing market for oil. We know if we say, we're going to go into Afghanistan and take over and bomb Afghanistan so we can control the oil pipeline that the public will protest. They will never agree. So we have to create a problem. We create a bombing of the World Trade Towers. We set the people into a panic and create the desired reaction. It's a terrorist group, and it's a terrorist group aided by the Taliban and headed by Osama bin Laden in Afghanistan, which is where we want to go.

We create the desired reaction. There never has been any proof in any way that Osama bin Laden is responsible for the World Trade Center bombing. No hint of Osama bin Laden since then has been found, and he has been almost forgotten. We would venture to say he is being protected by the American CIA somewhere in the world, kept under cover. It was the American CIA that created the Taliban in the first place. They created them in the seventies when the Russians were trying to overcome Afghanistan so that they could build a pipeline to get their oil out and profit from it. And the United States didn't want that to happen, so they created the Taliban and Osama bin Laden to destroy Russian control so the Russians couldn't get their oil out. This is why the Soviet Union collapsed. They spent twelve years fighting in Afghanistan with the opposition of the United States, the CIA, and the Taliban and went broke.

So you create a reaction, and you say, we have a solution. We bomb Afghanistan and we will find Osama bin Laden and punish him because he's responsible. And everybody says, yes, go get the bastard and punish him. So now we have the public in full support. But we have to maintain their fear to make sure they continue to support us and that we still have control. We want them to support anything we want because our ultimate goal is not to just take over Afghanistan. Our ultimate goal is to keep a belief in a war on terrorism going, to keep the people in fear so that we can attack any country that we want in the Middle East that has oil reserves that we or OPEC don't control. There are a few independent states left that hold most of the oil reserves that have not peaked.

We have to keep the people in fear so then we create the chemical scare. Remember the anthrax scare? The anthrax that was discovered was an American military variety. The information was reported in some newspapers, and then it disappeared overnight. Keep people fearful. Why do we want to keep them fearful in our own country? We want to keep them fearful so that we can maintain the war in Afghanistan, the war on terrorism, through the fear of our country being attacked by biological or nuclear warfare. We want to make sure the people stay afraid by a little scare here and there, so that, ultimately, we can make the country a military state. And so we initiate the Patriot Act. And we initiate something we call Homeland Security. Not much different than the Nazi Party.

Homeland Security and the Patriot Act basically take away all the rights of the American people should the government decide to declare a national emergency. And a national emergency can be declared at any time if there is an outbreak of nuclear war or a biochemical warfare scare or major rioting in the country, things like that. A national emergency can be called, Homeland Security takes over, the Patriot Act takes over, and basically, the Constitution is thrown out the window.

There is nothing in the Patriot Act to reestablish the Constitution. There is nothing within the agenda of Homeland Security to reestablish the Constitution. There is nothing to prevent them from taking over the entire country and putting it and all its people under military control. They have already been creating internment camps throughout the country in old military bases, old prisons and other places that have been deserted in preparation for a national emergency or a national panic at some time in the future where they can inter the minorities, the blacks, the Hispanics perhaps, and anybody else who falls into the category of, "if you're not with us, you're with the terrorists."

An interesting statement, was it not? It goes completely against the right to dissent declared by your Constitution, your democratic right to disagree with the government and the choices that it makes. If you're not with us, you're with the terrorists. Therefore, you are a terrorist. And in the Patriot Act, anyone who disagrees with the U.S. government can be labeled a terrorist, and they can be put away for any length of time without being charged and basically disappear. Just the way the Nazis did it during World War II. Time to wake up and smell the coffee.

J: What do we do, Gabriel?

G: What you do is you make people aware. You tell them about the books that are available. You make them aware of the decisions that are being made. You make them aware of what's happening to their Constitution. Make them aware of the new laws that have been put in place like the Patriot Act so they read it. And they then contact their representatives and say, no! All the senators and congressmen are still elected officials who vote upon these bills. The Patriot Act was voted on by the Senate and the Congress without your representatives ever reading it.

J: It was a fear response.

G: That's right. Same way the Federal Reserve took over the U.S. government in 1913. The president at that time pushed the bill through over the Christmas recess. Everybody wanted to get out, so they passed it and gave the U.S. Treasury over to the Federal Reserve, which is a private banking institution run by twelve families.

J: That was President Wilson. I majored in economics in college. I never learned that the Federal Reserve was a private bank, and I never heard anything about twelve families. I think of it as a national bank independent of Congress because Congress couldn't conduct economic policy.

G: The Federal Reserve is an independent banking institution. It has nothing to do with the government. The IRS is an illegal institution created by the Federal Reserve. The Federal Reserve created it so that the government and the people could pay back the interest that is owed it on the money that the government borrows. The Federal Reserve prints money at no cost to itself and then lends it to the U.S. government. Every dollar that you make, every piece of clothing you have, everything in your home is owned by the Federal Reserve, and it is on loan to you because the dollars you used to pay for them are on loan to you. The taxes that you pay are paying interest to the Federal Reserve on the money that is borrowed by your government and is borrowed by you through what you make in your jobs. That money is borrowed. It doesn't belong to you. It belongs to the Federal Reserve.

One of the reasons why John F. Kennedy was assassinated was because he had declared he was going to return the printing of money to the U.S. Treasury. The Federal Reserve didn't like that very much. He was going to return control of the monies of the government to the Congress because the Constitution says that only Congress may have the right to determine for the people how the monies of the U.S. Treasury are used for the people. Now they no longer have that right.

J: The Kennedy assassination was a government conspiracy?

G: Yes.

J: And the other deaths we have experienced, Robert Kennedy, Martin Luther King, and Senator Wellstone who was killed in a plane crash in Minnesota?

G: All very convenient. And Kennedy Jr. also.

J: Excuse me?

G: The junior Kennedy who died recently in a plane crash was also a conspiracy because he was thinking of running for office.

J: Pretty chilling stuff.

G: It's not a pretty picture.

J: The only way to deal with this is for the people to take back their government.

G: That's correct. They must wake up to the reality that is taking place and say no. There are more of you than there are of them.

J: It's true we're the only superpower, but the rest of the population of the world represents a formidable force.

G: And that formidable force, if you recall, tried to oppose the attack on Iraq. So what does that say where the change of consciousness is concerned? But the United States in its arrogance is so belligerent with its attitude of, I'm going to do it my way. It's already started to create its downfall.

J: The ones who opposed the war are beginning to look very smart and right.

G: Yes, so the change is already taking place. Now it just takes you and your friend and his friend and her friend and others to develop awareness and then make choices. Awareness isn't enough without choices, decisions, and action. You see, you will never change something by opposing the present system. How does peaceful protest stop war? It just brings more attention to the war. You've never stopped a war through peaceful protest. You will not stop this New World Order by opposing it. You will stop it by building a better model, taking responsibility step by step, person by person, choice by choice, connection by connection, to support the building of a better model. That is the law of resonance.

J: Don't we already have a better model? Our democracy is the model if it was working correctly.

G: That's true.

J: What confuses me is you counseled us to write to our congressmen and say no. Isn't that opposing?

G: No, that's saying, "I don't agree with this. This is what I would like to see." You have a right to say no—"No, I do not agree."

J: I guess I'm confused then by what you mean by "create an alternative model, but don't oppose them."

G: You're not fighting them. You're saying no. Then you offer a new solution, a better model, alternative choices, different choices. You say, this is not what I want. I want this. You get involved. You just don't say, I'm in opposition to war. What's the alternative you want to offer? What kind of life do you want to create? Do I want to take care of the hungry people of the world by being one of many millions that become involved and say, I don't want my tax dollars to be used for the military? I want my tax dollars to feed the hungry of the world.

J: We seem to be trapped in a system where concentrations of power grow and their influence increasingly overwhelms the rest of us.

G: You are trapped in a system because you participate in it, because you are dependent upon it. The less dependent you become upon it, the less you'll be trapped in it. The less dependent you are on your SUV and your cars, the less energy you will use. The United States comprises less than 5 percent of the population of the world, and it's using more than half of the world's energy! Why do you think they (the U.S. government) have such an agenda? Why do they need to control the world's oil? It seems pretty obvious to us.

J: Our entire economy seems driven by an incessant drive by corporations to keep pumping up their profits and stock prices. And millions of employees are hired and fired based on the bottom line alone.

G: It's about the product, not the people. The energy of the people is sacrificed to the product.

J: The earth has experimented with other economic systems, socialism and communism, and they don't work.

G: No, they don't.

J: What works?

G: A system of equity where people operate as independent individuals taking responsibility for their own reality and for the reality of their fellow man. I do unto others as I would have them do unto me. The good old Golden Rule. I do not make a choice that affects another that I would not like to affect me in that way. I operate through making choices and creating reality through the development of conscience. Conscience means I make choices that consider all concerned. I consider that as a soul, I am a part of the human family. What is good for me is good for all. What is bad for me is bad for all. We consider the soul of the individual rather than making the individual a part of the herd and keep them filled up so they don't protest.

J: What you're proposing is what all the spiritual teachers of the past have taught: love one another.

G: Of course. It starts with one person. Look at Jesus. Look at Buddha. Look at Krishna.

J: Well, we've known about Jesus and Buddha and all the other spiritual figures for centuries and …

G: And you still haven't gotten it. You have the path. You have the instructions. You have all the information. You just need to make the commitment to act upon it. But, you see, you must love yourself first. Love one another, he said, as you love yourself. If you cannot love yourself, you cannot love another because the relationship that you're having with another is the relationship you're having with yourself. So if you're not in harmony with yourself, if you're not in oneness with yourself, if you're in disagreement with yourself, you're going to be in disagreement with another. If you're in duality with yourself inside, if you're in separation with yourself inside, if you're in conflict with yourself inside, then that will be mirrored in your relationships with others.

Therefore, it comes back to taking responsibility for my relationship with myself. Then, and only then, can I be the example for another. Then and only then, by my example to myself and how I live my life, through the living of my life, through the action of it, through the demonstration of it, do I illustrate a new model, a better model that another can then look at and be inspired by to make a similar choice. But if I'm in conflict with myself, then I am creating a model of conflict, and I'm sustaining that model of conflict. It starts one on one. You are so used to looking at the problem from the point of view of "out there" rather than looking at where it starts.

J: All the powerful corporate and other interests are "out there."

G: Those are just structures. It's people who sustain them, and it's people who created them, and it's people that can change them. The object does not create your reality—the object merely reflects your reality, the reality you're committed to. In this case, the reality that is unconscious for most people is that they only want to receive the benefits of it in the periphery. They don't want to know what is behind it or what it's doing to them and to others and how it is robbing them of their souls.

J: It does seem to be robbing them of their souls.

G: Yes, it is. Because it keeps their focus outside of themselves on the objects, and they have to have more and more objects. That is why you are consuming more and more of the world's resources.

J: What's so ironic to me is that there is probably no more Christian nation than the United States that purports to believe in Jesus Christ and his teachings, and yet we are the perpetrators of everything that you're talking about.

G: Yes. They (many Christians) don't believe in Jesus Christ. If they believed in Jesus Christ, they would do as he illustrated. He said love one another. He didn't say, except if they're black, except if they're Jews, except if they're homosexuals, except if they're poor, except if they're this, except if they're that. That is not loving one another. He said the works that I do, ye shall do and greater than I have done. He left a promise of the fulfillment of the possibility of what he imprinted into the consciousness of the earth plane through his example.

You now are in the age of the Christing of consciousness. You're now in the age of the resurrection of the Christ. You are now in the age of the Second Coming. But it's not the Second Coming of a single man who is coming to rescue you. He already did that. He illustrated; he left you an example. Now you must lead by that example. You must do the works that he has done and greater than he has done. You must learn to love one another as you love yourself. You must learn to love yourself so you can love one another. You must do unto others as you would have them do unto you.

J: Is Jesus helping this process from the etheric?

G: Oh yes. He is one of the ascendant masters. He is the Sirian representative. His origins are from Sirius.

J: How would he be helping us through this process now?

G: By sustaining and maintaining the grid of what he put in place and influencing events in the etheric to bring about the initiation process. He illustrated through the initiation process, therefore, he sustains his work through the institution energetically in consciousness of the initiation process.

J: Last night public television broadcast an interview with a retiring Pentagon employee who has been a whistle-blower. He described our defense budget as "incomprehensible and unauditable." He said you can't track the money. There are trillions of dollars that no one can track. He claimed that hugely expensive defense systems are developed with little or no monitoring of their effectiveness and are sometimes put into the field before they have been perfected. He said it is a product of a "military, industrial, congressional complex" where each is rewarded by cooperating with the other. They're feeding their own needs, he said, not the American public's. It's just the kind of thing you have been warning about.

G: That's correct.

J: It seems to be a system that's impossible to understand or influence.

G: That's correct. You are constantly fed through the word they invented called disinformation. What does that mean? It means you are intentionally misinformed. You are constantly being deceived in order to maintain the shroud over what is happening, maintain the veil of illusion. You and most of the populace of the world are living in an illusion of reality where the physical world is concerned. You are fed disinformation to sidetrack you. As we said, the entire experience of 9/11 was disinformation. It was an illusion created to misguide you and misdirect you. It is the magician who makes you watch one hand so you don't see what the other hand is doing, distracts you with the left hand so that you don't see what the right hand is doing. That is what is happening. That's what this person was talking about on that television show.

Your world, as we have said, is creating a New World Order where the forces of duality are concerned, where the density of matter fighting for its limitation and control is concerned. It's creating a New World Order that involves the military industrial complex, a one-world government, a one-world economic system, a one-world monetary system, a world that is dependent upon and completely controlled by the international monetary system, the banking system through the issuance of credit.

Eventually, all money will be done away with completely and everything will be issued through cards and chips. The money chip will permit everyone everywhere to be monitored at all times as to what they are doing, where they are, what their business is, what they are purchasing, so that they can be controlled. This is the New World Order. All of the energy supplies of the earth are being controlled by what your U.S. government calls the war on terrorism. Whoever controls the remaining resources of oil controls the remaining energy resources and, therefore, also controls the food supply of the world in the future.

The television show that you saw, books that are being written, things that you are passing on to others, information on the Internet, revelations of the underground media, are all helping the body of humanity develop consciousness. As it becomes conscious, it can then develop a different system. It can then prevent the system to control the souls of humanity from being put in place. But it involves the cooperation and the desire of each human being that becomes aware to share that awareness with others. It is crucial at this time to spread that awareness around. The power of one. Because, as we've said, there are more of you than there are of them. They are a small group that has managed to gain control and power because of disinterest, because a bunch of children in adult bodies have given away their power by saying, you take care of me. You decide my fate.

J: We want to be happy with our toys.

G: That's right. Keep you consuming, keep you in fear, and keep you under control.

J: You have said that to change the collective consciousness, we have to change our own consciousness. It starts with us.

G: That is correct. What creates the collective consciousness? All the individuals who create it, all the individuals who embrace the herd instinct to fit in. Fitting in is a substitute for not belonging to yourself, embracing your individuality, being able to accept yourself as an individual.

J: You're saying trying to fit in is the opposite of loving yourself.

G: That's correct. If I cannot love myself, if I cannot accept myself, then I have to get somebody else to do it. In order to get other people to do it, I have to be like them, which means I have to give myself up. There is no unity in herd consciousness, which creates separation of self and alienation of self. For instance, the corporate structure is simply a mirror in the business world of what happens in the social world. There is no honoring the sacredness of individuality. The individual is subservient. The energy of the individual has no value except to produce the product and increase the revenues of the corporation. Therefore, individuals must give themselves up and their importance as individuals and their voice as individuals to become a part of the herd of the collective consciousness to serve the machine called the corporation to produce the product and raise the revenues.

J: What alternative model would you propose?

G: The honoring of individual expression and creativity within the corporate structure, the honoring of the substance and meaning and value of the individual who contributes to the whole. Do you see? But there is little of that.

J: That's what I was trying to accomplish when I was in the corporate arena doing management development work.

G: There are people now who are trying to do that. They're trying to bring meaning and value to the corporate world because the soul of the corporate world is dead.

J: Most people know it. They tow the corporate line, but they know it.

G: Democracies have fought things such as socialism and communism for years. But the corporation is a totalitarian system. There is no democracy. Democracy honors the power of the individual, the expression of the individual, the rights and sacredness of the individual; therefore, you do not live in a democratic society.

J: You have made very serious charges about groups you call the New World Order and the World Management Team, claiming they seek to destroy our democracies and conspire to control the world. People who read this could easily assume that these are the accusations of a fanatical conspiracy theorist. If you're going to make such charges, you've got to be able to support them. I admit it would be formidable to try to get that kind of secret information. There have been investigations with lots of resources behind them that have tried to get to the root of some of the questions you have raised and have come up with little. Still, how do you support these charges you're making?

G: Well, one source that perhaps would give you a good overview is a book by a journalist named Marrs called Rule by Secrecy. It traces the origins and development of the New World Order through the ancient orders of the Illuminati, the Masons, and many others. He substantiates the origins of the New World Order and how it is continuing today. That will give you a very interesting and plausible background for these things. The things that we say today are a matter of research. They are a matter of looking into these various companies, into the backgrounds of these various people, into the transactions that have taken place that have been reported in your local newspapers down through the years. It would involve a lot of research to get the information that substantiates these transactions. However, all the transactions have taken place, and the evidence is there.

J: You said that one of the motivations for the assassination of John F. Kennedy was that he wanted to take the printing of money away from the Federal Reserve and return it to the federal government. We know that there have been plenty of investigations of the Kennedy assassination and they've come up with very little.

G: Look what has happened with the investigation of 9/11 [as of 2003].

J: It's hard to understand just what is going on with that investigation. I've read charges that the Bush administration is stonewalling for supposed "security" reasons.

G: Nothing is going on. They're playing pretend. You see, this is the frustration of what you're up against. But, you see, you can substantiate some of these things by just looking at the Bush cabinet and then connect them to the corporations, the banks, the various financial institutions, and the various oil companies. If you look at the history of these peoples' connections, you have your proof right there. If you look at who in the Bush cabinet is connected to the Halliburton

Corporation, who in the cabinet is connected to the Carlyle Group. Who is receiving some of the big contracts in the Middle East right now for the reconstruction of Iraq? The Halliburton Corporation and the Carlyle Group.

J: Through my journalism studies, I always thought of the New York Times as the model of what a great newspaper should be. But I think of how long and hard they tried to make a scandal of a little real estate development called Whitewater during the Clinton administration. Frankly, I'm mystified why they seem to be ignoring the most blatant financial connections between nearly everyone in the Bush administration and what's going on now in the Middle East. There has hardly been a blip on the journalistic screen. It's very puzzling.

G: It's not puzzling. It's all controlled. When are you going to see it? When are you going to admit it?

J: Is the New York Times part of this?

G: Of course it is.

J: The Times was our bible in journalism school.

G: If you do some research, you will find that most of the important news reporters connected to the New York Times, the management, editors, etc. are members either of the Freemasons or the Trilateral Commission. The Trilateral Commission is completely about building a New World Order.

J: What is the Trilateral Commission? You have referred to it many times.

G: It is a commission that was created back in Nixon's time—through secret meetings around the world with some of these secret organizations—for the purpose of creating a New World Order. All the top dogs from all the financial institutions, the media, the corporations, all the military institutions, are all members of the Trilateral Commission. Research the people who are in Congress and in the Bush cabinet. You will find that most of them are members of the Trilateral Commission. All of their meetings are held in secret. They're not open to the press. If anything is leaked to the press, it is leaked very carefully. Yale's Skull and Bones club is another ancient order.

J: When you mention that group, people kind of chuckle that it's a fraternity.

G: It is a secret order. Many of the presidents, the top people in the big corporations, bankers, etc., have been members of the Yale Skull and Bones. It guarantees major positions of control where the operations of the world order are concerned. You have the little guys who quite innocently join many of these organizations because they are asked to, because they are let into the club. They have no idea what is going on at the top because what is going on at the top is held in absolute secrecy under the threat of annihilation and death.

J: Turning to another troubling situation, we have been hearing every day about those horrible suicide bombings in the Middle East. We have even been hearing reports of parents strapping bombs on their children, turning them into bombs.

G: That is not the problem. That is the manifestation of the problem. The problem is fear. Fear of difference, fear of oppression, fighting the feeling of not good enough. Basically the Israelis and the Palestinians are doing the same thing they've been doing for hundreds of years. Both sides are fighting the feelings of not good enough. Neither side is willing to relinquish that fight.

J: We're seeing it in Iraq too.

G: That's correct. The problem is not strapping bombs to your children and blowing them up to demonstrate opposition to something. The problem is the opposition to something. It always goes back to the very simple statement that you're so tired of hearing: what feelings are you in opposition to? Human beings make all of their choices based upon either moving toward a feeling or avoiding a feeling they don't want. That's how all their choices are made.

J: And you're saying the feelings they're trying to avoid are feelings of not good enough?

G: Yes, among others. Unworthiness, deprived, a mass consciousness of masochists fighting deprived and doing it beautifully.

J: So we try to address the problem with violence. Like invading Iraq.

G: Yes. You will never, never resolve a problem by avoiding a problem through defending against it. As soon as you try to get rid of anything you are aiding and abetting the very thing you are trying to destroy. What I cannot accept, I cannot love. What I cannot love, I will control. What I cannot control, I will destroy.

J: Translating that into intelligent policy ...

G: If I cannot accept reality as it is, then I cannot love it because love requires acceptance, acceptance of what is. You cannot deal with and negotiate with what is if you cannot first accept it.

J: Let's pretend that you are the Bush administration trying to create an effective policy for dealing with Saddam Hussein before the war in Iraq. What would be an example of employing what you're saying?

G: First of all, what was the problem that was perceived where Saddam Hussein was concerned? Address the judgment of this being and this country that are different than your own that says, you are wrong and I am right. There's the problem rather than approaching what you perceive to be the problem with acceptance and with love. Then there would be no need to control.

You see, the premise is false anyway because the motivation was not to better the situation. The motivation was entirely to gain control over the oil resources of the country. So there was no concern about Saddam Hussein, and there was no concern about the people of Iraq. The concern was about the oil reserves and who controls them. That is the bottom line. Therefore, the choice itself was made out of the fear of deprivation, the fear of being deprived of energy, of oil. So it was a fight of deprivation. And what is happening in Iraq where the American position is concerned? You are being deprived of autonomy. All of the insurgent groups are opposing your position of authority.

J: What is the solution to that?

G: Let them be.

J: Which would be what, withdrawing?

G: Yes. Let them be. The United States has imposed its will upon many different territories or nations since World War I. It has imposed its will, deciding it is right and it has the right to impose its will on other nations. It has created more dictators in doing so than there were before the United States started it. It has created more problems in more countries of imbalance and destruction and infighting than before it moved in on these countries. It has always had an agenda that was based upon its own greed, upon its own need to control something, because there was something it wanted.

J: We wonder why so much of the world is so hostile towards us.

G: The only dictatorship we see is the dictatorship of supposed democracy.

J: The dictatorship of democracy! Wow, that's what you're suggesting we are imposing?

G: Yes, you use that to give yourself a position of superiority and the right to impose your will upon others, believing that your imposition of democracy, as you call it, upon another nation is your right because it is democracy. In reality, it is not democracy at all. It is a form of imperialism not much different from the British form of imperialism in the previous two centuries.

J: In one of our earlier discussions you said something that I thought was very profound and eloquent, something like, "love one another as you love yourself is the earliest form of democracy."

G: That is correct.

J: That ties into a question I was asking in an earlier conversation when the tape stopped in the middle of your answer. I would like your exact words rather than my paraphrase. You were stating that all religions at the basis of their teachings say the same thing, love one another as you love God. I asked, what went wrong? You started to answer that people got hold of the teachings and used them as they had used the political system, and the taped stopped. I wondered if you would give a full response to that.

G: First of all, people misuse systems by turning them into absolutes, turning them into systems of rules and laws, which makes finite the experience that can be had within the system. Take, for example, the Roman Catholic Church. The basic premise of it is a separation from God. You are separate from God and you must earn the right to be acceptable to God and to have God embrace you in His kingdom called heaven. But you don't really have any chance of that because the very nature of who you are is wrong, bad, sinful, corrupt, and unacceptable.

Therefore, your life must be a life of despair and suffering in order for you to someday earn the right. But, of course, there is no indication of when that someday might be. That will be judged by that one called God, that ultimate parent figure. So, you are caught in a purgatory of constantly searching for what it is I need to be or do in order to be good enough, perfect enough, worthwhile enough, to have a connection to God and to enter his kingdom called heaven. And so it is a system that is set up as a system of shame and a system of resistance because in order to achieve it, you must constantly avoid anything that is not acceptable within that framework. Therefore, you must always resist anything that is bad, wrong, that is not within the limited criteria of what has been judged is acceptable in order to be acceptable to God. Therefore, it is not a democratic system but a rather dictatorial system

J: Well, the Catholic Church has reminded its membership rather frequently that it is not a democracy. I have spent the last few months steeped in books by various religious historians trying to understand the origins of the belief systems the Christian churches teach. I'm really surprised by the relatively small number of men who appear to have been involved in assembling what is known as the New

Testament of the Bible as well as the development of other Christian teachings that have influenced so much of the Western world.

G: Why are you surprised? All you have to do is look at your present reality in the United States. It is exactly the same.

J: What do you mean?

G: Look at the people who are dictating the belief systems of the whole and how the whole are reluctant to challenge it in any way, and just fall asleep under the hypnosis of you are right, take care of me as long as I don't have to be involved, make any decisions, or take any responsibility. There is your answer. That is why. Why should you be shocked? It is still going on.

J: To me it isn't as benign as people just falling asleep. People were punished for expressing a different point of view from the authority figures.

G: They're still being punished. Look at your policy called Homeland Security.

J: You're talking about the Patriot Act.

G: Yes. Have you read it?

J: Well, you have asked me that before, and I've learned more about it. I've learned how our civil liberties can be easily hijacked in a national emergency or if the President orders it.

G: Yes. Inherent in it is the punishment you are speaking of where anyone who opposes it is concerned.

J: As I have studied how our religious belief systems have evolved, I'm beginning to realize that the teachings of Jesus, whose birth you announced two thousand years ago, have sort of been hijacked by political systems called religions and our belief systems have calcified around the dogma they created.

G: Yes.

J: And I think when you connect that experience to our own times today, you're telling us that our own democracy has in the same way been hijacked by the powerful and the connected to serve their own ends.

G: Yes.

J: And we are under the illusion that we are in charge when in fact we're not.

G: That is correct.

J: That it is another small group of people who are running the show.

G: That's correct.

J: And there is a stated or unstated threat to challenging their control.

G: How easily the American public has accepted what they have been told, including and ever since 9/11.

J: What do you think of the 9/11 commission that is currently [April 2004] investigating the whole 9/11 event?

G: It is a puppet organization that will be allowed to function under certain conditions so that the public will be led to believe that justice is actually taking place. And it will, therefore, satiate and satisfy the limited amount of interest a few of the people bother to entertain.

J: Is the commission just creating the illusion of an investigation?

G: It is not about whether or not they are creating an illusion. It is about what will be allowed and what will not be allowed that will then determine the confines of the investigation. The government and the military can at any given time decide what is allowable and what is not allowable as far as classified information is concerned.

J: So you're saying that the information to which they have access is being restricted.

G: Exactly.

J: I am still so deeply troubled by your charges that our own government was behind the 9/11 event. What more can you tell us about how this whole 9/11 scenario unfolded?

G: Well, first of all the Bush administration is and was involved in the Carlyle Group among others that the bin Laden family was also involved in, which was headquartered in the World Trade Center. The SEC had given freedom from investigation to the Carlyle Group previous to 9/11 and had relinquished that freedom from investigation approximately three months before 9/11. They were, therefore, subject to investigation.

There had been some dealings where the Bush family was concerned related to the Carlyle Group and to Bush Sr., the former president of the United States, and his representation of the Carlyle Group as the senior international ambassador. There was some questionable business that had gone on there that was about to be investigated. The records and headquarters of the FBI were also located in the World Trade Center. Many other companies of questionable standing also had their headquarters in the WTC. There was a lot of stuff, so to speak, that could come down very soon. So that in itself was a reason to have an investment in the destruction of the World

Trade Towers. But the biggest thing was to create a problem/reaction/solution scenario.

The Americans had been pursuing the oil interests in Afghanistan for years, which is why they opposed the Russians in Afghanistan and built the Taliban to oppose the Russians in the first place. The Russian structure in the country broke down. The Iron Curtain fell in part because the United States helped stop Russia's efforts to build a pipeline that would get their oil through Afghanistan to the Indian Ocean. After the Russians were defeated, Unocal, an oil pipeline company, was negotiating to build the pipeline to get the oil out through Afghanistan. The Taliban controlled the country and were exerting various means of extortion that were extremely problematic to the building of that pipeline and also to the group that controlled the contracting of the pipeline.

Unocal, which is very closely aligned with the Bush family and other members of the Bush administration, had been struggling for years to gain a foothold there to build the pipeline, and it wasn't happening. Therefore, there was a need for the invasion of Afghanistan so that the foothold could be set in Afghanistan and the Taliban could be put under control once again. And the influence and interference of Osama bin Laden, who had been created by the government of the United States in the first place, could be laid to rest. To do that, you have to go to the people and say, look, we need to go in and invade Afghanistan. And the people would say, why? That's ridiculous. We'll never support that. Therefore, they resorted to an ancient ploy that governments have used since Roman and Grecian times, and that is called the problem/reaction/solution scenario.

You create a problem that is immediately threatening to the people in their own environment, the World Trade Towers collapsing. Then, in that scenario you create a reaction, and you direct that reaction to provide the solution you want. Osama bin Laden has attacked the World Trade Towers with his gangsters—so we must go and attack Afghanistan. And the people are willing to go, yes, Daddy, please, we have been threatened and you have found the enemy and the enemy is in Afghanistan. Therefore, go attack Afghanistan. Now you have the people agreeing to the very thing you wanted them to agree to. That is the problem/reaction/solution scenario. So you have the problem, you have the reaction, and you have the solution.

You hear little now, do you, of Afghanistan, of what is happening there. You have almost forgotten about Osama bin Laden, some legendary figure in the past.

J: We're supposedly searching for him in the Afghan mountains somewhere.

G: Ah yes, searching the mountains far and wide, yes.

J: Where is he? Do you know?

G: Osama bin Laden is very carefully being taken care of at this time. He is hidden out. So now, no one is paying attention to Afghanistan any more because now the problem/reaction/ scenario has shifted to Iraq. So now the right hand doesn't know what the left hand is doing once again. The magician is pulling his magic rabbit out of the hat, so to speak. And so now Unocal has its foothold in Afghanistan, and it's busily building the pipeline, and all of the Bush administration who are involved will profit greatly from it.

J: The pipeline is going from the Soviet Union to …

G: The Indian Ocean to be able to bring the oil through Afghanistan. However, the resources in the Russian sector were originally thought to be vast. They have since found those resources are not as great as they had thought. Therefore, it became increasingly important that they rush to control the oil resources in Iraq. Thus they hurried along the inception of the attack to get rid of that awful man who had all of those weapons of mass destruction holed up in Iraq, none of which has been found, have they?

J: Somehow they don't seem to exist.

G: They don't seem to exist.

J: Along with what you said about the oil reserves in Russia turning out to be smaller, Shell Oil recently reported that their oil reserves appear to be significantly smaller that they had thought. Estimated world oil reserves, in fact, may be smaller than previously estimated, which makes the Iraqi oil reserves even more valuable.

G: That is correct.

J: The Bush administration has minimized the importance of oil in Iraq.

G: Of course, because they must justify their cause.

J: You said that the extremes of duality would be revealed during this time. There are increasing numbers of books, articles, and groups challenging U.S. government policies and the real motivations behind them. Are they examples of what you have been forecasting?

G: Yes. They are the beginning of the evidence of light that is penetrating the darkness, penetrating the duality, bringing it into the light. All the secrets will be revealed, eventually.

Chapter 6:
Religion/Scripture/Spirituality

G: Duality is being revealed wherever it exists—just as it was last year in the Catholic Church, an example to show you the duality in the organized religious structures that have become corrupted.

J: By duality do you mean where the power and privileges rest with the few and most people are disenfranchised?

G: Exactly. The duality in the church, whether it be the Catholic Church, Protestant, or whatever it is, it doesn't matter. You see, as soon as you choose a figure to be your intervention between you and God to tell you who God is and to act as the intervener between you and God, you're in trouble. You're setting up a daddy figure, and you're remaining a child, not taking responsibility for your direct connection to your spirituality, your direct connection with your place with God.

J: That's what all religions do and teach, isn't it?

G: Yes, it is. So they are all in a state of duality.

J: What about the prayers and rituals that all the religions have developed? They all have them. Were they inspired by God, or were they created by man?

G: God has nothing to do with it. It's all man's choice. All duality has been created by man. Good and evil are created by man. The concept of the devil is created by man. The concept of the devil is simply man's inability to take responsibility for his own shadow and the actions thereof. And so he separates it from himself as another force that he won't take responsibility for.

J: There are going to be a lot of people reading this material who will probably consider what you just said to be outrageous, even blasphemous.

G: They certainly will. Thank God!

J: What would you say to the devout Christians, Muslims, Jews, and others who believe that they're honoring God through their prayers and rituals in the way God demands of them?

G: Do not give your power to beliefs. Beliefs are not truth. A belief is a doctrine. Belief is a dogma. It creates a limited frozen frame that can never grow. The truth is infinite. It is ever expanding. Do you not think that God, the Creator, is in a process of discovery and expansion all of the time in His infinite knowledge of His being, just as you are in a constant process of expansion and discovery of the knowledge of the truth of your being?

J: Most people think of God as being fixed and complete.

G: Of course. God is an old man on a cloud who is judging me. And if I'm a good little boy, he will reward me. And if I'm a bad little boy, he will punish me because God is in the image and likeness of the parent figure, the tribal figure. It started out with man worshiping the animals and the elements as Gods. Anything that they couldn't understand or that they didn't have power over that seemed to have power greater than them became the father figure who could reward or punish them.

All it illustrates is man's disconnection from his unity with all that is. And in his separation, he fears anything that is different or individual from himself because he has not yet learned to honor his individuality. Therefore, he cannot honor the unifying with the individuality of all aspects and expressions of who God is. Because every single human being, every grain of sand, every plant, animal, every oxygen molecule in the air is a piece of the consciousness and the expression of God. And all of it is one to make up the whole. One cannot be without the other. And when man disturbs the elements of nature, he is disturbing and distorting his connection with God and his connection with himself.

J: So you're saying God is still becoming.

G: God is always becoming because God is infinite. God is learning as you are learning.

J: It's hard to believe there is something God doesn't know.

G: Yes, it is. If God is infinite and immortal, then why would God be finite in his knowledge of himself?

J: Hmm. Good question. I'm still dealing with the statement you made earlier that the rituals and prayers practiced by the various religions were not inspired by God, that the things that have been created to honor God really don't honor God. Many people would consider that pretty shocking.

G: Religions were created by men. Religions in their earliest form were contracted from the earliest tribal ceremonies and rituals that celebrated the earth and the animals. You see, if you go back to the tale of the Garden of Eden and Adam and Eve thrown out of paradise, what they are talking about is how man first realized his separation.

When he separated his animal nature from the experience of unity with nature itself, with the natural elements, and became an individual reasoning being, began to develop the reasoning of the mind, he became an individuated being called human divided from the animal kingdom. He then lost his original unity with physical reality where nature was concerned and experienced separation for the first time. This is being kicked out of the Garden of Eden. This is eating the fruit of knowledge. And this is also represented by male and female and Adam and Eve, which became the separation of the sexes—the separation between the male and female within, between the assertive nature and the receptive nature. That is all that story represents, man's division from his unity.

Since then he has been seeking to resolve the problem of separation. That is man's task. And the only way that can be resolved is through the force of love, which is the force of the soul. Love reunites his physical being with his spiritual being. The soul is the connector because spirit is an unindividuated source. The physical is separate without that source until the soul is awakened, which becomes the integrative point. So the soul combines physical and spiritual to express the individual spark of being that is God in matter.

J: And that will happen as part of our evolution.

G: It is part of your evolution. You are part of a divine plan. You can either do it kicking and screaming, or you can do it willingly by following the plan consciously.

J: In other words, you are creating an alternative to religions.

G: That is correct.

J: As opposed to resisting them and fighting them and condemning them.

G: That's correct because then you'll just be in duality again. You see, there's nothing wrong with religions. The problem is in the way people practice them.

J: So let's make a statement about what can be helpful and constructive and useful about religions so that it doesn't sound like it's just an indictment of them.

G: The fact that all religions at the basis of their teaching say the same thing: "Love one another as you love God."

J: When you were talking about the birth of Christ, you said that we would be shaking up some sacred cows because the Bible as we know it is not entirely accurate. It has been translated many times.

G: Yes, it has. For instance, King Constantine took out all references in the Bible to reincarnation,

J: Can you make any generalizations about the value of scripture such as the Bible or the Koran?

G: All of these writings contain basic principles that are related to the divine order of life. But they have been distorted through the value systems of the people of those times who interpreted the information. And, also, understand that the Bible is a mystical writing that is not what it seems. It is interpretive. Therefore, it has stories that disguise ancient mysteries until you have reached a point of evolution where you can unlock its key or its code, just as the Koran has, just as other writings have. This was done to disguise the power of the universe so that it would not fall into the hands of people who would misuse it for their own use, so that it could be kept alive until humanity had reached a point of evolution where they could benefit from the true knowledge that was hidden within the mysteries.

J: You said that we are entering that age now.

G: That is correct.

J: But I suspect that since this is a new two-thousand-year age we have some time to go before the mysteries are revealed,

G: Yes. But some of the mysteries are being revealed now.

J: In what way?

G: Well, there are teachings of the ancient mystery schools such as the attunement program we believe you embarked on called Reiki that is a part of the ancient mysteries. The Light Ascension process is based upon the stages of initiation of the mysteries. And there are many other processes as well, for instance, the teachings of the Masons. The Masons were an early mystery school as were the Egyptian Left and Right Eye of Horus mystery schools. Those are ancient mystery schools.

But people have taken them and have distorted their rituals and the powers used in the teachings for their own purposes. This is why it is dangerous to give true power, the power of creation, to humanity because people misuse it. When they discovered the power of the atom, what did they do? They used it to destroy life, not to create life, not to restore life, not to foster life, but to destroy it. Do you see? This is why the secrets of the mystery schools have been held in secret through the ages and only a few have been allowed to be a part of them.

J: Religions and scripture are basically about honoring God. I want to ask you about a statement Jesus made that you quoted as: "Do not worship me, but worship the Father who is in heaven."

G: That is correct.

J: How should we worship the father?

G: In loving one another. In accepting one another through the individual expression of who you are. In seeing the value and the equality of each human being as the substance of God, God is all that is. To honor the differences of God's appearance and expression and being in every single expression of creation from the tiniest blade of grass to the tiniest cellular movement.

J: So worship has nothing to do with rituals and reciting words.

G: What good are words without action? Have words helped to keep harmony on your planet? Actions speak louder than words. Love is an act. Love is an action of will. It is not a sentiment. It is the expression of the will of being. It is the expression of the will of the individual to know life, not death, to know life in all of its forms. You have the opportunity as you look around you to look into the face of God in every form of creation that you see, in every human being you see. Yet, how many of them can you accept with love? Well, he has a different opinion than me. Or he's a different color than I am. Or he's a different social stratum. He doesn't wear the right clothes. Or he doesn't have the same orientation that I have. So you are constantly in the process of judging God. The entire opportunity to love and know God and communicate with God lies right here in your physical experience. You don't have to go elsewhere. When you have accomplished it here, then you will know God.

J: You said that the Bible was written in code because man was not ready to use the information.

G: Yes.

J: Have we reached the point where things can be revealed to us, or are there still things that need to be kept from man's knowledge?

G: There are still things in the ancient mysteries that would be misused by humankind if they were to be revealed at this time because man has not reached the point where he can deal with the power of creation in a way that is for the good of the whole. But this two-thousand-year cycle is for the purpose of establishing that point in evolution where all the secrets can be revealed. So over time the mysteries will be revealed as man evolves in his process to be able to handle them.

J: We're only in the first years of the new cycle, so we need a lot of time for the things you're talking about to unfold, I suppose.

G: Exactly, because the cycle is just beginning to initiate. As we have said, every cycle is governed by a ray of consciousness. The last ray of consciousness was the sixth ray, which governs the pairs of opposites. This cycle is the seventh ray, which is the cycle of spirituality that restructures form. It's also known as the seventh ray of the ceremonial order of magic or the cycle of ritual. Therefore, it involves the ritual of the ancient mysteries and the ritual of initiation. That's why in this two-thousand-year cycle man begins to evolve into his spiritual humanity through initiation.

In previous cycles he has remained in evolution through a process of aspirant and discipleship. Now he moves into initiate. He now begins to go through the initiation or the awakening of the soul consciousness because the soul consciousness is the accessible aspect of the divine in individual form. This new age begins the realization of the experience of the living Christ, the experience of the awakening of the soul, the experience of the awakening of love.

J: I would guess that the world's religions over the last two thousand years have helped prepare mankind for this time even though there have been plenty of problems and conflict.

G: Yes. You see, all religions were offshoots of earlier tribal customs and forms of worship. They also stem from teachings of the various schools of self-mastery, the mystery schools like the Essenes, for instance, of which Christ was a member. They are combinations of all those things, a lot of different things. Understand that man takes information and interprets it and distorts it for his use in a patriarchal system in which someone rules over the masses to keep them under control.

The earliest forms of religion were the earliest forms of government, the earliest ways of governing the people so that you didn't have chaos. You could control people if you could make them fear God, or fear the king. The king was just another form of the god of the land, a ruler of some kind, the pontiff, the bishop, whoever it is, because of man's infantile state of development. Man has remained in that infantile state of wanting that unconditional love from daddy.

So dad is created in the image and likeness of his tribal system, his patriarchal system. And that has based religions upon a system of morality, of moralism.

Moralism is a system that is based upon reward and punishment, right and wrong, good and bad. It's a system based upon duality; it's not a system based upon conscience. When you develop a conscience, all individuals are responsible for themselves. They are responsible for their acts. They are responsible for their development through trial and error. They are responsible for their development through the ability to experience remorse and to correct their mistakes and grow and discover from them and move on. They are able to take responsibility for their actions and the consequences of their actions. The consequences of their actions are not punishable—they are responded to. And through the education provided by the trial and error of their mistakes, they learn and grow. They cease to make those mistakes and they become more.

In a system of right and wrong, a system of moralism, you control people in a system that has only one choice available at any time. And that is the right choice. If you make the wrong choice, you are damned, bad, punishable. Therefore, you remain a child who must obey the parent, do what the parent says, always discern what would be the right choice to avoid the wrong choice to avoid punishment. So it is a system based upon reward and punishment, good and evil, right and wrong. It is not a system based upon taking responsibility for your actions and developing, instead of morality, a conscience.

A conscience is based upon equality, compassion, respect, and honoring one another. It's based upon honoring the individual, with the individual taking responsibility for who he or she is. If I were an individual, I should also take responsibility for the plight of others because I do unto others as I would have them do unto me. Therefore, I have compassion for the state of humanity. I do not declare war on a country and punish it because it is doing what I see as morally wrong, that it is doing the wrong thing and I am doing the right thing. If you are killing anybody, you are not justifiable in your morality. Killing is killing no matter how you do it. Taking a life is against the divine plan. Taking a life deliberately is against the law of the universe. The law of the universe celebrates life, supports life, has compassion for all life having equal value no matter what level it is at. The love of the universe supports the nurturing of life, not the destruction of it.

J: You told me that the primary purpose of this project was my own personal growth.

G: Yes. That's why you are doing it.

J: I can understand that's why I'm doing it. But with the billions of individuated souls who exist, I can't figure out why you would spend this much time for my growth.

G: Because it's not just for your growth. It is also something that you are, through your growth, seeking to find a way of passing on to others. So you see, the teacher is the student is the teacher is the student. The teacher is only as good as he is a student. The student teaches the teacher how to teach. Therefore, the teacher must be receptive to the student as a student in order to be able to teach the student. It requires a balance of giving and receiving, a balance of listening as well as giving out or speaking. The best teachers are teachers who know how to listen.

J: I spent a lot of time teaching in business organizations, and when I was at my best, I was doing that. I wish most of the teachers who I've had in my life could hear, believe, and practice what you just said.

G: Yes, because on average, teachers take information, make it dogma, and teach it as that rather than using the information to inspire and awaken themselves. That is the difference between a teacher who is a teacher technician and a teacher who is an artist.

J: And they don't involve the student enough in the process. They don't ask. It's nearly all telling.

G: Yes. Well that's the patriarchal system that leads into the educational process. My way is right. I know and you don't. It's the same as the religious systems. We know who God is and we have Him locked up in the church down the street here and you don't. One of the reasons that religion is the opiate of the masses is because the masses like to be told what to do. So religion is perfect for them because they have an elected official who will tell them who God is, what their relationship is with God, so they don't have to bother having a spiritual experience of evolution within themselves. Very little religion has a spiritual focus. In order to be a spiritual being, you must be willing to take the responsibility of finding the evolution of the God experience within yourself as an individual—how it affects you, how it awakens and inspires your individual growth and the individual path of the revelation of your own soul.

Each man is his own redeemer. A church or a religion cannot redeem you. Your redemption comes in the discovery and development of who you are and what you discover you are within for the fulfillment and the growth of your potential as a human spiritual being. That can only be done on an individual basis. It can only be done alone. The irony and paradox of unity is that until you are willing to be alone with yourself, you cannot be unified with all that is. Until you can accept and embrace all that you are within yourself, it is impossible for you to do so with all that is outside of yourself.

J: What do you mean, it can only be done alone?

G: Being alone with yourself simply means being willing to take responsibility for your own path, your own growth, your own development. That is what being alone means. Being alone also means finding the ability to accept all that you are, both what you judge as good and as bad, as part of the wholeness of who you are.

J: Learning not to condemn yourself.

G: Exactly. Why would you condemn God?

J: Ahhh. I grew up in a church where I thought I got redeemed through the sacraments, prayers, confession, and all those rituals.

G: Words. Words. Words.

J: Were they just created by men trying to control people?

G: Well, yes, to some degree. To some degree there is also purity of purpose in it. It was a way of trying to get people aligned in a certain way. Religions were the original forms of government, trying to create balance out of chaos, to create community and communion. Unfortunately, the concept got distorted into communion meaning sameness rather than communion meaning sharing the oneness of every individual expression of being and honoring the integrity of that individuality within the oneness.

J: Yes, some things got very distorted, and at times became very oppressive.

G: Yes, well, it's all a learning process. You see, what you call oppression is simply the embracing of one side and condemning the other.

J: It seems that in our age, finally, more people are willing to stand up to the institutions and authority figures and challenge them when they believe it appropriate.

G: Yes, that is happening because the consciousness of the soul level of humanity is beginning to awaken in this time of ascension, in this new age, this new two-thousand-year cycle. This new cycle is simply a period of evolution where you have reached a state of being where you are capable now of realizing the God self. Therefore, you are developing a new root race of human kind, a spiritual root race.

J: It's showing up everywhere. It's my impression that people are far more willing to challenge authority than perhaps any time in the past.

G: That is true. Because there is only one authority and that is you. You are your own authority. You see, as you embrace your own authority, you embrace the responsibility for that authority. You embrace the responsibility for creating your own reality. You embrace the responsibility of responding to life, responding to your own choices, to your own commitments and intentions, to taking responsibility for the consequences of the reality you are creating through your choices. If you want to know what people are committed to, look at what they have. You can always tell their commitment by what they have.

J: What do you mean?

G: Reality is based upon what you are committed to, what you are choosing. Therefore, if you look at what you have, you can always identify what your commitment is. If you don't like what you have, then change your commitment. Change your choices.

J: When you said that, I thought of material things. Of course, you must be talking about more than just material things.

G: Well, material things are merely a reflection of your inner values, your inner intentions, your inner choices and commitments. They're just merely a reflection. They are a process and an experience of mirroring back to you in the physical world how you're creating reality. That's their only purpose. They are the tools through which you get to experience the process of learning how to be a creator.

J: I guess as we express our individuality the way you are describing it, we are embracing our Godship.

G: That's right. God does not give someone else responsibility for its creation. It takes full responsibility for its entire creation. It doesn't say, oh, I don't like that part—I didn't create that.

J: I want to discuss something that we have talked about before because it has come up again in the news during the past week. It has to do with the issue of homosexuality. Homosexuals seem almost to be under siege. The Episcopal Church seems to be heading towards a major split over the election of a gay bishop from New England. The pope this week called homosexuality evil and condemned the idea of gay marriages. And President Bush seems to be pushing for a constitutional amendment banning gay marriages. He referred to homosexuality as "a sin." What would you say about all this?

G: Well, it's just another example of the duality of something surfacing in consciousness, seeing the opposition. The mainstream of collective consciousness is threatened by a group called homosexuals. Why are they threatened by them? Because they are different from what the collective consciousness accepts in the herd mentality because they are an individual group form, just as another religion is an individual group form. It's not something new. It's simply transferred to focusing on homosexuals. You see it with religious groups all over the world. What do you have? Religious wars. Christian groups against Christian groups, the Jews against the Palestinians, the Christian world against the Islamic world. You see—no difference.

It's about being able to embrace individuality. You see, the reason that there is duality is because each person in the collective consciousness is in duality with his- or herself. Look at the body of homosexuality. Homosexuals are in duality within themselves. They're in duality with their own acceptance of their own sexuality. What you call gay pride, for example, the Gay Pride parade in New York. It has nothing to do with acceptance. It has to do with fighting non-acceptance. So I put it in your face. You accept me because I can't accept myself. Let me show the extreme of my duality within myself, and if you accept it, then I'm acceptable.

What has to happen is that all homosexuals have to come to acceptance within themselves of their own sexual identity. Then there will be no conflict. There will be no opposition. The opposition is only being mirrored within the community itself. Why do you think the destructive force of AIDS is so rampant in the gay community? Because it is first chakra. It is a manifestation and reflection of sexual shame, an acting out of that sexual shame.

J: So each of us, no matter the issue, should accept and love ourselves.

G: Exactly. If you don't, nobody else will.

J: You've said often, you can't love another unless you love yourself.

G: That's correct. Pride is opposition. Pride is the defense of defiance where the ego is concerned.

J: The pope and the Catholic Church claim to be the voice of spiritual truth. So what would you say to the pope who claims to have infallibility with regard to matters of spirit?

G: You know nothing about spirit. Spirit embraces all being. It embraces the soul's individuation of being in all forms. The Catholic Church and all other churches to a great degree are nothing more or less than separated indoctrinations of ideas about the duality between spirit and matter, and they serve to continue to enforce that duality in the collective consciousness. You see, churches were the earliest forms of government before you had political systems of government, before church and state separated. If you go back to pagan times, early tribal belief systems related to spirit and God and early rituals related to the earth were the earliest forms of church. They were the earliest forms of governing the people. They used the symbolism of certain forms of nature and certain animal forms that they worshipped as Gods. Those deities had various qualities, and they used those qualities to bring fear to the people in order to control them, to govern them. It really has nothing to do with government. It has to do with control.

Government does not control. Individuality is government. Self-government is government. When you are able to take responsibility for yourself as an individual, your individual creation of reality for the development of a conscience in relationship to the sacredness of all life and the sacredness of the individuality of all life, then you are conducting government, the government of being. Anything else is a sham. So church was the earliest form of government. The Catholic Church is the largest and the richest corporate structure in the world. It has a lot to lose. The entire religion is based upon keeping the people down, keeping them under control, keeping them in fear, in fear of God, not in love of God.

That does not mean that there are not certain individuals in the Catholic Church who aren't like that. There are. But the body of government of the church as a whole is in duality and represents and teaches the duality between matter and spirit and uses it to produce fear and control. All of your forms of government are all forms of duality. Your laws don't tell you what you can do—they all tell you what you can't do. Your Ten Commandments in your Christian mythological book called the Bible are based upon what you can't do. Thou shalt not commit adultery. Thou shalt not kill. They don't tell you what to do. They don't empower you.

J: Where do they come from?

G: They come from an ancient system.

J: Moses didn't get them from God on the mountain?

G: Moses was the interpreter of information. Moses was a channel for his time, a time that lived in duality. What do you think the Egyptians and the Israelites represent, the Israelites wandering in the desert for forty years? They're still wandering in the desert. Israel represents the lower will of human kind that is still seeking to control in its separation.

J: What do you mean?

G: Well, look at how the Israelites see themselves, as the chosen ones. And, therefore, everyone else is not. The chosen one is representative of the lower ego, the lower self in separation that seeks to gratify its desires in its pride of being special. Why do you think you had World War II and the killing of millions of Jews by the Germans? Both sides were fighting the same feelings, the feeling of victimization and not good enough. Hitler was doing it by developing a super race, and the Jews were doing it by fighting their feelings of not good enough as the super race, the chosen ones. Both were committed to fighting the same feeling, and they did it beautifully. That's all that took place. If you want to fight a feeling, whether as an individual or on a collective level, you will find a partner who will be happy to mirror your commitment.

J: Whether we're talking about homosexuality, religion, racism, etc., to fight those who are trying to restrict or control us, you're saying we really have to address the feelings we have inside.

G: That's right. All you're doing is fighting the feeling of not good enough. And, therefore, you're seeing a feeling of not good enough everywhere.

J: And that is really the change of consciousness you keep talking about.

G: Correct. Look away from the form. Look at the substance behind the form. Look at the life that is imbuing the reflection in the form. The commitment behind the form is fighting the feeling of not good enough. Therefore, you will find a partner to fight it with you. You'll find the entire Catholic Church or you'll find the head of the government of the United States or whomever. Do you see?

J: So to change the collective consciousness, we have to change our own consciousness. It starts with us.

G: That is correct. What creates the collective consciousness? All the individuals who create it. All the individuals who embrace the herd instinct to fit in. Fitting in is a substitute for not belonging to yourself, embracing your individuality, being able to accept yourself as an individual.

J: That's really what loving yourself is.

G: That's correct. If I cannot love myself, if I cannot accept myself, then I have to get other people to do it. In order to get them to do it, I have to be like them, which means I have to give myself up. There is no unity in herd consciousness. Herd consciousness creates separation of self and alienation of self.

Chapter 7:
Jesus and Mary/Christianity

J: When you were explaining your mission as the Archangelic Realm of Gabriel you referred to the virgin birth of Jesus.

G: Yes.

J: Can you confirm that it was a virgin birth? As you know there is considerable controversy about that.

G: First of all, understand that spirit is not matter. What was being born in the birth chamber of Mary was the spirit of God through the revelation of the soul. That is the direct relationship with God. So what took place was the birth of a soul who was awakened, who knew and was conscious of his connection right from the point of birth directly to the divine plan and his purpose in it. That is the Immaculate Conception. Was the physical reality a part of that? Was there a seed that was planted, the sperm and the egg? Did that take place? Yes, it did take place to bring about the physical form. But it is not the physical form that this is about. This is about the immaculate form. It is about the form of a soul. That is the Immaculate Conception. So Mary was chosen as the host of the spirit of God for the Immaculate Conception of Jesus the Christ, the man of the soul.

J: So Jesus was conceived the way all children were conceived?

G: Yes. The virgin birth was the fact that this was the first child that was born as an awakened soul to bring about a level of consciousness imprinted into the earth plane. You see, the reason that there is so much dissembling about this is because, where humanity is concerned and where the Catholic Church is concerned, the whole idea of the virgin birth is all tied around shame where sexuality is concerned.

J: Not just the Catholic Church.

G: Yes, but the Christian church originated in its first form as the Catholic Church as an organization of some power. And so this is simply man's separation from his shame about his being a physical, sexual being. And, God, if it's connected to the physical act, is somehow tainted, dirty, wrong, and bad. The physical experience of love is just as immaculate and just as loving because it is an expression of physical beings' love and connection. But with most people, as the sexual energy is disconnected from the erotic force, the love force, it becomes an experience of shame.

J: You said, "The virgin birth is representative of the fact that the soul is not dependent on procreation where physical matter is concerned in order to find its existence or to be born." Could you explain that?

G: Physical matter does not create life. Physical matter is animated by life. Physical matter cannot be animated without the life force. The life force brings life to physical matter, animates it, gives it expression. That overall life force is the erotic force also known as the spiritual force, which is the main force of undifferentiated energy and consciousness that gives life to anything, whether it's physical or nonphysical, whether it's the smallest atom up to the largest physical form. The soul becomes the conscious experience of that animation that directs that animation in a specific way.

Without the connection to the soul and the body there would be no direction where the will for life is concerned, no individual expression of it. So matter, of itself, has no life. In other words, life does not begin in matter, does not originate in matter. It gets expressed in matter. But where physical beings are concerned, they believe that the whole force of life is in matter and that matter is responsible for life. Therefore, they fear death.

J: You're aware that in many places, Mary is as revered as Jesus.

G: Yes, we are aware of that.

J: What is your reaction to that?

G: Well, it's the same as people always do. They idolize symbols rather than embody what they teach. So they create an idol rather than take what that representative has taught them and put it into their lives. Christ repeated over and over and over again, "Do not worship me, but worship my father who is in heaven. I am but a man. Do not worship me." He said again and again and again. But yet people have not done that. They are worshipping the symbol rather than the substance.

J: I went twice to Medjugorje in Yugoslavia where the Virgin Mary reportedly was appearing to some young people there. And, of course, you know about Lourdes and so many of the other widely believed appearances of Mary. Millions of people have made pilgrimages to these sites. The young people claiming to see the apparitions quote the Virgin Mary as asking for prayer and recitation of the rosary and warning that she can no longer still the hand of God from punishing mankind for its sins, etc. What should we make of all that? Is she really appearing?

G: Yes, she is appearing as a collective thought form. She is appearing because of the desire of those who gather. You see, human beings create reality either etherically or physically through the strength and power of their intention. And their collective intention creates the manifestation that much more quickly and that much more easily. They are gathering together an astral thought form collectively because of their need and their desire to believe, and so it is so. Is it real? Yes, it is.

J: Is the message also created by the people?

G: Every message that is received by someone is the message that they collectively can understand or accept or are ready for.

J: Many people accept these messages as God's word.

G: Yes. Well, the interpretation by the priest is accepted as God's word too, is it not?

J: For many people it is.

G: The kingdom of God is within you.

J: I guess I'm really asking if this is divine revelation?

G: Divine revelation lies within you. That is why we say to you, do not worship Gabriel. Take what Gabriel says and use it to stimulate something within you, to awaken you to you, to awaken the divine within you. Otherwise, you are just worshiping something outside of yourself, whether it be Mary or Jesus or ... it is within you, dear one.

J: I realize God is within. But so many people are looking to these apparitions for wisdom and direction.

G: And they will continue to as long as they believe that they must look outside themselves for the answer. Then the answer will always appear outside themselves.

J: I know we're directed to look within, but it doesn't seem to make much sense that I ignore any wisdom that came to me just because it didn't come from within. I guess I don't know what to do with your answer.

G: What you do with it is you take it inside and you meditate upon it and you see how it connects to the truth within yourself. And if it does, then you know that it is a part …You see, it's all part of divinity anyway. It's all part of the spiritualization of being because everything is spiritual. Everything that takes place is spiritual because God is everywhere. So, yes, God is outside. God is inside. God is everywhere. So is that a part of a divine message? Yes, it is. What part of a divine message is that? Is it a good one? Is it a bad one? Is it neither? Is it a divine message that speaks to those who need to be spoken to in that way in order for them to sustain their faith and their belief in the divine? So, is it legitimate? Yes, it is.

What we are saying is that you do not have to look outside yourself. The same thing lies within you. Do you want to go to Lourdes to get it? That's fine. Do you want to go to Gabriel to stimulate your faith? That's fine. Do you want to talk directly to God? That's fine. Whatever you're doing, you're talking to God anyway because it's all of God. There is nothing that is divorced from God. God penetrates all, all that is physical and nonphysical. God is ever present, infinite, everywhere. Nothing is divorced from, separate from, God, whether you know that or not. God is ever present in everything.

J: In the Religious Science church they say God is all there is.

G: God *is* all there is. God is ever present in everything that lives. God is the very force of life itself. How can you divorce yourself from God unless you divorce yourself from the force of life? You can distort the force of life. You can separate your consciousness from it to some degree through fear and through the machinations of your personality and your belief in separation and isolation, but you still cannot divorce yourself from God.

J: Jesus gave us a prayer. It has come down through time to us as the Our Father. When I asked you how we should pray, you said to affirm what you want as already existing.

G: Yes.

J: Could you offer us an example of a prayer?

G: Divine love is ever present, all power, all life, truth and love over all and all.

J: Thank you.

G: You are most welcome, dear one.

J: Our country is predominantly Christian, and there is enormous curiosity and interest, of course, in Jesus. There have been so many documentaries on television this spring exploring what we know and don't know about Jesus and his times, the evolution of religion, etc. I would like to ask you some of the questions the programs have raised. One of the questions concerns his education. The Bible leaves a big hole from the time Jesus was a child until his ministry began when he was thirty years old. We don't know what happened during that time. You have said that he received a lot of training.

G: Yes. He was traveling in various parts of the East studying and learning from the various schools of mastery.

J: How did that come about? Was it known that he was to become what he became?

G: Yes, by various groups, the Essenes, the Left Eye and Right Eye of Horus schools of Egypt. Christ took his final initiation in the Great Pyramid of Giza in the King's Chamber.

J: I would assume he had been studying for years before that.

G: Yes, he was studying for thirty years from his birth. He studied in the Jewish temples as well as a child.

J: Was someone in charge of his education, guiding him through all these various mystery schools?

G: Many people. His guidance also was from within. He was guided through the order of the universe, the order of synchronicity as he was led. Each part of his process, each awakening of each initiation, guided him further to the next place, the next teacher. You have heard the statement: when the student is ready, the teacher is there.

J: So he must have been aware of his role from the beginning.

G: Yes.

J: Were Mary and Joseph aware?

G: They became aware. We made Mary aware before his birth so that she would be the host for what was called the Son of God.

J: I know we have addressed the issue of the virgin birth, but the Bible says that Mary was "with child" before she was betrothed to Joseph, that she was impregnated by the Holy Spirit, not by man. Is that true?

G: No. You see, they do not understand the concept of the virgin birth and what that is representative or symbolic of. You are all of virgin birth. You have all been conceived through a male and a female in physical form through the act of sex as was Jesus. However, the difference between you and Jesus is that the Immaculate Conception was the realization that what she was bringing into the world was the awakening of the soul of man. If you look at the other cosmologies, the Incas, the Egyptians, the Mayans and many other cosmologies, you will find that they all have the same story of the virgin birth. You will also find that the name of the virgin in each of the languages translates to Mary. The virgin birth is representative of the conscious awakening of the soul of matter. The name Mary means womb of matter.

J: So it has nothing to do with the issue of whether or not Jesus had a human father or that the Holy Spirit impregnated Mary.

G: No. The Holy Spirit impregnates all women. The act of conception, the coming together of the egg and the sperm, is the physical aspect that brings about the chemical interaction in the physical. But the spirit is what connects to the mother at conception, the spirit of the child. That is the Immaculate Conception. Without the spirit connecting to the fetus, there would be no life form. So the spirit that connects as each child is brought into conception is the Immaculate Conception. So each woman that brings about the birth of a child is Mary bringing into the world the birth of Jesus the Christ because Jesus the Christ means man of soul.

So the womb of matter brings into physical reality a man of the soul, a woman of the soul, a child of the soul. That is what these things mean. People take them too literally. But, as we said, it is not possible to bring life into the physical without the conception of the spirit. That is why, for instance, people will try many times to have sexual union and it will not bring about a pregnancy, why some people remain barren. Because the spirit cannot connect, cannot be awakened.

J: Why is that?

G: Many different reasons. On some level, they (the women) don't really want it. On some level, in their learning process, in their soul evolution in that incarnation, they are not meant to because not being able to is part of their growth cycle for that evolution. There is always a reason behind it on a spiritual level.

J: So for these so-called unwanted pregnancies, they were supposed to become pregnant?

G: Yes.

J: Was Mary betrothed to Joseph when she conceived Jesus?

G: Was she married? No.

J: That would have been very dangerous in those times. A woman could be stoned or put to death for conceiving a child out of wedlock.

G: That's true.

J: So you're saying they had sexual relations outside of wedlock.

G: Yes. And then they were wed.

J: So she did not say to you, as the Bible says, "How could I be with child when I have not known man?"

G: What you need to understand is when we spoke with her, we were telling her that this was preordained, that she was chosen, that the soul of Jesus had chosen her, and she had chosen the soul of Jesus. This was the Immaculate Conception. This is always the Immaculate Conception. The Immaculate Conception is not based upon the choices of the personality, two personalities who get together and decide to have sex based upon their attractions and their impulses. Having sex doesn't guarantee anything, anything sacred, any real union or the production of life.

What guarantees the production of life is the Immaculate Conception, the spiritual conception. It is the conception of the soul's choice, the union of souls. You see, there is a union of souls when a child and a mother come together in conception. There is a union of souls when a man and a woman come together to produce the phenomenon of life. Why does it not take sometimes? Why does it take at other times? This is the great question. And doctors don't entirely understand this. They can explain it from a point of view of hormones and from the point of barrenness and weakness in the production process and all that sort of thing. And all that is partially true. But what it comes down to is, it is a soul choice to create life. And the problem with these scholars is that they're focused on the physical.

J: How important is the ceremony of matrimony in the world of spirit?

G: It's not ultimately important at all. It's symbolic. It's ritual. The ritual of marriage does not in any way guarantee union. The purpose of the institution of marriage originally was to guarantee the ongoing reproduction of the life form and reproduction of the species. And it was also created to align certain families with other families because, originally, where marriage was concerned, that choice was made by the parents. The unions came through the parents' choices because they wanted to align certain families to increase their power and wealth.

On a spiritual level marriage is two souls coming together as one, souls sharing the truth and revealing and surrendering the truth of who they are and sharing that with one another. That is the union of marriage, a marriage of two souls.

J: In our culture, we pronounce both a marriage and the children who come from it as legitimate or illegitimate based upon whether or not the parents engaged in a religious or legal ceremony.

G: Yes, well, that is all based upon those ancient needs of preservation of the species, of communities, of ideals, of certain religions, of ways of governing people and bringing them out of chaos. Also, it has its good points because it is a way of teaching people on a physical level about commitment and how to take responsibility. But on a spiritual level, marriage is a communion of two souls.

J: How would you respond to people who might express shock at the idea that Mary and Joseph had sex before they were married?

G: Too bad. Grow up!

J: Well, what about the taboos of their time? Did they go ahead because you advised them that they were supposed to have a child together?

G: We did not advise them that they were supposed to have a child together. We said that she would bring into physical life the Son of God. What we were saying is that she would be responsible for bringing the awakening of the soul of man into the physical experience. Now, broaden your view for a moment. Look at the earth as the body of Mary. Look at the earth as the womb of matter that supports all physical life and, in supporting all physical life, contains within all the souls who exist upon the earth, contains the union of God in physical form, the revelation of God in physical form, the revelation of the soul of God in the physical experience. So, the earth, Gaea, is the Immaculate Conception.

Did the earth have sex to create life? In a sense, yes. Sex on what level? On a molecular level, on a level of atomic structure, a level of magnetics, a level of gravitational forces, a level of cellular forces, a level of DNA? All of those forces contain the celestial forces of the body of Mary bringing about the Immaculate Conception because all physical matter is of God. All physical matter is the expression of spirit. All physical matter contains the soul of God's expression. All individuated forms are individual souls expressing all of the parts of God in communion in the physical world. And the womb of Gaea, the womb of Mary, brings that forth in the sexual union. Two cells come together to create life. How is it different, we ask you?

J: All these rigid attitudes flow out of religions that have set rules of right and wrong.

G: Exactly. You see, the whole controversy based upon Mary and sex and spirit and why the Immaculate Conception took place without sex is because of the shame that mankind has for the idea of sexual union in the first place, that somehow the idea of sexual union is not spiritual.

J: That attitude still prevails today.

G: Of course it does. It's simply an illustration of the three forces: the force of sex, the force of love, and the force of Eros, with the force of Eros being the force of spirit. The force of love being the force of the soul. The force of sex being the force of the physical. When the soul awakens the force of love, it brings together the union of Eros with the individual physical expression of sex. The will of God in Eros individuates into physical form through the physical relationship of sex and contains within it the awakening through the love force of the individual expression of God's being. And until that is realized, you will live in separation and shame. The lower self will always be separate from the higher self. The physical will always be separate from the soul. And the soul and spirit will be separate from the physical. None of them is separate. They are all one. They are only separate in your consciousness.

J: Some biblical scholars have speculated that Jesus was born in 6 BC about April. Is there any way to confirm that with you?

G: No. No, there is not because the calendar has been changed many times. You now operate through the Gregorian calendar. So there is a lot of speculation. When was he born? What month was he born? What day? That sort of thing. Because of the way in which they changed the calendar, none of the speculations is accurate. Let's put it this way—it doesn't really matter. What matters is what he did. What matters is what he illustrated, what he taught, the legacy that he left. That's what matters. It doesn't matter when he lived. It doesn't even matter so much how he lived. What matters is what came out of it. What matters is how his life was an illustration for all humankind.

The same with you. It matters not how old you are, when you were born. It matters not so much the choices you make. It matters what you do with those choices, how you direct those choices. It matters what you learn and what you are able to share that is of value to humanity and to yourself. That is what is important.

J: In an earlier discussion, you said that what matters is how we're being while we're doing whatever we're doing.

G: Exactly. Well, how you are being is how you are valuing your life process, how you are using it, what you are bringing to it, what you are doing to it. That is all the state of beingness. You see, you can have a state of beingness where you are complaining, "Oh, I'm a poor victim. Nothing ever works for me. I'm never going to make it in life. None of it matters. It's all a waste of time. Nobody loves me." You see, that is a state of being. That is a choice like any other choice.

It's never about what is happening in life. It is what you are doing in it. How you are using it. What you are using it for that determines your state of being in that life. It's never about the circumstances and the situations of life. It's about how you're using them for your growth, for your understanding, for your illumination, for your evolution.

J: And isn't it all tied to the purpose of life, which you have said is to learn to love more?

G: Exactly. And all learning to love more means is learning to be more, learning to embrace more of your being, learning to express and experience and share and give more of your being.

J: You said that the details of Jesus's life are basically irrelevant as it's what he illustrated and taught that is important. However, details of his life are of great interest to many people. I wanted to ask a few more questions about Jesus because the Bible is somewhat sketchy and there are some differences among the gospels about the details of Jesus's life.

G: The Bible is a book like any other book that was written by people. People have agendas according to the events and consciousness of their time. The Bible has been distorted and edited and reworked many times over the centuries. There are seven books of the Bible that aren't even in the Bible.

J: Do they still exist?

G: Yes. Tablets that were found in the ancient caves that have never been brought to the light of day. They are controlled by the Catholic Church, controlled by governments. Lots of information. The Bible has been translated over and over many times. There's the modern version, the King James version, the Aramaic version, this version and that version. It has been interpreted this way and that and, as we have said, much of it is also encoded. And so the accuracy of it is questionable.

J: That is why I want to get your version of a number of things. There is some speculation about Jesus' race. What were his racial origins?

G: He was darker skinned than Caucasian, more Middle Eastern.

J: How was he chosen to fulfill the mission that he filled on earth?

G: It's a soul choice. The soul of the one that was chosen was at a stage of evolution where it had moved from adept in the evolution of lifetime after lifetime to master soul. Master soul is the last level of incarnation that will ever happen in the earth plane. Most of the time master souls do not reincarnate. A level of adept is usually the last incarnational cycle in physical matter in a body.

J: Could you explain more about that?

G: Adept is the level before master. That is the level at which the soul achieves mastery in form. It no longer incarnates once it has mastered the physical. The only time a soul will incarnate in a physical body is if it chooses of its own volition, having achieved adept level, to return for the service of the divine plan for humanity. It usually does so to achieve or institute a cycle of evolutionary development where the divine plan is concerned—to set a cycle in place, which is why a master will return in physical form. Then that master in physical form must illustrate through the (physical) form what it has come to teach. The master must lead the students by demonstrating in its own experience the steps and stages to imprint it into the consciousness of the group. That creates or sets the energetic emotional and mental imprint into the consciousness of humanity or a great part of the collective consciousness of humanity.

The imprint of Jesus the Christ demonstrated his mastery through the awakening of the soul. That was the imprint set for this age. So he agreed to do that at the soul level. Since then he has not incarnated in physical form. He remains as one of the ascendant masters governing the divine plan from the etheric.

J: You have explained that he did that by managing the energy forces.

G: Managing the energetic grids. You see, the energetic grids are what gradually bring consciousness into matter. They create the energetic forces that shift and change the evolution of form. Everything begins energetically. Energetic grids are grids of intention that are put into place. Those grids can be accelerated. They can be interwoven in various ways to produce an energetic or consciousness blueprint. Remember, everything begins in consciousness. It begins as energetic grids. Then it translates into awareness. Awareness becomes experience.

During his lifetime, Jesus the Christ developed the energetic grid of the seven levels of initiation that awaken soul consciousness in matter. He wove the imprint of that energetic grid into the consciousness of his own body through demonstrating and going through the stages of evolution of the initiations: the birth, the baptism, the transfiguration, the renunciation, the crucifixion, the resurrection, and the ascension. Those are different stages of self-mastery that all masters must go through in the school of self-mastery, the school of learning.

He illustrated in his life the movement through the Hall of Learning into the Hall of Wisdom as a demonstrated force, a blueprint into the consciousness of humanity set for this time. He set the energy grids in place to be awakened in the Age of Aquarius. Now that awakening is taking place because the grid has been set in place. He and the other ascendant masters are interweaving the grids in the etheric to bring about the evolution of its process in the physical where the mass of humanity, of collective consciousness, is concerned in this two-thousand-year cycle.

J: You have said that there is a unique convergence of energetic forces coming together now.

G: They are unique to this system, to this particular configuration, because you are unifying twelve systems, not one.

J: Because that is a bigger challenge.

G: Yes. You see, you are unifying twelve archetypes of God into ascension.

J: Please explain to me again. What did God want to achieve by bringing the twelve together as it is the first time it has been done?

G: To bring more parts of itself into configuration, into experience and communion simultaneously, through the physical form. God has been examining and experiencing parts of him/herself ever since the beginning, which is the alpha and the omega. There is no beginning and there is no end. Therefore, this is just another aspect of its own evolution, which is infinite. Do you see? The alpha and the omega have no beginning and no end. There is nothing but infinite consciousness. Consciousness is always becoming.

J: I would assume then that there will be more configurations as God continues to experience itself.

G: At some point in evolution, where the experience of your solar system is concerned, there will be the development of intergalactic awareness, which will bring about the ascension of your entire galaxy as well as the ascension of interrelated galaxies. The one and the whole are all the same. They are all interacting, interrelating all of the time. They are already at one. But God consciousness, in this solar system, is simply a way of focusing on twelve aspects and studying the experience of twelve aspects of its being and then billions of fragments of the expression of those twelve aspects through individual soul fragments. And then archetypes of those soul fragments as they are studied through the oversoul of the combination of all the fragments of an individual soul in all lifetimes. So God gets to discover and explore the experience of him/herself in many ways at once because it is all simultaneous.

J: That begins to describe infinity on a truly vast scale. [Laughing] I don't pretend to comprehend it all. It's awesome to say the least. Amazing.

G: Yes.

J: Coming back to our discussion about Mary, can you tell us specifically what you said to her and what her response was?

G: We had simply awakened her consciousness to remind her that when she had come into this physical form, she had chosen at a soul level to be the one who delivered the birth of the one who would bring the example to humanity for this time. And that she, in doing so, was realizing and fulfilling her sacred purpose as a soul. You see, it was also to show that the feminine aspect, in separation from the male aspect, is there to bring about the birth of the divine child each time a baby is born, that the divinity of God is born in the physical each time that a child is born. Do you understand? Now, that divinity is seldom realized because of the way in which the adults, in their lack of parenting skills, pass on their separation to the child, rather than, as Christ said, to learn from the little children. To become as a child allows you to enter the kingdom of heaven, to realize the advanced idea of God.

J: Because children embrace everyone? They don't see themselves as separate or make judgments?

G: That is correct, because children are not separate. They have not developed the skills of separation, the skills of defense. They have not yet been wounded.

J: The Bible says that you had to explain to Joseph what was happening to Mary because she was pregnant out of wedlock. Based on what you have told us, that doesn't appear to be accurate.

G: The way the story is told in the Bible is to convey symbolically the divinity of the birth of the soul within. So, because of that, they've (Biblical authors) misinterpreted the idea of the Immaculate Conception by discounting Joseph's part in it. They've had to say, well, if this is an Immaculate Conception, a divine child born, then it must be born independent of that experience called sex. So therefore it was written in that way. We in no way have ever said that Joseph did not have sex with Mary to bring about the birth of Jesus Christ. As we said, the Immaculate Conception is not the conception of a physical child without sex. That has been the main distortion the Christian religion has used to control and, therefore, make the idea of sex sinful and an antithesis to the virgin birth of Mary. They have completely misunderstood the whole concept of what that was and what it meant and what it was for.

You have to remember that the Bible was written by men, and it has been rewritten by men many times according to what is convenient for their understanding. Therefore, what is in there and the words that are in there are not entirely accurate. What they represent symbolically is accurate. They are an encodement. The code has never been broken because it has never been understood. This is because man has never been ready for it to be broken, has never been able to conceive of and to understand and to put into action the meaning behind the form where the Bible is concerned. The Bible is symbolic. It is a set of codes.

So did Mary conceive immaculately without the experience of sex? No. Now, this is going to put everybody up in arms because it destroys the belief system to which they've been adhering for thousands of years that has simply kept them separated from themselves. It has kept them in shame where the divinity and the physicality of their being is concerned, creating separation between their sexual nature, their sexual force, their divine love force, and their erotic spiritual force. The three forces are meant to be in communion with one another. It has also created the separation between male and female and the idea that physical form is "conceived in sin" as they say.

The only thing that is conceived in sin, because all sin is simply ignorance, is your belief systems that have remained in limitation. That is the only sin there is. It is your own belief systems that have kept you in limitation and separation in order to control your separation from God. Because if you look at your Christian mythology, you will see that it is entirely configured to keep you separate from God.

J: It seems to be about all the things we have to do to connect with God and how we need the church to make that happen.

G: And yet it still plays upon your separation in order to do that. You must separate from your physical sinful self when in reality, the only way you can awaken in your spiritual self is by holding the temple of that spirit (the physical body) sacred in wholeness and total acceptance and celebrate its aliveness and make it fully conscious as the vessel of your being. Therefore, your physical body is sacred. It is not sinful.

J: I wanted to ask about Jesus's personal life. Did Jesus have any brothers and sisters? The Catholic Church maintains that he did not.

G: Yes, he had two brothers.

J: What were their names?

G: One was named Joseph and the other was named John.

J: Were they involved in Jesus' ministry? Were they a part of his discipleship?

G: Yes, they were.

J: Were they two of the twelve apostles?

G: They were disciples of Christ, but they were not part of the twelve apostles.

J: Jesus' father, Joseph, is discussed very little in the Bible. It says he was a carpenter. Is that true?

G: As far as what he did for a living, yes. He built things, which was a very useful occupation back then.

J: Did Jesus' family play any significant role in his ministry during his life or after?

G: The role they played mainly was to support and administrate.

J: Jesus had no sisters?

G: Not that we know in that life.

J: An interesting answer. When you say not in that lifetime, as he did not incarnate again, he may have in previous lifetimes?

G: He had many previous lifetimes, thousands.

J: How old was Mary when she married Joseph?

G: In your time frame she was about seventeen and a half.

J: And how old was Joseph? He supposedly was much older.

G: He was around twenty-seven, closer to twenty-eight.

J: How old was Jesus when Joseph died?

G: Jesus lived to be thirty-three years, which was the master number. Joseph died about seven-and-a-half years previous to that.

J: And Jesus became the head of the household at that time?

G: Not really, because he was well on his path of learning, so he was not, as they say, home that much. He was doing a great deal of traveling. Very little is spoken of his interim years. All that is spoken about really is the beginning years and the last three years of his life, the years in which he put his ministry in place. The years in between were used in learning. They were used in mastery of self. They were used in going through the cycles of learning in the schools of self-mastery where the initiations and the preparations for the initiations were concerned. So they were his training process.

J: Where did he go for that training?

G: Various places. He spent time training in India, Tibet and Egypt. His last initiation was in Egypt in the King's Chamber of the Great Pyramid.

J: Who were his teachers?

G: Various teachers.

J: Were they taking him to these places, or was he seeking them out himself? How was this unfolding?

G: Both. Part of it was a journey of self-seeking that enabled him to make certain synchronistic connections, which was a part of his training, was always a part of the training of an initiate. That happens in the earlier stages. In the later stages, he is chosen. And then the teachers appear and seek him.

J: I assume Mary and Joseph were supportive of all of this travel and study.

G: They didn't have much to say about it. They realized it was a divine plan and that they were a part of that divine plan.

J: There is speculation about whether Jesus married. Did he ever marry?

G: He did. He married Mary Magdalene. He had two children.

J: Whatever happened to those children?

G: They grew. They prospered. They continued to be a part of their father's teachings. One of them emigrated to another part of the country. One stayed pretty much close to home.

J: What were their sexes and their names?

G: They were two boys. One was called Saul, and one was called Simon.

J: Mary Magdalene is portrayed in a very negative way in the Bible. It refers to her as a prostitute and a sinner. She supposedly was reformed by the teachings of Jesus. Is that accurate?

G: Nothing that you read is entirely accurate. All of it is according to how they wished to depict the story and how they wished to have you receive it and be influenced by it. You could interpret Mary more as a woman who, for her time, was very individual, who was very much her own person, who did not adhere to the rules of the male patriarchy of the time. Because of that, she was condemned. Christ recognized her intelligence, her individuality, her desire to serve, and her ability to embrace new concepts, which he was bringing about or evolving or coming into awareness of himself in his learning process. This drew them very close together, a mutual soul connection and understanding.

J: It seems incredible to me that his marriage and children would be left out of the Bible.

G: Well, if this were included in the Bible, it would throw out the whole concept of the idea of sex versus the purity of the idealized form of Jesus. If Jesus were just a man, like every other man, there goes that superior concept of divinity. And yet Jesus said over and over, "Worship not me but my father who is in heaven."

J: Of course, we're taught to think of him as being God.

G: Yes.

J: So if he got married and had children, I would think that would kind of confuse things.

G: It certainly would because then it would say that every man is God. You wouldn't want that because you could no longer use the concept of the birth of Jesus to control the people. You could no longer punish them with the idea of his dying for their sins; therefore, they must serve in penance with their unacceptable physical selves, sexual beings that are disgusting and simple, you see. It would throw that concept out the old window, wouldn't it?

J: The whole basis of Christianity is that Jesus died for our sins. He saved us.

G: No. You see, the whole concept of Christianity, particularly from the Catholicism point of view, focuses on the crucifixion rather than the resurrection. The resurrection is the awakening of the soul within. The resurrection is the joy and the freedom of God within the physical form. But what they focused on was the struggle, the suffering of the cross, dying for our sins. The Catholics struggle with duality between spirit and matter. Until you can realize the Christ within, the soul within, that God exists within you, you will not be free of that concept of duality. You see, the Bible was written and conceived during an age of duality. If you look at the commandments, they're all about what you can't do. They're the beginning of the age of duality.

J: We're taught in the Catholic Church that Jesus ascended into heaven, bodily.

G: He did, right here.

J: He did right here?

G: That's what the resurrection is about, bringing heaven into earth.

J: You know what I'm saying, that he physically elevated into heaven.

G: He went somewhere else.

J: Yes, exactly. Heaven's up there somewhere.

G: Somewhere up there, wherever there is. Yes, having a hard time finding heaven, somewhere other than within yourself. Heaven and hell live within yourself. Heaven and hell live within your mind, within your emotions. Hell is you trapped in the desire body, in your own mind, in your own duality, holding onto your separation and fighting for it. That is your hell. Your heaven is the awakening of the consciousness of your being without duality, the communion within, the awakening of the soul within. That is the Immaculate Conception. That is the resurrection. That is the ascension. That is heaven on earth. He promised you, "The works that I do ye shall do and greater than I have done."

J: And that referred to the awakening of the soul in all men?

G: That is correct. That was his promise to you. That was his promise of celebration and joy of a heaven on earth.

J: The Catholic Church celebrates a holy day of obligation where the ascension of Mary is celebrated, and, of course, again, it's depicted as the physical ascension of Mary into heaven. What would you say about that?

G: The ascension of Mary is the surrender of Mary to the birth of the soul through the birth of the divine child. Her ascension took place in giving birth to this divine being in physical form in her place of service to all humanity. You see, ultimately ascension is giving up the separated self. That's all it is. All you're talking about in awakening the soul is giving up the separated self, giving up your fight for separation and acknowledging your unity within.

J: What would you say to the Christian churches that celebrate the life of Jesus and his meaning for mankind, but whom you claim have distorted things a great deal? How would you counsel them?

G: Give up your need to control one another. Allow all human beings to evolve on their own paths to awaken their spiritual experiences within, and support that. Support the investigation and the discovery of each individual experience within. You see, the temples you have created, the graven images you have created outside—your churches— are simply distorted substitutes for the church within. Your body is the church, the temple. You build elaborate buildings to house beings coming together in worship. The purpose of those temples ultimately is for unity, not to preach hell and damnation and separation.

J: Surely they have things to teach that are worthwhile.

G: Everything is worth something to somebody, depending upon the person's level of development and where he or she is. Everything speaks to someone; therefore, it is all worthwhile.

J: If they are teaching things that are not consistent with the message and purpose of Jesus' mission, is that worthwhile?

G: To someone because that is that person's process of learning. If you must learn how to contact God through separation from God and eventually get it that way, then so be it. That's a choice. If you want to do it the other way, fine. That's a choice too. Is one good, one bad? No. They are just different choices, different methods. All that is created is of God. Everything that lives, moves, and has its being is of God. Therefore, all of it is perfect, already, just as it is. Can I bring my presence of being to the essence behind the form, the life behind the form, that which informs it, rather than getting hypnotized by the form it takes? Instead of being hypnotized by the dogma of the religious form, what is the substance behind it?

J: It just comes down to love one another. There is nothing else, is there?

G: Basically, that's the message.

J: And that's where it all started.

G: Exactly. Love one another as you love yourself. Imagine God saying to himself, herself, itself, love one another as you love yourself. He would be speaking to all parts of himself that are in fragmented experiential array in the universe.

J: What a powerful image. You have said that the twelve apostles have ascended and have become a part of the planetary hierarchy of guidance.

G: Yes.

J: To me, that brings up the question of Judas. Is he one of the twelve who ascended?

G: Yes.

J: How do you explain Judas in terms of each one of us incarnating with a soul mission? The Bible says Judas betrayed Jesus. He is vilified in Christian theology.

G: Yes, vilified by those who interpreted his task. The task of Judas is simply the task of each human being that when you come face to face with your own resistance to standing alone, there is always the betrayer that is reflected in another, that is reflective of your inability or resistance to facing yourself. The betrayal of Judas was necessary in order for the ego (of Jesus) to surrender its control, the ego that was betraying the true essence of the journey of the Christ Consciousness through the one Jesus the Christ. The betrayal is a part of the renunciation process of the lower will. The lower will is the betrayer. Judas represents the lower will. He is an archetype of that lower will. And in the process, in the Garden of Gethsemane, in the renunciation, the one Jesus the Christ announced, "Thy will, not mine, be done." The surrender of the higher will of the soul, finally. But yet He had to surrender completely upon the cross yet again. "Unto thee do I commend my spirit," were His words.

The complete surrender of the body to spirit and, therefore, for the purpose of resurrection of the soul thereafter.

J: Did Jesus expect that after his ministry a church would be formed?

G: Yes. But as with all churches he knew that it would be distorted because people would be running it. And he said over and over to people. "Do not worship me. Do not build a church around me. Do not worship me, but worship my father who is in heaven."

J: When he referred to the Kingdom of God coming, what was he referring to?

G: He was referring to the awakening of the soul, the Christing of consciousness in this age. This is the Kingdom of God. What do you think this is? It has always been the Kingdom of God. You just don't have the awareness of it because you live in separation because you have not awakened the soul, the Christ Consciousness within, to become the example of the Kingdom of God.

J: What did he mean, "Receive ye the Holy Spirit?"

G: You receive the Holy Spirit through the awakening of the soul in physical consciousness, physical experience, physical action, in physical response.

J: When the apostles were in the upper room and they began speaking in tongues and they talked about having received the Holy Spirit, what happened? Had they received the Holy Spirit?

G: All they're talking about is the downloading of the light body into their consciousness that brings in certain what is sometimes called "light language." It is simply the inability of the conscious mind to distinguish its own way of understanding its own language, the information that is being passed down. So it's called speaking in tongues.

J: And did that inspire these men, who after all were not particularly educated? They were simple people by our standards, yet they were able to go out and preach across the world to spread the message of Jesus.

G: You don't need to be intelligent to be knowledgeable or to be wise. As a matter of fact, intelligence usually interferes with it because intelligence is trying to control everything and understand everything and put it into a category. Intelligence is no criteria for wisdom. Many intelligent people have no wisdom whatsoever.

J: I wasn't suggesting they weren't intelligent—I was just observing that they were simple men who were not educated by today's standards, yet they were able to spread their ministry throughout the world.

G: Yes, because they spoke from their heart. You don't need much education to speak from your heart. All you need is willingness. You see, the heart is the organ of the soul, the doorway to the soul. If you awaken the heart, you will have all that you need because the Christ Consciousness lives within the force of love within the heart. And the truth of being lives within the force of love within the heart. The truth of the individual aspect of spirit expressed through the physical lives within the heart. So, as the heart is awakened and opened, the soul speaks forth through the heart through the revelation and expression of the truth of being.

J: In a way, it seems like what happened in that upper room is happening now throughout the world with all mankind.

G: That is correct, gradually. These are the preparatory steps. Once these seven levels of each of the seven initiations have been initiated into the earth plane in consciousness, then you will begin to see major changes and shifts of integration begin to take place in physical matter. You are still in the process of the initiation of the initiations.

J: Are you talking of the process completing in 2012?

G: More or less, yes.

Chapter 8:
Love/Creating Reality

J: We are engaged in a series of interviews in which I can ask any questions I wish and come back to ask follow-up questions. Is this a unique experience with your level of consciousness, or has this happened before?

G: As far as we know, there have been no books produced based strictly upon our information.

J: I'm curious how this project came about, certainly not just because I chose to do this.

G: Understand that all things that take place are taking place on some level in the divine order of things. Everything operates through resonant causation rather than cause and effect. When you are at a certain level of soul development, you operate through a different frequency from other souls. Therefore, you begin to operate through the law of attraction or what is sometimes called the divine order of synchronicity. But synchronicity is not really synchronicity. It is the laws of attraction based upon the laws of quantum physics that when an energy of a certain level maintains a field, it begins to create a resonance that attracts things of similar resonance into its field. Therefore, as a soul you're drawn to a particular field of energy. So you were drawn to the channel, for instance, through various coincidences or synchronicities. But those synchronicities were based upon people who maintained like frequencies that created the connections. So if you maintain that and if you maintain that space in your consciousness, then everything that happens can operate through that law of the universe, which is that like attracts like based upon its frequency.

J: Synchronicity was one of the first words Robert said to us when we called about Reiki training. He was about to start a group. There were a number of synchronicities that led us to that phone call and, ultimately, to this book.

G: Yes, synchronicity is the law of the order of the universe. When the lower human will is in operation, then man is separated in isolation and he is operating through that lower will and imposing that lower will upon circumstances to control them because he doesn't trust his connection to the universe. The laws of synchronicity operate perfectly in nature, so the laws of nature operate in synchronicity with one another.

Because of his individual choice, man is the only one who gets out of synchronicity. When he is in the flow, trusting his place and his connection to the universe, the law of synchronicity can be in operation. Then all kinds of things happen that you call coincidences that create those connections. But most people don't recognize those connections when they have them because they're too busy trying to control things. They have a certain agenda about how things should be. My will, not thine be done. Do you see?

J: How do we get into that flow so that synchronicity is working for us?

G: By operating through the heart. The heart is the synchronistic pattern of the soul. Everything in the earth plane is synchronized to the heartbeat of the earth. The heartbeat of the earth moves at a certain number of hertz or vibrations per second. And the human body, based upon the heart, is synchronized with the heartbeat of the earth. That's why when you go into nature you calm down and you feel at peace. The heart feels at peace and opens because you are synchronizing with the heartbeat of the earth. So allow your heart to lead you because the heart is the doorway to the soul. The heart is the intuitive organ that relates directly to communication from the soul. The soul is the divine aspect of being that governs the law of synchronicity in physical matter.

J: That sounds wonderful, but many of us who follow our hearts can get into a lot of trouble.

G: No, because sometimes you think you are following your heart, but you are following emotional attachments instead. There's a difference between emotional attachments and the heart. The heart speaks to you from within based upon your connection to your inner knowing, into your intuitive divine factor. Emotion is something that operates through the lower self. So sometimes people let their feelings create their attachments to ideas, concepts, situations, or persons. They project their feelings onto events, circumstances, and situations, and then they say, "I'm following my heart." Following your heart is a very quiet, powerful, all-knowing experience. It is a place of silence in the center of your being. It is the connection to the core of who you are. Feelings are all over the place.

J: We can get caught up in our hormones and think that that is our heart.

G: No. That has nothing to do with your heart. That has to do with your sexual organs.

J: Sometimes it's hard to know which is which.

G: Yes, because human beings tend to interpret their sexual attractions as love. They tend to make sexual attachments related to desire and interpret that as love. You see, the heart operates through the love force. The love force is the expression of the truth of your being that comes from the core of you, your soul. So in your love you are in the revelation of the truth of your being, and you are exposing that revelation of the truth of your being and using that as your guide. When you connect that to your sexual energy, that can direct your sexual energy. The truth of your being directs your sexual energy, rather than your sexual energy directing the truth of your being, interfering with it and distorting it.

Most people use sexual energy to create an attachment or to use someone as an object to gratify a desire, to release a little tension where their sexual organs are concerned, and that produces a yearning and an attachment. All desire produces attachment. Attachment has nothing to do with connection. Connection has to do with fusion. It has to do with two beings who are able to surrender themselves to themselves and, therefore, to one another.

J: You're talking, of course, about love. I'd like to read two of your definitions of love and ask you about them. You said in our first conversation that we humans are all here to learn to love. Then you define love as "a force of creation, a force of being. Learning to love means learning to awaken, realize, accept, express and experience in the fullest way possible the experience, expression and potential of your being as an individual." And another time you said, "The divine plan is to learn to love, to learn to embody love by expressing the truth of your being as an individual in all of its knowledge, all of its expression, all of its experience and all of its form."

G: That is correct.

J: I guess my definition of love would have been something like "a very strong affection for someone or something."

G: Yes. That has nothing to do with love. That has to do with projection and attachment.

J: If most of us don't know what love is, which is the goal of the divine plan, how can we ever achieve it? Most of us would define love very differently from the way you've defined it.

G: Yes. Most people define love as a feeling of affection or a sentiment. That's love attached to a feeling. That is part of what love is. They're in the process of expressing love, expressing who they are. You connect with others, and in that connection you feel certain feelings. You may feel compassion, affection, tenderness, closeness. Those are all attributes of the experience of love. But they are not what love is. They are all feelings that you experience in the expression or the experience of love, but they are not what love is. The core of what love is, is the expression of your being, the revelation of your being, showing and sharing all of who you are with life, with the world, with every other human being, with one individual human being. All of that is love.

J: I don't think that's what most of us understand when we try to follow what Jesus taught about loving one another.

G: That's true, because you see, most people are locked in a stage of development that remains in infancy. They are locked in a codependent stage of development that has to do with motherly love, which is the expectation of unconditional love no matter what I am or what I do. So mother's unconditional love teaches an infantile love. I am loved and therefore I love.

But that's dependent upon if I am loved. If you remain locked in that condition, you remain in a state of narcissism where love is concerned. I have to be loved before I can love. Therefore, love is not dependent upon me. It is independent of me.

It relies upon someone else to make me feel that I'm safe, loved, cared for in order for me to then feel I can love the object in return. That's infantile love, a state of narcissistic love. It's just the beginning of learning what love is that the infant experiences, which makes the infant feel safe in the physical environment for the first time.

Then you move beyond that as you grow in childhood to learn what fatherly love is. Fatherly love teaches the child, under ideal circumstances, I can give love and by giving love I can produce love (which hardly ever happens because the father hasn't learned what love is either). The father is the one who takes it into the world and shows the child how to give of himself and share who he is, and by doing that produces the act of love, produces a reciprocal cycle.

Then moving into adolescence the child learns, under ideal circumstances, the experience of brotherly love. Brotherly love is the love of equality, the love of two individuals. Brotherly love says: You are an individual. I am an individual. I respect you as an individual and love who you are as you are, and you respect and love me as I am. I love you for your individuality, your individual expression, and I can love you because of who I am as an individual. And by loving you through my individuality and by sharing who I am, I then produce the experience of love in you, and love awakens in you. And you give love back to me by honoring who I am as an individual and sharing yourself with me as an individual. So the combination of those three types of love then produces the wholeness of love in your being. But most people remain frozen in one or more of those stages of love and never get to the point of integrating all three of them.

In Western civilization, most of you live in a state of infantile love. Look around you and see a bunch of children who have their arms and mouths open saying, "Give me love, fulfill me." It's all about me. It's all narcissistic. The world is centered on me. I don't produce love. I don't give love unless I'm first satisfied, unless you first love me, unless you validate me, unless you respond to me, so I feel safe enough to then love you in return. So my love is determined by the unconditional love that I receive from my caretakers. And now my projection of mom gets projected onto the world, and I want the world to take care of me, my government to take care of me, my economic situation to take care of me. I want all the amusements to take care of me. I want my job to take care of me. And I'm not willing to exercise my individuality in that. As a matter of fact, in order to remain a child, I must give up my individuality. I must fit into the herd consciousness. I must remain as a child.

J: Synchronicity is related to how we experience reality. You said, "Human beings create reality either etherically or physically through the strength and power of their intention." I would guess that most people believe that fate or God or forces greater than them play a greater role in creating their reality than they do.

G: Well, dear one, as we said, where their development is concerned, the majority is at an infantile level. In order to believe you create your own reality, you have to take responsibility for its creation, for your choices. You have to be aware of how your choices are creating consequences through cause and effect. You have to have some sense of the fact that all reality is interconnected. Therefore, every choice you make, every thought you think, every feeling you have is resounding into the universe and interacting with all reality all of the time.

But people don't believe they have that power. They believe they are separate from the universe, from God. Therefore, God is like a parent who is watching them and guiding them and either rewarding them or punishing them. That is how they prefer to think of it because they have never moved to the state of development that has allowed them to move out of the idea of a patriarchal God, father, mother figure that is in charge. Therefore, they have no responsibility, and so they are just the victims of fate. They have never come to the point of realizing they are responsible for their own actions.

J: Would you simply and clearly explain how we create our own reality?

G: You create your reality through what you think, what you focus your intention on, where your thoughts are concerned, and how you attach feelings to those. The thought process is male or assertive energy that goes out into the astral plane. The emotional is the receptive energy that attracts. Therefore, whatever feelings you hold inside that are related to certain thought patterns and the repetition of those thoughts strengthens the intention of the creation of that reality. And as they are repeated again and again and again, it sustains and maintains or draws to you that reality.

J: In a previous discussion you said, "You are now shifting into quantum physics. You're shifting into the idea of maintaining a quantum field of energy and operating through resonant causation rather than cause and effect. Resonant causation is when humanity evolves through knowing and is able to maintain and sustain a certain vibration and frequency overall to shift evolution consciously rather than through unconscious choice."

G: Yes.

J: I know this is an evolutionary process and it's not going to happen right away, but that seems to be such a momentous shift. Our learning up to now has been through cause and effect, which, to me, essentially means that we take an action and there is a consequence. We assess it, make a judgment about it and base our future actions on the consequences. So we learn through trial and error, cause and effect. What I understand you to be saying is that we are going to be shifting into an ability to just operate out of knowing by being in consonant energy with others.

G: Cause and effect, first of all, is created through unconscious choice and consequence. In other words, it is created through a survival process of unconsciousness or ignorance. You take an action. You are not aware of what the consequence will be. The consequence results. And because you were unconscious, you do not respond or take responsibility for the consequence; rather, you react to it in a survival manner. Therefore, you are not able to respond to it. You're not able to see the value of it, take responsibility for it, and then learn from your actions so that the next time you are more conscious and you make conscious choices out of a place of knowing. Cause and effect is learning through trial and error because you're not conscious enough to learn through conscious choice.

However, through resonant causation I know this choice I am making is going to produce this result or that this is going to happen if I make this choice. It's going to affect me this way and others that way. And I take responsibility for that. Or, if it's not something for which I'm willing to take responsibility, I reevaluate my choice. When you operate from resonance, you operate at a certain vibration and frequency of reality. You are maintaining and sustaining a certain reality through the particular vibration. You resonate with the reality. Therefore, the choices you make contribute to that reality. You're not doing it haphazardly. You're not doing it through trial and error.

Resonant causation means I resonate at a certain vibration and frequency of consciousness, and there is a certain knowing connected to that. I operate through a radiatory resonance of energy. I resonate with the reality I'm creating and with the choices I make. And I am making choices that have value, meaning, and purpose that are for the highest good for myself and all involved. I consider all parts of reality as to the effect or consequences that my choices may produce. That doesn't mean I always know exactly what's going to happen, but I'm in the ballpark. And I know my choices are not going to cause unconscious harm to someone.

J: It sounds to me as though you're talking about moving from unconsciousness to consciousness. Isn't that what therapy work with the Robert Bakers of the world is designed to do?

G: Yes, the whole purpose of the work is to make you conscious—conscious of what you're doing, conscious of what you're not doing, conscious of what is taking place where your unconscious choices and actions create unconscious cycles of manifestation and reality in your life. So you can change and shift those. But you can't change and shift anything you're not conscious of. As you become more conscious of how you are making choices in the subconscious without knowing it, then you will become more aware of the effect on your reality. As you become consciously aware, you can make conscious choices and can, therefore, create a conscious reality. You can manifest consciously, rather than making choices that are based upon defenses of which you're not even aware.

You see, you create reality through what you resonate with anyway. But most people don't know what they resonate with. And most people resonate at a very low frequency based upon all their resistance, all their trauma, and all their stuff that is stored in their nervous system in the emotional and physical bodies. For instance, when you say "I want this" and the opposite happens. What that is illustrating to you is that you are unconsciously resonating with something that is the opposite of what you say you want, something that lies in the unconscious or the subconscious of which you are not aware.

Often people will say to us, "I want this, Gabriel." And we say, well, what are you doing about it? They say, well, I'm doing this. And we say, well, that's not going to get you what you want. Are you willing to do this, this, and this—take these steps towards what you say you want? And they say, well, what if this happens, or that happens, or I'm afraid or I'm this or I'm that. Therefore, they don't resonate with the reality they want. They resonate with the reality they want to avoid, which is why they have it.

To resonate with the reality you want, you have to be conscious of the reality you want to avoid. You have to release that avoidance in order to move towards what you want. The only reason people don't have what they want is because they're not available to it. They don't resonate with it.

Any given reality is available to you, anything that you ask for because the universe is a benign, neutral energy that says, yes. Your commitment determines what you manifest. If your commitment is to avoid something that you don't want, then you'll manifest that because that's what you resonate with. All your attention is focused on avoiding what you don't want. So doesn't it follow that you will have what you don't want? Because that is what all your attention is focused on.

You see, if you want to avoid a feeling—let's say you want to avoid a feeling of being deprived. It's like ringing up the universe on the cosmic telephone and saying, hello universe, I would like to avoid the feeling of being deprived. I hate this feeling. I don't want to be deprived. And the universe says, all right, that's your commitment.

We'll support that. Here's a way you can fight deprival—by giving you something when you're deprived so you can fight it. And then you say, well, now I really hate this feeling, and I really want to get rid of it. And then the universe gives you more extreme ways to fight it, more extreme circumstances until you are willing to see what you are doing and change your commitment.

J: How do we manifest what we want?

G: By being aware of your feelings and of whether you are accepting those feelings or resisting them. If you are resisting them, you are fighting them. You're keeping them in place, and you need circumstances to fight them with. You see, if my fear in intimate relationships is the fear of rejection or abandonment, I will always attract someone who will reject and abandon me because that's my commitment. I want a relationship where I can fight this feeling, this fear of abandonment and rejection. So I'll always attract someone who is unavailable who abandons and rejects me. So I can maintain my commitment. Do you see?

J: Yes, but what is so frustrating is that people are affirming all the time what they believe they want: "I want a loving, fulfilling relationship." And they're getting the opposite.

G: That's right, because fighting abandonment and rejection are more important than having a loving relationship. Their commitment is not to having a loving relationship. If they were committed to having a loving relationship, they would have to first accept their feelings that they want to avoid so they can move toward being loving. If you're fighting abandonment and rejection, you're not committed to being loving. You've committed to destroying something.

J: So what do we do?

G: Accept the feelings of abandonment and rejection so that the feelings are felt. Move through them and release them so that they're not held inside to draw, attract, or magnetize circumstances to them so they can continue to fight what they're avoiding. That's why we spend so much time emphasizing accepting your feelings because your feelings are the magnetic property. They are the negative polarity of creation. Your thoughts are the positive polarity of creation, the male energy that goes out into the universe, creates the grid work in the etheric, in the astral. The emotions pull them back to your reality. If you're resonating with the emotions of deservability, of acceptance, of love, then that's the reality you will attract. If you're resonating with avoiding feelings of being deprived, inadequate, unlovable, then you will attract circumstances to mirror that reality. It's not a big mystery. People get what they're committed to.

J: It seems hard, and I don't know if I can explain why it seems so hard.

G: It's difficult because you're not used to flowing with your feelings. You are used to resisting them through the armoring in the body. Very few people have a steady flow of feelings. Most people, if you ask them what they feel, will categorize them into two feelings, good and bad. What does that mean?

J: OK. Let's say I feel rejected, and I feel the feeling.

G: Yes.

J: I'm experiencing the feeling.

G: If you experience that feeling, it will immediately change to another feeling.

J: And that is what you are advising that we do.

G: Exactly, so that you are fully flowing with your feelings. You're not focusing any attention on fighting one because then you're only giving it more power. Whenever you try to destroy something, you're aiding and abetting the very thing you are trying to destroy.

J: So I'm not fighting the feeling of rejection, and I'm feeling it. Then what?

G: You just feel it, and it changes to another feeling. You will know you are feeling it because it will change. If you are resisting it, it won't change, and it will be painful to one degree on another, depending upon the amount of resistance. Emotion is the expression of the feeling. The emotion is how the feeling moves. If you're having the emotional experience of pain, there's a lot of resistance to whatever the feelings are that are trying to move. If you're having an emotional experience where the feeling is experienced, felt, expressed, then it changes immediately into another feeling. There's no resistance. Why do you think that nobody resists happiness? Nobody resists happiness because they think of it as a good feeling. Now why doesn't happiness ever last? Why doesn't the feeling of happiness last?

J: Because we don't resist it.

G: That's right. It changes to another feeling. Why does the feeling of sadness last? Because you resist it. You keep it in place.

J: I can relate to that. My beloved partner died. It took me years to recover. I obviously didn't know how to deal with it, but I wasn't aware that I was trying to hold onto anything. I was trying to move past it without a whole lot of success.

G: No, you were trying to move past it. That's the key. Trying to move past it meant you were resisting the feelings that were there because you didn't want to feel them. So if you could move past it, you could avoid the feelings that were coming up. So the feelings stayed, and you got stuck in them for years. If you had been able to accept the loss and feel the loss, it would have lasted for a short time and you would have moved on. But you had a lot of feelings invested in the relationship. Do you see? A lot of feelings that you didn't want to feel—probably loss, abandonment, feeling unloved, disconnected, inadequate without the person, loneliness—all of that. You were feeling the pain of resistance to it. If you had felt the feeling of loss, it would last [snapping fingers] and be gone.

J: Like most people, I think I would need help with that.

G: Well, you are beginning it. For instance, what are you feeling at this moment?

J: A mixture of pleasure and pain.

G: All right. How does that make you feel?

J: I believe I'm learning, so I'm feeling content.

G: When you feel content, how does that make you feel?

J: Happy.

G: And how does that make you feel?

J: Joyful, relaxed.

G: You see, what we're illustrating to you in this exercise is how feelings move if you accept the feeling that is there. Right now I feel content. How does that make me feel? Open. How does that make me feel? Delighted. How does that make me feel? Sad. How does that make me feel? Angry. How does that make me feel? Strong. You see? Each feeling, if you accept it, will allow another feeling underneath it to unfold. As a matter of fact, all of your feelings are going on simultaneously. When you resist one, you block all of them. Sometimes you can experience more than one at the same time. Sometimes you can experience sadness and joy at the same time. That's an example of the simultaneous action of feelings.

J: We were talking about resonant causation.

G: Yes.

J: I certainly want to get to that place. I guess I just have to be patient with the process.

G: That's correct. You have to be in the process. The easiest way to get there is through acceptance of where you are. Enlightenment is being in the now, fully present.

J: Is that all it is?

G: That's all it is.

J: I suppose I would define enlightenment as knowing.

G: That's what now is. If you were in the now, you would always know because you're there. Only when you're in your head, in your thoughts and your feelings, are you out of the now in the past, so you don't know because you're not present.

J: Do you have any sense of how difficult that is for humans as you haven't been one?

G: It is extremely difficult for humans because they're ruled in the third dimension through the illusion of time and the illusion of the mind. The thought process of the mind is a total illusion of reality. It's a description of the reality that has passed. When you are in the now, there are no thoughts. There are no feelings. There is only being. There is only presence. Then thoughts and feelings are transformed to the higher aspect of the mental, emotional body, which is intuition and knowing. You have direct access to the reservoir of your divinity because you are here now.

J: So to get to a place of resonant causation we have to?

G: Learn to still the mind. Still the emotions by accepting them so they become neutral. So one is not more or less important than another, which is what creates duality. You see, the desire body is created through the illusion of time. The desire body is created to long or yearn after something in time. It is illusion created by the ego that attaches its sense of self and well being to objects in the physical world. Therefore, it is devoid of any consciousness of the life behind the form. The life behind the form is the experience of now.

J: Thank you for all that.

G: "More confused than ever, Gabriel. Thank you so much."

J: [Laughing] Thank you so much, Gabriel.

G: You are most welcome, dear one.

J: In one of our discussions, you observed that when we can look around and recognize others as aspects of ourselves, we will have achieved a certain level of growth.

G: Everything that you see around you is an aspect of you. Everything that everyone experiences you can identify with on one level or another. Now you can accept it or not according to how you are able to accept and integrate it into yourself. So, in other words, when you can accept all of your feelings in yourself, then you are no longer ruled by your feelings or your emotional body because you are no longer trying to avoid anything, which then keeps it in your face as resistance and produces the pain of avoidance.

If you are able to accept all of your feelings within yourself, then you have no problem in relationship to others because you will not be using them to either get rid of a feeling or give you a feeling. Therefore, you will no longer be creating desires and attachments with other people for them to determine your experience of reality, your feelings or lack of feelings, your positive or negative feelings. When you can accept all of your feelings and take responsibility for your own behavior, your own choices, so that your choices are not determined by someone else, then you don't make someone else responsible for the experiences that you have in life.

You are responsible for your own experiences in life by what you choose, how you choose and through what kind of commitment you choose. Whether it is to try to avoid something or whether to accept and love something. That makes you free. Every aspect of another human being is an aspect of yourself because you are a part of the collective consciousness and you are a part of every experience that every human being has. And you will go through all the growth patterns that they go through. And they will experience the same thing with you because everything that you see around you is a part of your growth process, your learning process, your unification process.

You will then see where you are able to unify within yourself or not according to what you are able to accept within yourself or not as you see mirrored around you. For instance, you know that if you are fighting a feeling, you will have people and circumstances around you that will give you the opposition necessary so that you can continue to fight that feeling.

J: So if I don't like certain people, they'll keep showing up?

G: Oh yes, because it'll be based upon the feelings they evoke or seem to evoke. It's not that you don't like the person. It's that you don't like how you feel when you're in relationship with him or her. You don't like the things the person does that evoke certain feelings with which you're not at peace. You can't love that part of yourself or accept that part of yourself; therefore, you're not going to accept that behavior in the other.

J: So help me deal with that. You may have explained it, but obviously I haven't quite gotten it yet.

G: Well, in any given situation all you need do is ask yourself: how do I feel? Then when you ask yourself how you feel, ask yourself: am I honoring what I need in this situation—or not? Now, based upon how I feel, if it's a negative feeling that comes up, obviously there is something within yourself that you are not honoring because it's evoking a feeling you are having a difficult time accepting. So you need to ask yourself, what is it I need in this circumstance? What is it I need but have not expressed that is taking me out of balance, is making me resistant to what feelings are coming up? Because those feelings are coming up for a reason. They are coming up to indicate to me that there is a need behind this feeling that I'm not acknowledging. Behind every feeling you have is a fulfilled or unfulfilled need. If it is a negative feeling, then it usually is evocative of a need that has not been exercised, fulfilled, and/or identified.

For most people it is a need that has not been identified. So maybe somebody is dominating the conversation and I feel left out. I feel unheard. I feel unseen. What is the need behind those feelings that I am making the other person responsible for? The need for me is to speak up, to express my feelings or my opinion or my point of view or what is important to me in the situation, to give myself equal space and time in the situation to express who I am.

J: I am trying to link the idea of loving one another as you love yourself with the idea of as you see others, you see aspects of yourself and then loving all of them as you would yourself. In many social situations I find myself gravitating to some people and avoiding others. I feel as though I should learn to love them and not pull away. And I feel a sense of guilt about it.

G: Well, again, you see, it's about selection. It's about choosing that which honors your resonance. You see, everything seeks its own level. That does not mean that any of it is good or bad. There's nothing bad about this group of people or that group of people. It's simply that it's a certain level of experience and learning that sustains and maintains its own level. People enjoy and revel in that. They support one another and gather together to create that resonance and that reality.

Within all the different levels of reality available to you, you have freedom of choice as to which levels of reality you wish to participate in and which ones you don't. And that is your right and that's quite all right. But it's not about making them bad or wrong, good or superior or inferior. It's simply about choosing what you resonate with and honoring your own resonance.

For instance, why is it that you choose one person to be your friend as opposed to another person? You choose a person because there are certain things that you resonate with together and because you experience a certain communion, a certain something in common. Just as, for instance, when you put out the material of Gabriel, not everybody is going to resonate with it. There are people who are going to go, "I have no idea what that means, and I have no interest" because they don't resonate with it. They're not at that level of understanding that it means anything to them or it has any attraction to them whatsoever.

J: There's nothing wrong with that. They just don't resonate with it.

G: That is correct. They just don't resonate with it because it's not at the level of learning with which they relate because they are just at another level of incarnational development. Therefore, it's very important to understand that all of the different forms that are available where teaching and learning and participation and all that sort of thing are concerned are not right, wrong, good, or bad. They're all there for somebody's commitment.

Chapter 9:
Health/Healing/Living/Immortality

J: When discussing the DNA molecule, you said that so far eighteen to twenty on sites are connected, but scientists have never understood what the other forty-four are for. What do you mean by "on sites are connected?"

G: There are sixty-four on sites in the DNA. An on site is a place in the DNA molecule where a wave form moves across it connecting two points. In connecting those two points, it produces the amino acids needed to create the chemical interactions in the endocrine system to bring strength and balance to the immune system and reproduction of the cells to restore the life, balance, and harmony of the physical body. It regenerates life. Without those connections, life in the physical would not continue, and your body would not be able to restore itself.

Your body renews all of its atoms every year. In other words, your body is completely renewing itself once a year. Every few months your skin renews itself. Every few months some of the organs completely reconstruct themselves on an atomic level. In order to do so, cells must go through a production of mitosis and reproduction. That happens through the instructions of the DNA molecule because the DNA molecule instructs organisms through the genetic code. And so when the on sites connect, producing those amino acids, it restores health, well-being and balance to the physical body, and it recreates the physical body.

J: And it does that with only eighteen or twenty.

G: That's correct.

J: You said that there are forty-four more. What could happen if more were connected?

G: The connection of all the on sites in the DNA would bring about the experience of immortality in the physical.

J: In other words we could recreate all components of our body so that we could keep it forever young?

G: That is correct. You could keep it at any stage of age or growth that you wished to simply with the thought process, simply through willing it.

J: So what is it going to take to connect more of these sites?

G: Well, sometimes more than twenty connect when people experience a faith healing. They experience a total recovery from a life-threatening disease. The body is meant to be healthy and well all of the time. Disease is a distortion of the processes of the physical body. It is a distortion of the physical, emotional, and energetic processes.

The physical body is much like an earthworm. If you look at the body of an earthworm, it has segments. And those segments are there for a purpose. They're energetic diaphragms. When the earthworm is alive, there is energy from the sexual force moving from the tail up towards the head. And there is a force of energy from the erotic force moving from the head down to the tail. When the energy moves unimpeded through the segments, it creates a pulsation wave throughout the earthworm's body that creates the sensation of excitement for life, desire for life, passion for living, and, at the same time, pleasure in the sensation of life through the sexual force. And that causes the pulsation wave of movement through the body that allows the earthworm to be able to move across the earth.

J: So it's not just humans who experience those energetic forces.

G: That's right, the crudest forms. If you go down to the amoeba, you will find the same thing. The human form has three diaphragms. It has an energetic diaphragm in the anus, one in the solar plexus, and one in the throat. One spiral of energy moves up from the base of the spine to the crown, the kundalini sexual spiral. The other, the erotic spiritual spiral, moves down from the crown to the base. When those forces are unimpeded, it creates a wave called the orgasmic wave through the body, an experience of orgasm that creates a sensation of pleasure and excitement in the body.

When you are born, to some degree you have this if you have not been impeded and armored in the birthing process too much or in the gestation process during pregnancy. That's why children are so open and available, and they experience on so many different levels and dimensions at the same time. As they grow through the modeling of the parental units, that ability shuts down because they develop armoring in the body.

As we said, the body is segmented like the earthworm and the currents are going vertically from head to tail just like the earthworm. Only difference with the human is that they develop an individual sense of things, and they begin to interpret through their feelings the sensations of life, the pleasure and excitement that moves through them. When they experience pain or trauma, they begin to shut down in their ability to experience those waves of pleasure and excitement for life in order to get rid of or avoid pain. When that happens, they begin to develop armor rings of blocked energy and blocked emotions in various layers in the body like layers of the onion. These are horizontal rings chronically impacted in the muscle tissues that prevent the movement of the pulsation wave up and down in the body to create that sensation of life and pleasure and excitement and passion and fusion with life inside.

There's an armor ring that happens in the ocular layer around the eyes and the cheekbones; another armor ring in the area of the jaw, lips, and tongue; another in the throat, upper shoulders and neck; another in the chest and arms; another in the solar plexus; another in the upper abdominal region; and another in the pelvis and legs. Thus there are seven rings altogether.

These all develop at various times during childhood phases of development, creating experiences of shutdown with the sexual energy, the erotic force, and the love force, restricting the ability to experience the flow of life through the body. It creates the disconnection from the soul and the armoring of the defenses of the personality or ego. The ego then maintains those layers of armored defense chronically in the body. The body becomes more self-contained as life goes on. You grow into adulthood, and you shut down more and more, experiencing less and less pleasure and excitement for life, limiting your life force and life experience more and more into a comfort zone where you are living or responding to very little of life.

The nervous system then becomes an editing system that edits out everything except what the ego has decided is safe. And so you live through the illusion of the ego. And you are in a constant process of defending yourself against life, which stops the flow of energy of those three forces. It stops the flow of balance between giving and receiving where love and the expression of being are concerned because the love force is the truth of the expression of being on a soul level.

J: I know you have trained Robert and Ron Baker to work with these issues. Do most psychologists and psychiatrists understand this?

G: Some of them do. Most of them don't. More and more understand the importance of the physical body and the emotional system of the body in the prevention of disease, the harmony of experience, and the expression of the wholeness of being.

J: The experiences you are describing are so widespread and harmful, I can't think of anything more important than to train people to do this kind of work.

G: Absolutely. It is absolutely essential. The body is the vehicle through which the spirit expresses itself when the soul is awakened. The soul cannot be awakened if the body is armored to its processes. You see, the soul is always there. The soul is not something that is outside of yourself. It is inside yourself at the core of your being all of the time, but it's not awakened because there are so many layers of defenses between you and it.

J: You have said that we create our own reality. Does that mean we also create our own diseases?

G: All disease is created by you. All disease is simply caused by imbalance in the functioning of the organism based upon imbalance in the organism emotionally, mentally, and energetically. Until you understand that life force interfered with or interrupted is what creates disease, you will never be able to conquer the illusion of disease in which you believe.

J: The life force interrupted? Please explain that to me.

G: Life force interrupted occurs within a physical body when you have rings of energetic and emotional armoring in the tissues of the body that prevent the life force from flowing freely through the body up and down. That energy has to go somewhere. If it is confined in a limited space, it attempts to move and interferes with the organs or the area of the body where it's trapped.

J: Does Reiki help open that?

G: Absolutely, because in Reiki you are learning how to get in touch with the flow of the life force.

J: How would you explain how Reiki works?

G: It's very simple really. Reiki is really just another word for life force or God, which is the energy that makes up all living things in the universe. When the system is fully available to that force, that is Reiki—that is a perfectly balanced state of being in physical reality. So the purpose of Reiki is to help to balance the life force in the physical body and its flow.

J: When we're giving Reiki the energy is flowing through us. What is actually happening in the body of the recipient?

G: The body of the recipient is receiving the flow of that energy in a communion between the two souls. If both are open, there is a reciprocal engagement of giving and receiving. The blockages of the recipient will determine the amount of life force it is able and willing to receive and the amount of healing it is allowing itself to effect.

J: What could we be encouraging the patients to do or think to enhance the effect of the Reiki treatment?

G: Participate in visualizing the energy flowing through them, imagining it as a golden light. Golden light is a good light because it is the energy light of the soul, the energy of the second ray. Allow the energy without impeding its flow in any way, opening more and more to just receiving and trusting the flow of it.

J: I've been asking for your help when I'm giving it to people. Does that have any effect at all?

G: Of course. You are calling upon our energies to help. Call upon all the help you can get.

J: What else can you tell us about the connection between disease and the imbalances in the flow of energy?

G: Your medical community has no cognizance of the fact that energy is the source of creation. Therefore, what happens with energy is what creates disease, not what happens with the physical body. The physical body doesn't create disease. The physical body simply registers disease because the physical body is simply a hologram or a barometer of what is happening in the areas of creation that produce the physical body. So all disease starts energetically, emotionally, and mentally. Then it is translated into the holographic reaction of the physical body. So the physical body simply registers symptoms.

Therefore, the medical profession treats symptoms. Its practitioners try to get rid of symptoms. But they don't get to the source of the disease because they don't understand energy. They don't understand how emotion creates the movement of energy, and, therefore, creates the balance of the immune system and the balance of the conditions of the physical body. And most don't understand how mental belief systems impact the body.

J: Unfortunately, the medical profession would react to your explanations much like the Catholic Church reacted to Galileo when he said the Earth went around the sun instead of the other way around.

G: Of course.

J: How does what you're saying apply to a serious health issue such as AIDS, which is affecting much of the world, especially Africa? It's considered incurable. Can people cure themselves?

G: Of course they can. But you first have to get to the source of the problem. AIDS or any immune deficiency disease is created on a cellular level. It involves the cellular reproduction of the body. Therefore, it is a disease that, at the source of it, is a problem or a trauma that basically involves shame of self on a very primitive cellular level. And that shame of self is related to the sexual identity of the person. When we say sexual identity, we are talking about the way in which people use the force of creation in their lives to experience and express the power and identity of who they are. That has been shamed to a great degree. This creates blockages in a very important part of the body, which is where the sexual creative energy comes from. That is the pelvic region of the body.

That's why, for many, AIDS is a sexually transmitted disease because it is related to first, second, and third chakra issues that are related to your sexual identity in the physical. And it is related to energy that is blocked, that does not allow the cellular memory of the body to reproduce itself at a rapid rate. It influences production of the T-cells. The T-cells reproduce the physical body.

AIDS is a disease that is a deterioration of the physical body based upon shame of self at the core. Therefore, to cure it, you must get to the core. You must get to the issues of shame that exist on a cellular level where the right to be, the right to have life, the right to be you is concerned. And those issues have to be cleared. The traumas involving them that are locked in the pelvic region of the body have to be cleared. The energy then has to flow through the body because the energy flows in the body determine the rate at which the cells can reproduce themselves.

All of the emotional memory of shame of self is programmed into the spiritual aspect of the DNA at a very early age. That is encoded in the DNA, which is what makes it a cellular disease, which makes it a disease of immune deficiency because immune deficiency comes from the inability of the connecting points in the DNA to connect. When this happens, they can't produce the amino acids to create the chemical interactions in the body needed for the reproduction of cellular memory to restore the physical body. When that process breaks down, when the sense of self is shamed, it affects the immune system.

The immune system is not created to fight anything. It is created to assimilate the experiences of life. When it is forced to fight, it breaks down. This affects the production of cells. Therefore, the source of the shame of self has to be gotten to. There's a reason it is such a rampant disease in your society. It's based upon shame of self that produces shame of intimacy and connection.

The reason it is so prevalent in the homosexual society is because it is a group of people who have a great deal of shame about their sense of self. And so they act out that shame with one another. It is a mirror of the collective consciousness of shame of self, shame of sexual identity. They play roles in their community and with one another. A lot of them tend to see themselves and identify themselves based upon their sexuality—"I am a gay man or a gay woman"—and that becomes the prevalent aspect of their identity. They are trying to prove their right to be that or to find acceptance for that within themselves and with others in their community with whom they interact. And so they're acting out their shame of self rather than realizing their sexuality, their sexual expression, is simply a minute aspect of the wholeness of who they are.

J: The whole thing gets out of balance.

G: Exactly. The whole thing gets terribly out of balance, and so they are using one another to validate themselves as a man or a woman.

J: So how should AIDS be treated from an energetic perspective?

G: It has to be approached emotionally, energetically, and mentally where collective belief systems from the family system are concerned that produced the shame in the child.

J: So working with the kind of programs that Robert conducts would be therapeutic?

G: Yes, exactly.

J: Generally, how does the therapy affect the patient?

G: It creates the flow of energy through the body by releasing the emotional programming that's trapped in the muscle tissues and in the organs of the body that create the energetic armoring that blocks the energy flow throughout the body.

You see, each energetic construction is based upon where and how the energy is armored in which layers in the body. As we said, there are seven rings of armoring in the body. Each one of those layers is related to a state of development in childhood. Each of those armorings has consecutive layers of energetic armoring that creates tension and stress in a certain area of the body physically and energetically that blocks the flow of energy there. When the energy is blocked there, it can't flow through the body, so it literally explodes in that part of the body because it's locked in. That creates a predetermination of what areas of the body later in life will probably break down in disease—whether someone is going to have heart problems, prostate cancer, digestive problems, problems with their eyes, arthritis in the joints. It depends upon where the predominant layers of armoring are based upon the particular defense structure of the person and on which levels of emotional development the child got locked in.

J: What role do vitamins and good nutrition play in good health? Is it all about energy?

G: They help the interrelationships of the chemical reactions in the body and the way in which energy is stored in the body. Therefore, they help on a physical level to restore balance. Again, you are dealing with the symptoms so that they don't get any worse or perhaps improve, but you're still not getting to the source of the disease. Therefore, it could return or come back as something else. You see, most people don't die of old age. It's almost impossible to die of old age. People die of disease, not old age.

As for the specific value of vitamins, it depends upon what vitamins you're taking and how they're produced. If vitamins are irradiated, as most of are, they are of little or no use whatsoever. You will get 10-15 percent of value out of them, if that, because their value has been killed through the irradiation.

J: I didn't know vitamins were irradiated.

G: Yes. Most vitamins you get over the counter are irradiated. Also, you need the flora factor that produces the natural bacteria in the body to be able to absorb the vitamins. Otherwise, they just pass through the system. Most of the vitamins on your commercial shelves are irradiated because most of the herbs and minerals imported into the country are irradiated in vast amounts for sanitation purposes. Therefore, their natural processes have been killed. Also, make sure you have good antioxidants along with your vitamin intake because they help process the vitamins in the body.

J: If disease is about energy imbalances, why would drugs such as antibiotics have such a quick impact on something like bronchitis and other infections?

G: Because antibiotics work on the microbes that are in the body to kill the bacterial imbalance in the body. On a chemical level, they knock out the bacteria. Remember, your body is a system of chemical interactions, electromagnetic interactions and fluid interactions as well.

J: So the fact disease occurs on an energetic level doesn't mean that drugs aren't useful.

G: No. You see, human beings deal with disease on a physical level. So they deal with it on a level of microbes and viruses and cellular balance or imbalance and things like that because that's the way in which they understand it. What they don't yet understand is that if they could get to the source of how disease is created from the perspective of movements of energy, they wouldn't have to work with physical symptoms. They could just work with the flows of energy, and they wouldn't have to have disease at all. Eventually that will take place in your evolution.

J: I suppose in another hundred years or so, our current approach to disease will look pretty primitive.

G: Yes. You see, as human beings begin to understand the functioning of DNA and how to manipulate its functioning, they will be able to eliminate disease altogether. Remember that DNA is the cellular structure recording all the information that moves through the body. The DNA holds not just the physical genetic implications, but also the emotional and energetic patterns. Basically, DNA is a blueprint of patterns that the RNA has sent it. RNA records the information from the body and sends it into the DNA. The DNA unscrambles it and sorts it into blueprints or patterns. In the past, the RNA molecule has been functioning in one way only. It sends information into the DNA from the body system and through the endocrine system. As you begin to open up the spiritual aspect of DNA, it begins to operate as a two-way system. In the future it will begin to send information it has recorded in the DNA out into the consciousness of the organism. So you will be able to access what is recorded in the DNA on a conscious level and begin to manipulate that.

J: As the medical profession doesn't understand the source of disease, what can we who do understand do to heal ourselves?

G: What you are doing, and that is gaining a greater understanding of how your own physical body operates and taking responsibility for balancing its energy flows. Then, by example, you can raise the vibration of the body and you can overcome disease and maintain the body in balance and health. And you can also begin to disseminate to others what you know. For instance, studying the energetic process of Reiki is one method whereby you begin to understand energy—how to access it, how to make it flow, how to balance it. That is a step towards taking responsibility for learning the dynamics of the way energy creates the life and flow of the physical body and how to restore that balance.

The more people investigate the origins of life from the energetic standpoint, the more it becomes something that more people embrace, the more it becomes common knowledge and less mysterious. When things are first introduced, they seem mysterious and people treat them as if they were myths because it's not the status quo. It's not the standard they've been taught. For instance, when you were a child, you were taught that germs create disease. Is that true?

J: Yes.

G: Since then, science has reversed that. They have said germs do not create disease. Germs can contribute to creating imbalance, but they do not create disease. You are exposed to germs all the time, everybody is. You have germs in your body all the time. Why do some people take those germs and create disease and other people do not? It has nothing to do with the germs; it has to do with how the body is responding to what is taking place, how it is using it. Take the immune system, for instance. People have thought the immune system is used to fight disease. The immune system does not fight disease. When the immune system has to fight, it breaks down. The immune system is used for bringing balance to the body. When the immune system is balanced, there is health and well-being. When it is out of balance because it has to fight, it breaks down and disease occurs because it becomes weakened.

J: As far as maintaining maximum health is concerned, beyond studying Reiki what general counsel would you offer?

G: Reiki is a method of learning to use the universal life force of energy. But that in itself is not enough. You have to also have an understanding of your own personal process. So what you are doing in therapy is also an absolute necessity because the vehicle must be clear in order to sustain the movement of energy. One of the reasons there is so much disease on your planet, so many immune-deficient diseases, is because it is showing how great an imbalance there is in the physical system.

The energies of the planet have been raising their vibration over the last fifty years, but particularly since 1987 when the Harmonic Convergence occurred. It created a massive stepping up of that vibration. Then the 1994 Jupiter occurrence and other occurrences and alignments have taken place. Each one of those has created an infusion of higher vibration of consciousness and energy into the earth plane and into the bank of DNA around the earth. So it is creating a mutation of the planetary DNA, and it's also creating a mutation of the human DNA as a direct reflection of that in the microcosm. Because of that and because the forms (our bodies) are so polluted or so blocked, when the vibration is raised that immediately starts an entrainment process that brings up everything that is diseased in the body, everything that is out of balance, everything that is in resistance, everything that is in conflict. And the body simply becomes a mirror of the conflict.

So if you are working consciously to clear the vehicle, then you are in charge of the process. Then you can take greatest advantage of the process, of these energies as they come. Then you're not a victim of them because you learn how to clear yourself consciously. You can then embody the higher vibration with more ease rather than disease.

When you start the process, all of the stuff that is immediately there on the surface starts to come up and all the toxins start to surface, so you go through kind of a healing crisis because you are disturbing energetic blocks within your body that have been there for years. And you've learned to live with them, with a certain degree of stress and shutdown, and you have accepted that as normal. The experience of humanity is not an experience of becoming more open and available to life. The process of living, aging, and getting older has become a process of gradually shutting down to life. And that has become the normal process, quite the reverse of what it should be.

There is no reason why the body has to age and fall apart. The only reason it does is because as you grow older, because of the defenses, because of your survival system as you develop inside, you shut off to more and more of life. And you create a smaller and smaller frame of reference for living, for embracing the pleasure and excitement of life. So you shut out more and more of it and you limit your experience and confine it to a tiny framework. Then your defense says: "This is all that I am capable of experiencing. And I have to fight everything that opposes that. I have to fight change, fight development, and fight growth because it doesn't fit within the confines of the limited perspective I have given myself, that I have conditioned myself to accept."

You see, human beings very easily accept limitation rather than growth, expansion, and development because change is threatening to them. But the process of living is the process of changing. The process of living, from the soul perspective, is the process of growth and development. That's all the soul is interested in. The ego is interested in confining, limiting, keeping things within a safe perspective, a comfort zone that it can understand and control. Being open to change frees you to be available to the areas of life where what you seek is available. Holding onto the past keeps you trapped there until you can let go and make space for something you cannot see or experience or be accessible to where it is available.

J: You're suggesting we make space for what we don't know is coming.

G: Yes. People are reluctant to live in the emptiness of the void. And this is the place where creation exists. You see, in every breath you take, there is a space between the in breath and the out breath. That space is the space of neutrality where the letting go takes place and the freedom to fill the space in the next in breath takes place. And that is the place of neutrality. That is the place of the void.

J: That's where we should be willing to be?

G: Yes. That is the place of surrender. Because when you are breathing in, you are receiving, you are being receptive. When you are breathing in you are taking in new life from the point of view and the perspective of the breath. You are also always breathing in the previous cycle, the previous experience you just had. Then breathing it out means letting it go. That space in between is the gestation period where the assimilation or the integration between the breathing in and the breathing out takes place, where you take from the old that which is of use, and you release in the next out breath all that is not of use. That's where the cycles of growth and understanding and development take place.

But most people hold onto what they have breathed in and refuse to let it go. When they intend something by breathing out, they don't really breathe it out because they don't really let it go. They still hold onto it. Therefore, it can't be made manifest. You must be able to let it go completely. That is why we suggest the mantra, "I know what I've given you. I don't know what you've received, and it's none of my business." That puts you in a state of neutrality where you truly let go of the manifestation that you seek. Allow it to go out into the ethers and form its grid work and then come back to you. And hold that place of emptiness as a place of faith, as a place of trust, as a place where the higher good of self resides in the absolute neutral place of knowing that what is for the highest good will be made manifest.

J: So the breathing almost becomes a metaphor for the process of life.

G: It is an exact metaphor. It is not just a metaphor. It is that which allows you to experience life. How much you are able to breathe in will determine how much of life you feel you deserve. How much of life you are able to receive. It is a direct indication of your receiving pattern. How much you breathe out is going to be determined by how much you breathe in. So it is an exact indication of your ability to give of yourself, to share yourself, to expose yourself to life.

J: So how we breathe is the key to how we live?

G: That is correct. That is the fundamental key to the universe. It is the key to life.

J: You have been saying that, haven't you?

G: Yes, we have, again and again. But you are finally hearing it.

J: Say it again, if you wouldn't mind, for extra emphasis here.

G: As much as you are able to breathe in is as much of life as you are able to receive, that you feel you have a right to receive. Therefore, you will limit yourself to receiving in life according to how much you limit your in breath. If you limit your taking in of life, you will also be limiting what you feel you have to give to life, what you feel you can expose to life, what you feel you can give to life without feeling you are giving something up or giving yourself up. Giving and receiving are an exact mirror of one another. Giving and receiving are the same thing. As I give I receive. As I receive, I give. If I am only breathing out, only giving, I will die. If I'm only breathing in, only taking in, only taking, I will die. I must be able to breathe in and breathe out. Try it. Try just breathing in without breathing out again. Try it right now. Breathe in. Just keep breathing in. Just keep breathing in, no breathing out. It's impossible.

J: Is that what most people do? Try to hold onto the past, in essence only breathing in, too afraid to take in new experiences by not letting go and taking a new breath so to speak?

G: In a sense, yes. The fact that most people utilize only 15-20 percent of their lung capacity is an indication of how much they feel they deserve where life is concerned.

J: So we're living only about 20 percent of our life potential.

G: That is exactly right. Therefore, you are literally living a life of starvation. You are starving the brain of oxygen and its capacity to function as a physical functioning unit to be able to interpret and take in consciousness. That's why most people are not very bright where conscious awareness is concerned. They are asleep because the brain itself is not oxygenated, so it cannot fire. It cannot function. It cannot produce its chemical processes properly.

Being able to breathe in or not able to breathe in also interferes with the functioning of the endocrine system, the glandular system of the body. The endocrine system is the distributor of energy to the various chemical processes that nourish and nurture the various organs and systems of the body and also accesses the different minds of the body. The endocrine system is the doorway between the conscious mind, the subconscious, and the superconscious. The endocrine system controls the functioning of the nervous system through how it balances or distorts the serotonins and various chemical processes that are produced in the brain. Therefore, the breath is the source of all of that.

The breath is also the source of the reproduction of life on a cellular level. As you breathe in, you breathe oxygen into the body. You accelerate the reproduction of cells, the renewal of life. As you breathe in only this much, you are not oxygenating very much of life. You are not reproducing very many cells very rapidly. Therefore, you are shutting down your ability to regenerate life.

You see, you have been given the gift of life in the breath, the secret of life in the breath. If you use that secret of life, you have the ability to regenerate life endlessly. The one thing that keeps you from regenerating life and reproducing it, which results in aging, disease, and death, is the fact that less than 1 percent of the body can reproduce itself. The cells of the body are programmed with messages of trauma that don't allow the body to reproduce itself without aging, disease, and eventually death. If you are unable to access those traumas and therefore stimulate the release of the emotional charges held in the body that keep the damaged areas in place and, therefore, don't allow the life force to fully stimulate the regeneration of the body, you will always have the process of aging, disease, and death. If, on the other hand, you are able to free yourself of your personal history in the body, you have the potential of immortality in the physical body.

In the DNA itself, in the forty-four on sites that have never been stimulated, what the scientists call the junk DNA, they're beginning to understand it is not junk DNA. It is spiritual DNA. It is the potential for immortality in the physical. As they have uncovered the secret to the DNA molecule, they are now actually predicting the possibility of the average life span increasing to two hundred years over the next fifty to one hundred years. And within the next two hundred to five hundred years, they're predicting the average life span increasing up to five hundred or more years.

Those are speculations based upon what they have discovered so far. However, those speculations fall far short of what is possible. Look at the cases where a life-threatening disease has had an instantaneous healing. That healing happened because more than twenty on sites in the DNA were activated. By activating a few more on sites, the disease was eradicated from the body instantaneously. If you were using ten more of those on sites on a regular basis, think of what would be possible.

J: Stimulating these on sites, I think you said, involved dealing with our personal issues and breathing.

G: And breathing accesses what? It accesses the sensation of being. This is why human beings don't breathe. That's why they stop breathing because breathing produces feeling. And feeling is the sensation of the movement of the life energy through the body. When the movement of that life energy through feeling is associated with pain, human beings begin to stop the breath process to stop pain. It happens very early in childhood and gradually increases into adolescence and adulthood. So by the time you are an adult you have pretty much begun a slow movement towards your annihilation simply through the process of shutting off feeling.

The DNA molecule is influenced by feeling. It holds all your emotional patterns in place, all your emotional patterns of resistance and of acceptance. When you are holding feelings in the body, you are holding the life force and preventing it from movement, preventing it from having expression. When that takes place, it creates a length of wave form in the DNA that misses connecting the on sites in the DNA. Therefore, it does not produce the necessary amino acids and chemical productions in the endocrine system that bring about the balance in the immune system and in the body. So when you are holding emotions, when you are suppressing emotions, then you are having a negative experience of emotion because holding or suppressing creates resistance, which creates pain. Pain creates fight, and that form of fight or resistance stimulates a closed system, a system that is feeding upon itself. Therefore, it breaks down.

When however, the DNA is affected by a wave form of a movement of feeling, which means that you are accepting and experiencing your feelings moment to moment, it produces a different length of wave form. It's a matter of allowing all feelings, negative as well as positive. The DNA is stimulated by the allowance of all feelings. When there is a flow of feelings, it produces a length of wave form that connects the on sites in the DNA molecule. Connecting those on sites produces and stimulates the production of those chemicals needed to bring about the balance of the immune system and, thus, the physical body.

J: That whole process starts with the breathing.

G: Breathing is the source. Without breathing you cannot think, you cannot feel, because breathing awakens the consciousness in the physical body. When you breathe into the body, you stimulate awareness. You stimulate life. You stimulate consciousness. So the physical body, the emotional body, and the mental body are dependent upon the breath. Everything in life is dependent on three things: the breath, movement, and sound. Life is movement. Resistance is nonmovement, which is death, destruction.

J: So the awakening of the soul is all about breath, movement, and sound. Those are the three elements that make up the energetic exercises we're including in the book.

G: That is correct.

J: You stated that instantaneous healing occurs because of the connection of more on sites in the DNA. Robert Baker tells a pretty dramatic story about how his bones were crushed in his legs and spine when he was a child. He says he was brought to his grandmother who was a healer, and he had an instantaneous healing. She wasn't trained in Reiki. What is the missing ingredient between someone who is practicing Reiki and may have a mild effect on the client versus someone who has a powerful effect such as Robert's grandmother?

G: The ability to know the perfect state of being and to hold that perfect state of being unflinchingly without a doubt. To hold it with the wholeness of your being with the absolute knowing of the perfection of that state of well-being and health. To focus, not on the disease, but on the healing. Not even on the healing so much because when you focus on the healing, you are focusing on the expectation of process rather than the knowing of the state of being. All healing is a manifestation of knowing on some level.

J: So let's say we're dealing with a serious chronic disease that the AMA may not be able to help with very much such as cancer. How would you counsel us to approach this client?

G: Allow yourself to embody the truth of that life force, to embody it by becoming neutral and taking it within and allowing it to pass through you and allowing it to radiate forth to those who will receive it. When there is a communion between two souls, which was the case with the one, the Christ, where there was no doubt in the mind or in the feeling, thought and feeling become one energy that sustains and maintains the inception of that healing. Seeing that being in perfect health, in perfect balance with no doubt whatsoever.

J: I read that Jesus could not perform miracles in his hometown.

G: There is an old saying that a prophet is not recognized in his own home. In other words, human beings tend not to value what they take for granted because they tend to create ideas and freeze frame people, events, and circumstances according to those ideas. The hometown is really representative of the collective consciousness of any given state of being. When there is a collective consciousness that sees things one way, it cannot recognize anything else. It cannot recognize the possibilities of change, of miracles, of other realities because it holds so dearly its attachment to its own collective belief system.

J: Doesn't this relate to what you were saying earlier about healing when there is no doubt? So healing is undermined by the doubt of the collective consciousness.

G: Yes. For instance, where the channel is concerned, the advice that his grandmother would give to him regarding healing was: Tell no one of your disease. Do not lend it to those minds that will not hold it in well being and health. Do not give it to the worriers who will further exacerbate the problem rather than support the solution. Therefore, share it only with those who you know will hold it in the highest light of well-being. That creates a resonance of solution and healing.

J: That's good counsel for anyone struggling with disease.

G: Exactly, or with anything. Any problem whatsoever because the worriers will attach to you. They will help you to maintain and sustain that state. There is a statement that says birds of a feather flock together. And they certainly do.

J: I have a cousin who has breast cancer. She said she was feeling the burden of her family's worry. I think you're saying she is right.

G: That's right, because the worry simply adds to the problem. It simply sustains the breast cancer.

J: So what can we counsel people who are struggling like that?

G: Worry is not love. It is fear.

J: So we're bathing them in fear.

G: You're bathing them in your own fear. Worry has nothing to do with love.

J: So to help these people we must …

G: You must see them in their perfect state of being, unwaveringly. You see, you are dealing always, dear one, in the realm of the quantum field of possibility and probability. The quantum sea, as they call it in physics, is the pregnant void of creation. It is the place between the in breath and the out breath. It is the place of all probability and possibility that exists simultaneously at all time. When you dip into the sea of possibility and probability where reality is concerned, be sure you dip into it with a very clear focus of that intention so that you pull from it the probability that you want to create most specifically.

J: How do we do that?

G: Focus your consciousness and your feelings, your intention and your feelings.

J: So I have cancer, let's say.

G: You don't want to focus on the cancer. You want to focus on the healing, on the solution.

J: How would I do that?

G: You can surround the cancer cells with absolute love. Embrace them with absolute acceptance, nurturing, and love so that you are not fighting them. Because the minute you have to fight anything you're aiding and abetting the very thing you want to destroy.

J: Can you suggest an affirmation that would help with that focus?

G: Well, there are many, but keep it simple: I am in a perfect state of health and well being. It is my divine right, and I demand and declare that it is as it is. I am perfect here and now. Divine love always has met and always will meet every human need.

J: Thank you. Your teachings about health and healing seem pretty clear and understandable, but putting them into practice seems challenging.

G: Because that's where you challenge the comfort zone of your thoughts and your feelings that might be contrary to them.

J: The affirmation you just gave helps me focus my thoughts and intentions.

G: Yes. We have created a very effective tape of affirmations—affirmations of abundance as the channel has called it that you might want to listen to. You will find it very helpful in affirming the mind and the emotions. It is about abundance in all areas. Life is abundant. You see, it's about declaring life, dear one. Go back to the breath. How much life am I declaring at this moment? How much life am I breathing in? Take a deep breath.

J: You have said this over and over and over again. I know it, but ...

G: There is a deaf ear to life for the most part. People constantly fight for their death. They constantly fight for their limitations because they constantly fight for the comfort zone of what they think they know as that makes them feel they're somehow in control of life. Our question is: why would you want to control life? The only reason we could see that you might want to control life is that you don't trust its existence.

J: We want to stop bad things from happening.

G: Bad things don't happen in life. Bad things happen, as you call them, in resistance to life. So give up your resistance to life and you give up bad things as you call them. What do you think of as bad?

J: Well, for example, ill health, the death of a child, people killed in accidents.

G: Why is that bad?

J: It doesn't feel good.

G: Ahhhh. "I can't accept how I feel about it."

J: Yes. The feeling of loss is painful.

G: You are not in a lot of pain because you are experiencing loss. You are in a lot of pain because you are resisting experiencing loss.

J: And you're saying that is what we're all doing when we say bad things are happening.

G: That's correct. That which you call bad things has nothing to do with the experience. It has to do with resisting the experience. It has to do with judgment about the experience of life.

J: So we should just accept.

G: What a good idea! In doing so, you might then approach life in a different way. In doing so you will approach life in a way that has faith in life, trust in life and that honors life through the choices that you make in life that are different from the ones you are making now.

Chapter 10:
Death/Spiritual Realms/Guidance

J: In our first conversation, I told you that Phillip and I had lost our mothers in the past few years, and I asked what you could tell us about them. You said that they were in the mid-range of the astral plane.

G: Yes, in the mid-range of the fourth level.

J: Where is the astral plane?

G: The astral plane exists in the same time and space as the physical plane. Without the astral plane, there would be no physical plane. The astral plane is the fourth dimension of energy that holds thought forms and feeling forms in place, which is what holds matter in place. For example, if every human being for one second were to forget that the earth existed, it would cease to exist.

J: You said that on one of your tapes. That's hard to understand.

G: All matter is held in place by the vibration frequency of consciousness.

Physical consciousness is held together by the comprehension of thoughts and feelings. Feelings are the attractive aspect that creates the attachment to the physical world. Thoughts are the aspect of the physical world that describe its form and the reality of it. Without the description and the attachment, there is no physical form. So it is the comprehension of thoughts and feelings that enable you to keep physical reality in place.

The physical body has seven levels of consciousness. Those are the seven chakras that correspond to the seven levels of the astral plane. The seven levels of the astral plane are various levels of refinement of energy related to the journey from the physical into the causal plane or the soul plane. The astral plane is the intermediary or the space between the physical and the soul plane, even though it's not a space in reality. But we describe it as that for you to understand it in a physical way.

J: So it's not some far off place.

G: It exists in consciousness. You would not be alive in a physical body if you did not have an astral body to contain your soul body and your physical body. In the third dimension, you have a physical body. In the fourth dimension, you have an astral body. The astral body is the container that is a holographic energetic duplicate of the physical body. It is made of bioplasmic matter, which is a less dense form of matter. It's a kind of iridescent light, a vibration frequency. That bioplasmic matter is connected to a silver cord that is connected to the physical body. The silver cord attaches to the physical body at the point of birth when the umbilical cord is cut. It replaces the umbilical cord, and it allows the individual to have life independent of the mother.

Up to that point the life force is being fed through the mother's umbilical cord. The silver cord of the astral body is attached to the mother's astral body when the infant is still attached to the mother's physical body. Once the umbilical cord is cut, the astral cord connects to the physical body of the infant and contains the infant's physical body and contains the soul body within the astral body in the physical body. So the soul body is trapped in the astral form. At the point of death, the astral cord disconnects from the physical body with the soul body and they are both released into the astral world, into the astral level of consciousness, the fourth dimension.

The physical body then dies and deteriorates and goes back to the atomic structure from which it came. It no longer has the astral body to maintain and sustain its connection to the physical world, so it deteriorates. The astral body, in the meantime, holds the soul body in seven levels of refined forms of energy. The first level is very dense and very connected to the physical world. This is when you sometimes see what you call ghosts or spirit apparitions. These are apparitions who often are not yet aware that they are dead or are still very attached to physical reality emotionally and mentally with a lot of unresolved issues. So they stay around and they can be perceived by beings in the physical world.

J: How long does this last?

G: It can last a few hours, days, months or it can even last hundreds of years with some people. It depends upon the person's attachment to the unfinished business in the physical world, particularly if the death was sudden through an accident or something like that. For instance, the 9/11 incident created a lot of astral bodies who hung around that area for a period of time. Some are still hanging around, and they are gradually dissipating into the other levels of the astral.

J: Phillip's twin brother was killed in a motorcycle accident. His mother claimed he appeared to her shortly after and told her that he was all right.

G: Yes.

J: So that's possible?

G: Yes, because he's still directly connected to the physical world. Also, spirits can connect to and possess physical bodies. This is sometimes called spiritual possession. If people in the physical bodies have a connection to a person that they are not able to let go of in the mourning process, sometimes they'll keep them attached. As you progress through the astral world, as you begin to let go of the physical world and your emotional and mental attachments, the levels of the astral body gradually disintegrate. They're like shelves of energetic bioplasmic matter. Each one is a higher vibration than the last one. The highest vibration is the seventh layer of the astral world, the final layer of bioplasmic matter at a high vibration that still encloses the soul body. When that has deteriorated, the soul leaves the astral realm and goes into the causal plane, which is the soul plane.

Once it has left, the soul is free of the physical world until it decides to reincarnate. In the soul plane, you connect all the dots, so to speak. In other words, you get to connect to your oversoul. You get to look at the whole plan and evaluate it—to see how the oversoul plan of all your soul fragments interweaves in its connections, interactions, and purpose with all the souls where the planetary logos is concerned, the entire Akashic. Then you decide from there what would be the best kind of soul fragment to create for yourself for the next stage of soul development, where and how you can best serve it. Then it will gather together a specific astral body based upon the type of life it has chosen to embody and its level of soul development. It will then reincarnate again in the physical, and it will go through the same process again.

Some souls, as we said, remain trapped in the astral world for years. For instance, Queen Elizabeth I spent about three hundred years in the astral realm because she couldn't let go of trying to control the government of the United Kingdom. And so she stayed attached for that period of time. She has finally left the astral world and gone into the soul plane.

J: I would think there would be spiritual assistance for souls like that.

G: There is, but you see, human beings have freedom of will. They are free to make choices based upon their belief systems. For instance, the Catholics have something they call purgatory. Now they don't entirely understand what that is when they speak of it. What it actually is: souls who remain trapped in the first two levels of the astral world because they are taught that when they die, Christ will come and resurrect them, so they must wait to be redeemed by Christ. Often beings of light they have known in other lifetimes, who have transcended the astral world, will come from the soul plane to take them on to the soul plane, to take them out of the lower part of the astral realm, or to educate them beyond those lower levels. But they refuse to go to the light because they are waiting in this state of purgatory to be rescued by the Christ. So because of their belief systems, they remain confined in this purgatory, in this kind of living hell, where they're caught between the physical world and the nonphysical world.

J: So that is their own creation.

G: Yes, how they create the astral world is based upon what they believe and how they saw reality in the physical world. They just create an exact duplicate in the astral world except it's not solid.

J: What about hell?

G: Hell is a level of consciousness. Hell is based upon attachments that desire has not fulfilled in the physical world. So hell is people who are in unfulfilled desire constantly seeking the physical world for their sense of identity, their sense of self, their gratification, and their fulfillment. For instance, let us say you have an alcohol addiction and your body dies and you go into the astral world. If you have not satisfied that addiction, you will still have it in the astral world, except you will have no way of satisfying it. You will recreate the alcohol in astral form, but it is in astral matter. You will still have the thirst, but the thirst cannot be quenched. So that's kind of a living hell.

Bars frequently are filled with lower level astral spirits that attach themselves to the energy fields of alcoholics and feed their addictions. They are feeding off the addiction of the being that is sitting there having the drink trying to get satiated. It's a form of astral possession, which simply feeds the addiction of the physical being.

J: What help is available for these souls?

G: Gradually they will come to their senses, so to speak. They may meet other beings in the astral world and connect with groups, with teachers, that sort of thing. Gradually they will work their way through the different levels of the astral world and free themselves from the astral possession in the astral plane, Therefore, it's so important that in the physical world you find freedom from the astral body, from your astral attachments, your emotional glamours, your mental illusions. This is why we emphasize always that transcendence and awakening of the soul can happen in the physical body. You do not have to wait to go into the astral world to transcend the astral world. At this time the astral world is gradually disintegrating and dissipating. That's why people are finding less and less satisfaction in the physical world, less satisfaction in their attachments, in their consumption, less satisfaction in their focus on the physical world as the source of their sense of self and their being.

J: I have to confess that your description of what happens to us in the astral plane after we die sounds more than a little cold. I'm not hearing anything about love or joy.

G: Well, there is no love in the desire elemental. The desire elemental operates through survival and fear and is governed by the astral plane. The desire elemental is all of your emotional, physical, and mental desires that are attached to the physical world as the source of your sense of self and source of reality. Once you make an inner connection to the soul, you then govern the physical world through your inner self, through the connection to the truth of your being. Then you're not attached to the world to gratify and satisfy you. You use the world simply to grow, to gain experience, and to learn. But the source of power and sense of self comes from your divine connection inside. You're not seeking it from the outside. This is the transition that you go through now in this two-thousand-year cycle, the transition from your outer illusion to your inner reality. You then begin to direct the outer reality based upon the inner reality.

J: When I referred to love and joy I was thinking about when I die. It's a comforting thought to think I'm going to be greeted by souls I love. Many spiritual writings indicate that is what happens. What happens when we die? Are we greeted by souls we love?

G: It depends entirely upon the person and the person's intentions. If that's the intention you set, then that's the reality you will have. It is important to understand that reality is not something that is arbitrary—it is something that you create. How you motivate and move your consciousness, what you feel and what you believe, is what creates your reality. For instance, take people who grew up in the East Indian religion. When they go to the astral plane, their idea of heaven is based upon their archetypes, the things with which they grew up. So that's what they will experience because that is their reality. Whereas, what you might experience in creating heaven in the astral realm would be based upon your beliefs related to the Christ. So whatever you have created in the physical world reflects your belief system because the physical world is created through beliefs, not necessarily through truth, but through collective belief systems.

The astral world contains the collective belief system of humanity and what it perceives as reality. What you perceive as reality as an individual is also how you will experience the astral world, just as you experience the physical world. At the death of the physical body, you simply continue on from the moment that you left the physical body in consciousness exactly as before. That is why we encourage everyone to do your transcendence here in the physical world, to find reality here in the physical world, to connect to your soul consciousness here in the physical world. Then when you move into the astral world, you will be directing your reality consciously. You can also transcend death altogether, and you can decide to recreate and reform the physical body any way you like because it's just energy, molecules moving in space.

J: When would we be able to do that?

G: Not for awhile.

J: So at some future time, some members of mankind will be able to do that?

G: Eventually all members of mankind will be able to transcend the physical altogether. There will be no need for it because the physical world is simply a state of consciousness used for the purpose of experiencing the evolution of the soul. So the soul's evolutionary or growth experience—how the soul grows, expands and deepens its consciousness and awareness of itself—is the purpose of the physical plane. No other purpose. Through experience, God, God that is all there is, gets to experience him/herself in something called a remembering experience of all the different parts of him/herself through all the different aspects of humanity in the physical world, as well as the animal kingdom, mineral kingdom, and plant kingdom. And now you are entering into the divine kingdom in your evolution. It's all very complex.

J: Yes, it is. But you are helping me expand my understanding of what being a creator is.

G: Yes.

J: Phillip wants to know if you can use energy to fax a visual description of some of the concepts you're talking about.

G: We cannot because you are not at a vibration to be able to comprehend it. You see, you must be aligned. We can only bring in a limited amount of information, for instance, through this vehicle (Robert Baker) because he is only aligned to a certain degree. If we were to bring in more of what you call infinite power, we would blow up the vehicle.

What you are talking about is psychic phenomenon, which is based upon manipulating magnetic attraction in the physical world. That is lower psychic energy. Lower psychic energy is based upon the manipulation of matter related to the lower self. It's what you call psychic magic and that sort of thing. That is of the material world. Could we do that? Yes. What purpose would it serve?

J: Well, a picture can be worth a thousand words. We just wondered if it were possible for you to supply some visual depictions that would clarify some of the more complex concepts we have been talking about.

G: They are not physical concepts, so they can't really be described or depicted visually. You could make drawings, for instance, of the geometry of what holds physical matter in place. Basically, physical matter is held in place by three forms, the circle, the square, and the triangle, which make up the double tetrahedron, which encloses the physical reality or the etheric body in the physical world.

J: Would you be able to provide a visual of that?

G: Well, you can do that yourself now. Take a pencil and draw two triangles right on top of one another.

J: So I have a Star of David?

G: That's correct. That's a sacred geometric of all things in the physical world. That's the double tetrahedron.

J: And it holds everything together?

G: That's right. It is the geometric that makes up all platonic solids.

J: How does that relate to molecules and atoms?

G: It encloses them in a form. So, in other words, you have that double tetrahedron around you and through you. That's why you are able to maintain yourself as separate in form. Once you awaken that double tetrahedron and learn to spin it, you will able to bring spiritual power into physical form. That is the process happening now. The tetrahedron is beginning to awaken, gradually, slowly.

J: Are those some of the mysteries that are being withheld?

G: That's correct.

J: Have we been able to do that in the past?

G: Some have, yes.

J: In Atlantis?

G: Atlantis understood the concept, but they misused the power.

J: I want to refer back to our discussion about the astral plane. It sounded a little cold. And when I asked about love and joy, I was a little confused by your response. Can our mothers still feel love for us?

G: Yes. Love is interconnected and interwoven throughout the entire universe. It is the glue of the universe because it is the essence of all souls. So on a soul level you are interconnected in love, not with just your mothers but with every soul in the universe. But in order to experience love in the physical plane, you must be connected to the soul's consciousness, which means you must be individuated. And you must be in charge of the lower self because the lower self is connected to survival and fear in the physical plane, and it is connected to attachment to the physical world, which disconnects it from the individuality of its being.

You see, the love force is the force of the soul. The experience of joy is when the soul is awakened in the physical body. Happiness is something experienced by the lower self. Happiness is fleeting and temporary. It's something you constantly seek, which enables you to constantly be moved towards more—moved towards growth, towards experience, towards embracing change in seeking happiness. It's sort of a joke of the lower self that stimulates the desire for more.

The force of love is the force of the soul awakened. The force of the soul awakened is the expression of the individuality of who you are in this incarnational form with all of its parts expressed, experienced, shared, and awakened. So as you awaken to more of yourself inside and learn to express, experience, and share that, the more you awaken to the love impulse of the soul, the more you awaken to the possibility of the experience of joy of living. Because as the soul awakens, it brings its light into the consciousness of the physical body.

In order to do that, you must quiet the lower self. You must quiet the emotional body with all of its dualistic, separated, categorized feelings that it determines are negative and positive. You must be able to still the mental body in order to focus it. You must be able to move beyond thought into the direct perception of knowing. Once the emotional body is stilled, then you can awaken to the presence of the intuitional body of the soul, which then connects you to the direct knowing when the mind is stilled. Then the emotional and mental bodies are able to be directed by the soul and the personality is directed through intuition and knowing. That is the state of the I Am of beingness of the soul.

Then the love force is awakened. Then you experience the joy of being. But as long as you are attached to separated feelings and descriptions of reality through thoughts, you will never be able to awaken that sense of connection to your soul. There is nothing that keeps you from it except your own busy thoughts and feelings attached to the physical world as your sense of self. This is why Christ said be in the world, not of it.

You have to release yourself from the three worlds, physical, emotional, and mental where the attachment of the lower self and the desire elemental is concerned. You see, desire is of the lower self. Desire is a substitute for the passion and excitation of the erotic force of the divine that is not yet able to connect to the conscious awareness of the lower self. Once that conscious awareness is there, you no longer operate through desire. Desire becomes transformed into the desire of the soul, which is the expression of being.

J: So our concerns about our mothers are really coming from our lower selves.

G: Yes, from the desire elemental. As the lower self, you interpret love as a sentimental feeling of attachment. That's not what it is.

J: We've talked about that, and I still have trouble fully understanding it. For example, when Jesus said, "Love one another as I have loved you," it's hard to separate that from emotional attachment.

G: Of course, because as a human being who sees your reality in the hands of other human beings, you are always outer focused. This is the focus of an infant who has never moved beyond the infantile expression of unconditional love of the mother. And the infant is still seeking it co-dependently in relationship to the world because it has never moved beyond that infantile connection to mother to become an individual and find within itself. Therefore, you have a world that is confined in infancy where its emotional development is concerned, for the most part.

Most human beings are confined to an infantile or an immature state of development. In the infantile stage of love, the infant receiving the unconditional love of the mother says, if you love me, I will love you. In the immature stage of love development, fatherly love, around age eight to nine, it is: I need you, therefore I love you. When you reach a mature stage of love, there are two individuals who love in equality. That means they are able to respect and love each other for who they are individually. The mature stage of love is: I love you, therefore I need you. Not I need you, therefore I love you. Mature love integrates motherly love, fatherly love, and brotherly love.

J: It might be helpful to have a workshop on love.

G: Yes.

J: There's an awful lot to know about it. If most of us are stuck in infancy, we have a lot of work to do.

G: That is correct. Your entire Western society is stuck in infancy.

J: What about the East?

G: Well, parts of that as well. You cannot separate them now because, basically, the world is influenced by the consumer attitude of the West.

J: During our discussion about the astral plane, I was thinking about some current American television programs in which mediums supposedly communicate with the spirits of loved ones who have passed on who are related to people in the audience.

G: Yes, that's true.

J: That's valid?

G: Yes, you can do that. Why you would want to, we don't know. But you can do that.

J: I can understand it if people have a strong emotional connection to someone or when there is a tragic circumstance. For instance, if someone has lost a child and they want to believe the child is in a good place, I can see why they might find some comfort in that.

G: Yes.

J: When I watch these programs I'm aware they are mostly about getting clues to establish the spirit's identity—like grandma was wearing a brown dress when she died. There doesn't seem to be any wisdom or teachings coming through. Is it because they don't have any?

G: Well, they're dealing with lower psychic energy. You see, when connecting with the spirit world, you are dealing with psychic energy. You're not connected to soul energy. So, you're connecting to the thought and feeling forms that are connected to the energy fields of the person you are reading and that person's attachment to the person in the astral world. So you're dealing with lower psychic energy. Psychic energy has nothing to do with soul energy. Soul energy has to do with direct intuition and knowing that connects to the causal plane, to the soul itself. What they are connecting to are astral entities, to spirit forms.

J: Do souls in the soul plane communicate with souls here?

G: Yes, of course. You have many types of guides. You have guides that are angelic presences who are aspects of your soul group that have moved beyond the soul plane and into the lower areas of the angelic plane. These kinds of angelic presences act as guides and guardians. They help guide certain aspects of the connection between your soul fragment in this lifetime and your oversoul plan. And so they act as guides and as guardians to keep you on the path, keep you safe. They give you clues along the way, but they will not interfere. They will not tell you what to do. They will offer guidance.

So always be wary of anyone who says he or she is an angelic presence, one of your guides who is telling you what to do, because anyone who is telling you what to do is probably not an angelic guide. It's probably some spirit that you're picking up on in the astral realm that is falsely representing itself to you. Astral beings do that occasionally because it gives them some attention and glamour, and it allows them to make a connection to you.

J: How can we know what true angelic guidance is?

G: By not telling you what to do but, rather, guiding you so that you are empowered to make your own choices and decisions. If it interferes with your freedom in any way, then it is not higher spiritual guidance. It is probably guidance from the astral plane. You also have guides who sometimes come from the astral plane that are beings with whom you've been in touch in many, many incarnations. They are there to guide you in the astral plane because they have not taken physical form, but they are acting as a guide for you because they are connected to your soul's journey and they owe you one from a cycle of previous lifetimes. So they're paying off their karmic debt to you, and they can give some good guidance.

J: How can we better connect with the guidance?

G: Your soul fragment is guiding you, and your oversoul is guiding your soul fragment. But most of the time you are not aware of it because you are not sensitive enough to pay attention. You're too distracted by everything in the physical world and all your worries and all your ways of controlling everything, trying to figure everything out, all your emotional attachments in the physical world. So you never get still enough to notice the synchronicity of your soul's guidance.

J: So stillness is critical.

G: Absolutely. The most critical thing is to become still within, to still the mind, to still the feelings, so that you can begin to experience that guidance. So you can begin to notice how your soul is guiding you this way or that way, how it is connecting you with this person or that group or situation. What it is teaching you. What learning experiences it is introducing you to. For instance, your connection to us has been your soul guiding you. Do you see?

J: Yes. We have talked about the synchronicities that led to this project. You said that mediums who claim to speak to spirits were connecting with lower psychic energy from the astral plane, which has nothing to do with soul energy. Are you saying that there is no wisdom on the astral level, that psychic energy doesn't have value?

G: No. All we're saying is that if you are connecting with spirits, you are connecting with spirits who are still trapped within the memory and the attraction to their physical forms. That's why they're still in the astral. That's why they're in spirit form. That means that, for the most part, they have not advanced that much because they have not yet thrown off the shell of the astral form to allow the soul to be revealed. They're not able yet to connect with their soul consciousness and the wisdom it contains.

So the purpose of psychic energy and the connection to the astral world is simply to bring some contentment to people in the physical world who have lost loved ones. It also allows them to realize that life does not end in the physical. It allows them to reconnect in some way, and it gives them comfort and help. All of which are very important. But understand the connection to the astral means you are simply strengthening your desire elemental connection to the physical world.

J: Do we experience learning and training in the astral realm?

G: You can, yes, if you are operating through the higher levels of the astral realm. There are seven levels of spiritual refinement. If you are in the lower two levels, you are still where you're not really cognizant of anything other than your emotional and mental attachments to the physical world. And you just keep trying to recreate those. Even in the third level of the astral world, you'll find people recreating their reality and living it out exactly the way it was in the physical. They will create astral duplicates of the way they lived.

J: So they're recreating in the spirit world the same environment they left?

G: Exactly, because they never moved beyond that. They're still trapped in that consciousness.

J: There must be many souls that can move through that pretty quickly.

G: Yes. There are many who do. It depends upon the level of soul development they have come into in the incarnation, how much awareness they have of other dimensional consciousness, how much work they have done in the physical plane to release their emotional and mental attachments to the physical world as the source of their sense of self.

J: You have said many times how important it is to attempt to awaken the soul here.

G: Yes, exactly.

J: Not long ago we learned that one of our friends was critically ill and not expected to live. Despite all that we know about spiritual matters, we have this deep feeling of sadness.

G: Well, of course, because, where your humanity is concerned, that sadness is related to the loss of a piece of physical reality to which you are attached. The sadness is about loss. It is about the concept of death because human beings believe the only life there is, is the life in the physical body. They do not believe the life force itself is a force independent of the physical body, and that the physical body is simply a vehicle through which life expresses itself in individuated form for a period of time. And so that period of time is something that you get encapsulated in, and then you describe yourself as that period of time in the physical body. Because you are confined to that belief and because of the limited degree to which you are able to perceive the living force of life, you believe that once the physical body is gone, life is gone as well.

J: I know that the life force continues, so I guess I just have to take control of my feelings.

G: Well, it's important to allow yourself to have the feelings. You have sensory awareness as a human being so that you can distinguish the different degrees of relationship and experience, which is how you grow and learn about parts of yourself and learn how to love.

J: That's the reason why we've come here.

G: Yes. So sadness is a part of loving. Anger is a part of loving, Joy is a part of loving. All of it is a part of loving because all of it is an expression of who you are. And the force of love is who you are.

J: I was thinking and wondering about what our friend will experience in the astral plane when he passes. You said a lot of what we encounter depends upon what we expect and how much we've evolved before we pass over.

G: Yes, because your experience in the astral plane will be exactly the same as it was the moment before you passed from the physical body. So nothing changes. The only thing that changes is the physical form. You no longer have the physical form to encapsulate the astral body in the soul body.

J: You said that we are surrounded by the same environment in death as in life.

G: That depends upon how attached you are to that environment. If you're attached to that environment you will recreate that environment in the astral.

J: So I could be in the same house with the same furniture and the same people?

G: Yes, That's why astral beings often remain connected in spirit form to a place. That's why you have what you call ghosts within a place. It's the astral body of a person who has been unable to let go of his or her original form of life in the physical. And so the person continues to haunt it, to inhabit it. Often, beings who have passed over, depending upon how they've passed, sometimes don't have an awareness that they have passed. So they continue to live as though they were living in the physical. They continue to attempt to interact with beings in the physical, but they become confused as to why the beings aren't responding to them because they are talking and acting as if they are still relating on a physical level and don't realize that they have passed.

J: I would think it wouldn't take long before they would catch on.

G: It depends on how ensconced they are in their illusion.

J: Once they do catch on ...

G: Then they go through the process of gradually letting go of their attachment to the physical world.

Chapter 11:
Abortion/Homosexuality/
Death Penalty

J: Abortion is a major issue in the United States and around the world. Many religious groups consider abortion a sin against God and want to make it illegal.

G: Man has freedom of will. That is his divine gift. Therefore, he has the ability to decide whether life will continue or whether it will not. And he is making that decision even now as we speak where the planet and individuals are concerned. So he has the power to abort life or the power to allow it to come to fruition. That is a part of his growth process, a part of his learning about the sacredness of life, about choice where life is concerned, and about the quality of life he wants to create in the physical. Therefore, his ability to decide whether to bring a child to term or not is a part of his freedom of choice.

Understand, it is not just the parent, but it is also part of the evolution of the soul of the spirit that is coming in or is aborted. It's a part of that soul's decision as well. Many times the spirit decides at the last minute, well, I've changed my mind. I'm not going to come into this host. There is another host that will better serve me. Therefore, these spirits will choose a different host and incarnate with someone else because the spirits have decided it would better serve their incarnational process.

J: In that case, I could understand that a fetus might then be born dead. But how does that relate to the idea of a parent deciding to abort a child?

G: It relates to the spirit not connecting to the physical.

J: And somehow that has influenced the decision of the parents?

G: Yes, because, you see, part of the experience of the spirit connecting is there has to be a desire on a soul level where the parents are concerned and particularly where the host, the mother, is concerned. No matter how that child is brought up, even if that child is put up for adoption, is abandoned at birth, that mother on a soul level has chosen and that soul has chosen that mother. They have chosen to come together for the purpose of setting up the lessons for that soul and for each other. So adoption and abandonment are not arbitrary choices. They may seem arbitrary at the physical consciousness level, but on a soul level they are not.

J: So the circumstances of life including parents are chosen before we come here.

G: That is correct.

J: We're not really victims.

G: That is correct. The general overview of the design of the soul plan for an incarnational cycle is decided before the incarnation is chosen. Within that are variables based upon choice. The main lessons are set up by the parents who are chosen and the particular spirit who chooses those parents—the particular ethnic group it has chosen to incarnate into, the particular location, social, and economic background. All those sorts of things are part of the choice. That sets up an overall arc for the soul's design for its growth pattern for the incarnation. But to be in control of the experience, each soul has freedom of choice in order to learn and evolve experientially.

If you did not have freedom of choice, you would not learn and evolve experientially. This is essential to the soul's development. The soul must feel it is autonomous in its growth and evolutionary experience, that it is not being interfered with by spirit. Therefore, the aspect of spirit it contains has freedom of will. This is the gift God gives to each part of itself so that each part of itself can evolve consciously through freedom of will, freedom of choice.

J: If a society legislates against abortion and makes it a crime, it is then limiting the freedom of choice of the individual soul.

G: That is correct. It's limiting the freedom of the capacity of that soul to choose and, therefore, to grow through its own will and purpose. But, then, even that imposition becomes a part of the evolutionary process, the learning process, of the whole of man. Every choice you make is perfect for the commitment of evolution in one way or another.

J: I want to ask you about another controversial subject. The U.S. Supreme Court recently ruled that states cannot ban private sexual conduct between consenting adults. The particular case involved homosexuals, although it applies to everyone. Some people have likened homosexuality to bestiality and other immoral or criminal activity. What do you have to say about homosexuality?

G: Well, it's just a different form of expressing who you are. That's all. It serves a purpose like any other combination of relationships.

J: What purpose would it serve?

G: To balance out the distortions in the way in which you perceive your sexual identity as a male or as a female. What determines if someone is heterosexual or homosexual or bisexual or whatever is simply an influence of certain conditions in childhood in relation to the development of one's sense of identity. What tips the scales, whether it determines if someone is seeking sexual expression as homosexual or heterosexual, is determined by the modeling of the parents. For instance, if someone is a heterosexual, it's because a balance has taken place between the relationship of the mother and the father. Where the heterosexual is concerned, the sexual identity is learned from the person of the opposite sex. In other words, the male learns his sexual identity from the mother. The female learns her sexual identity from the bonding with the father.

Now what determines that distortion or shift that creates homosexual leanings rather than heterosexual? Usually what happens where the male homosexual is concerned is that there is an overpowering relationship with the mother and a lack of relationship with the father. Therefore, the male doesn't get the sense of his sexual identity. His sexual identity is overpowered by the mother, and his feeling of identity as a male is withdrawn or absent where the father is concerned. Therefore, in his sexual attraction he leans towards that which was missing (the relationship with the father), and pulls away from that which was overpowering, which was the relationship with the mother. That is the attraction toward males.

Now where the female homosexual is concerned, the opposite is true. She usually felt overpowered by the relationship with the father and felt frustrated in the absence of the relationship with the mother.

So she is drawn towards the mother to seek her sexual identity. And that is the attraction towards females.

From a higher perspective, it is also an opportunity for souls to be able to examine with a person of the same sex the male and female within themselves, to find that balance between two people of the same sex rather than through a person of the opposite sex. It all serves as a learning process. It is all a process of growth and development. All souls experience all kinds of interactions and interrelationships with persons of the opposite sex, same sex, as brothers, sisters, all of that, throughout their incarnational process. So they have, in the recording of their holographic consciousness, an understanding of all relationships.

J: Is sexual identity chosen before we incarnate?

G: All your types of relationships are chosen. In other words, the overview or the basic through line of what it is you're going to set up for yourself is chosen before the incarnation. And then you select the players who will best serve setting it up for you in the physical.

J: Would that explain why you might have several children who grew up in a family under the same conditions, but their sexuality developed differently?

G: Exactly. But you must understand that each incarnation is individual. An individual soul chooses a particular way of learning. And depending upon how those souls interpret and internalize the experiences they have and how they adjust themselves to their own traumas as a result of the parental modeling will determine how they perceive it, how they internalize it, and how they respond to it. So that will determine what kind of an experience they have.

All people are individuals. Their nervous systems are influenced by their individuality, how the particular soul has set things up, what it is they decide to learn, and how they decide to learn it. So you can have three kids in the family with the same parents, and they will all experience a different reality. Or two of them will experience a similar reality and one will be totally different. You see? It depends.

J: Homosexuality seems to be one of the last targets of discrimination.

G: Homosexuality is no different than anything that is different, that is not a part of the status quo, that is threatening to the comfort zone of the collective consciousness. For instance, look at it from a more neutral perspective. Let's take it away from homosexuality and look at it from the point of view of when people believed the world was flat. If anybody said to them, no, the world is round, they would say, you are crazy. That is not true. And they would have condemned the other person until someone proved the world was not flat—it was round, and people were not going to fall off when they sailed to the edge of it. Then all of a sudden the entire consciousness changed. But human beings change gradually because they are afraid of differences. They like the comfort zone of their collective reality, their collective belief systems, that they can all agree upon because it makes them feel connected. Limitation and sameness makes them feel connected.

J: Many critics have made it a moral issue and condemn homosexuals as immoral.

G: Yes. Well, you see, moralism is the system of duality. Moralism is based upon right and wrong, good and evil. And that is based upon the domination of a collective consciousness. It's based upon a patriarchal system, the male energy that says, I know and you don't. My reality is the best reality, the only reality, and yours is not. As long as you have a patriarchal system based upon right and wrong, good and bad, you will be in duality. Until you learn to develop a conscience as an individual and take responsibility for that conscience, take responsibility for your own choices, take responsibility for your own creation of reality through conscious choice, you will continue to operate through right and wrong, good and bad and morality as a substitute.

J: Capital punishment is another polarizing subject in our country. The United States is at odds with most of the Western world over capital punishment. We have many people on death row even though there is so much controversy about the reliability and fairness of our justice system.

G: Your prison system has become a welfare system paid for by the taxpayers. That is simply an example of lack of education and taking responsibility for life.

J: Lack of education on the part of the people in prison, or of the population who wants to imprison them?

G: The lack of education that does not see the value in taking care of its (our nation's) people by educating them responsibly and providing equally for all with compassion.

J: The Supreme Court is considering a lower court ruling involving the death penalty for teenagers. What is your view on the whole idea of the death penalty?

G: The death penalty is simply another illustration of resistance to life. Why would the death penalty be a requirement in the first place? Because there are those who take human lives. There are those who destroy because of their pain, their suffering. You are coming to a point in your evolution now where you have synthesized the lower self and you have a greater understanding. And you move toward the heart, the heart of the soul. And the soul does not invoke destruction of life. As a matter of fact, it is the repository of life.

As the soul grows in its influence, the desire to punish others for their actions will no longer exist because souls will begin to establish their integrity, the sacredness of their being, their honoring of all life. Therefore, there will no longer be the extremes of polarity that produce the duality of the death penalty. Because you will begin to take care of your prisoners early on in their lives so they do not have to put themselves in such incarceration where the resistance to their feelings is concerned and where the lack of nurturing of their being is concerned. You see, where murderers are concerned, they are acting out extreme pain. They will begin to realize that there is no ennobling reason to destroy life or attempt to destroy a life-form, because you are destroying just a life-form—you are not destroying life. The life of that person goes on. It continues. You cannot destroy life because life is energy, and energy cannot be destroyed, although you can destroy the physical body.

The magnetic poles are shifting by degrees. Gradually over the years, you will find the gravitational force less dense and the magnetic force almost nonexistent. When that takes place, it will provide an opening in duality. The soul will then reveal itself as the solar force, the energy of the sun, the sustainer and source of life. When that happens, there will no longer be things such as the death penalty. There will no longer be the need for a central government because souls will have learned how to take responsibility for and enjoy the experience of being empowered.

J: When will we get to such a place?

G: That is up to you. It is all up to you.

Chapter 12:
August 30, 2003: Martin Luther King, Jr. /John F. Kennedy/Middle East/World Government/Democracy Revisited

J: Last week was the fortieth anniversary of the march on Washington in which Martin Luther King, Jr. gave his famous "I have a dream" speech. I heard the whole speech for the first time and was very moved by it. It reflected your teachings so clearly that we are all one. Was Martin Luther King a spiritual messenger with a special mission?

G: Martin Luther King is a soul who is at a certain level of development. When souls incarnate at a certain level of development, their place of service is donated to world service in some way. Therefore, they become a messenger because they have reached a state of development energetically and in consciousness as a soul where they are able to reach out and contact soul groups and bring them together at some level.

Souls come in particularly at times of preparation. The time Martin Luther King came in began the preparation for this age. From about the 1960s onward was an accelerated time that was preparing for this millennium, preparing for the raising of consciousness. And so there were souls coming in at that time for that purpose. Those souls served a specific purpose to mark a time and to create an impression. Gandhi is another example. He came in at a certain epoch to make an impression, and that impression has stayed. The same with Martin Luther King.

At that level of soul development, they have access to the universal truth that souls at a lower level of development don't have conscious access to. It's not that they don't have it available to them, it's that they haven't reached a state of development in their conscious being where they can contact it readily. And so he had that, as do others. In a sense, they become channels connected to their higher selves, to their soul essence. The higher the level of soul development at which you incarnate at in a lifetime determines the vibration that comes into the body and how easily the body and personality are able to access the essence vibration, so there is no blockage between the two.

Now, that doesn't mean they don't have problems in their personal lives, that they don't have challenges like any other soul. They're working on their own passage, their own individual growth, but at the same time they have a higher purpose that has to do with the planet or has to do with large groups of people. For him, his purpose was to bring attention to the black situation and to the separatist situation and to continue the healing of that segregation. The beginning of the last century was the beginning of the healing of separation on the planet, particularly the beginning of healing of separation in this new world, the North American continent. This particular continent is acting as an archetype to bring together all peoples. That is why you have such an influx of all different ethnic groups into the country called the United States of America. Its original purpose is to create a unified field. It is, as they call it, the New Jerusalem.

J: Yes. You said that when we discussed that the letters USA were the central letters of the word Jerusalem.

G: Exactly. It's the New Jerusalem. So it is the place that brings the children of Israel out of bondage so to speak.

J: In this past century were there other leaders helping to bring about this higher consciousness?

G: John F. Kennedy is one, and he was thwarted in his process.

J: Was his brother Robert also?

G: A part of the legacy, but not so much, not the same level of soul development or evolution. Now these souls sacrificed themselves, very much a part of the Christ legacy. They are examples of how mankind still believes that the only way they can surrender through spirit is through pain, suffering and separation. You now are at the time of the cross, the time of the crucifixion, the time when the soul awakens, and matter surrenders to spirit through the soul, and spirit surrenders to matter through the soul. That's what this era is about. So it is the time of the crucifixion.

Now the crucifixion can be experienced in two ways. It can be experienced through duality, through pain and suffering, which is how it was illustrated to you, how you were doing it in the last millennia. That was the struggle of the two sides of duality, the celebration of duality. Therefore, the crucifixion illustrated to you during that age was surrendering to spirit and surrendering to matter through pain and suffering.

But it doesn't have to be done that way. It can be done with ease. It can be done with the forward movement of the flow of life and the embracing of life rather that the struggle, the resistance to it. So it doesn't have to be an experience of suffering. It can simply be an experience of ease and surrender. Mankind always views surrender as a struggle because people feel they're giving something up rather than giving in to include something.

So man fights for his separation, fights and struggles for his duality, for his limitations. He fights to remain ignorant, to remain separate. The very thing he doesn't want he fights for. The very thing he most abhors is separation. The thing that causes him the most pain and suffering, he continues to fight for. And the reason he does that is because he has not developed to a point where he realizes what true individuality is. Until the soul awakens, he will not know that and will continue to struggle for individuality through separation. Separation is not individuality.

In becoming a homogenous society, it is a fight for separation because it alienates you from yourself by trying to fit in with others. Fitting in with others is not communion, is not unity, is not oneness and wholeness with yourself. Individuality is. Standing alone within yourself and having ownership of this whole self then enables you to be able to reveal it, to share that whole self with others. So it's an ironic paradox that in order to be unified, you need to be alone with yourself. But being alone with yourself is not being separate. When you are not alone with yourself, you are separate because then you are focused out there through the desire body to fit in, and you are alienating yourself from yourself.

J: So we can't all come together until each one of us deals with our personal psychological issues?

G: Exactly.

J: That's a big job.

G: Yes, it is. It's a huge job. But you need to understand that you are moving into the time of resonant causation. You're moving out of cause and effect. As the sixth ray diminishes its influence, as it moves out and the seventh ray comes in, you move more into quantum physics. You move more into the process of creating a group consciousness, which then produces a ripple effect of quantum physics. Therefore, when a certain mass of people reaches a certain vibration or level of consciousness, it begins to create an immediate shift in consciousness. Do you see? This is why over the past fifty years, for instance, you have progressed more than you've progressed in the last five thousand years. In the last ten years you have doubled that progression. That's an example of quantum shift.

J: So I guess our consciousness has shifted a great deal.

G: Yes, consciousness has shifted very much. If it hadn't, you would not see the struggle before you that you see. It's the remaining time of the children of Israel wandering in the desert, so to speak, symbolically. And, of course, this is why you continue to have the struggles in the Middle East because the place called Israel is representative of the lower will of man. And the place called Palestine is representative of the lower emotional body of man, and there's that constant struggle between the two, between the mind and the emotions in the lower self.

J: The whole world is fixated on it. And I guess there is a lot of despair right now because none of us sees any way out. The conflict just goes on and on and on.

G: Well, you see, mankind must eventually realize that struggle doesn't work, that struggle, itself, is futile. It is embracing, it is acceptance that creates ease. Struggle creates destruction.

J: How could these people resolve this eternal conflict?

G: By giving up their fight of separation. What is it derived from? Separation of religious beliefs, separation of economic functioning, separation of political hierarchies. It all involves the fight of separation. Ultimately, it involves the fight of feelings. Both sides are fighting the feeling of not being good enough. Just as the Jews fought the feeling of not being good enough with the Germans back in the Second World War, and the Germans fought it with the Jews. Hitler was fighting the feeling of not being good enough with the Germans by wanting to build a superior race, to avoid feeling not good enough. The Jews have been fighting not good enough for thousands of years. They did it with the Egyptians. Then they did it with the Germans. And they've been doing it with others in between. So as long as you continue to fight a feeling on a mass scale, you will find another group that will be willing to fight it with you to mirror your commitment. That's all that's taking place.

All that is ever taking place in manifestation is either acceptance of a feeling or fighting a feeling because human beings experience through feelings. Manifestation of reality is created through feeling. It is the feeling body, the emotional body, the negative charge, that draws the manifestation into the physical. It's the thoughts that send it out into the astral that begins to design the mental grid. And the emotion holds it into the physical as physical form. Therefore, if you are fighting feelings, you will always create what you are seeking to fight or to avoid, so you can continue the commitment to fight it.

J: So what should …

G: Accept their feelings of not good enough. That's all. Very simple. If the whole group on both sides would stop and take responsibility for their own feelings and say, I've been fighting the feeling of not being good enough. Let me embrace that feeling. Let me embrace that wound within myself as an individual, myself as a country, and take responsibility to respond to those feelings. Everything would change. Everything would shift. Hard to believe isn't it? Hard to believe that all the problems in the world exist because of wounded children inside the subconscious fighting a few feelings and making all of their choices based upon that. That is the origin of all of your duality, separation and suffering and pain—simply fighting a feeling or several feelings.

Look at the United States doing the same thing. Fighting the feelings of imperfect. Fighting the feelings of not enough. Fighting the feelings of deprived. That's why they're out there fighting to gain control over the rest of the world. Never get enough. Fighting deprivation, fighting unsafe and fear of annihilation, fighting the war on terrorism. Interesting, isn't it?

J: I guess so. But it makes it all understandable at the same time. You have said that everything is energy and consciousness.

G: That is correct.

J: I don't know how to define consciousness. What is consciousness? Is it directed energy?

G: Sometimes. Consciousness in its pure sense is formless. Consciousness, where the mind of God is concerned, is undifferentiated. It's all inclusive. It's infinite. It's all awareness simultaneously, undifferentiated, undivided, unseparated. Consciousness becomes differentiated when it becomes an expression of individuality. Then it becomes differentiated as a soul. A soul inhabits a portion of consciousness and brings that portion of consciousness into living form of some kind. And that livingness of form becomes an incarnational experience that is a fragment of consciousness.

For instance, you in this physical body are a tiny fragment of consciousness, but you contain within that fragment the wholeness of consciousness. However, you've chosen to take that wholeness and confine it to a fragment for the purpose of experience. So you confine it to a body, to a time, to an experience, to a certain relationship of expression, to a certain set of challenges, ideas, and concepts to enable you to induce an experience called growth, development, and evolution.

J: Although we're really just remembering.

G: You're remembering through one fragment of your being when, in truth, you are the wholeness of being. You are God. The container you've chosen has chosen one fragmentary aspect of God to experience, one speck in the cosmos, one cell in the universe.

J: And the value is the experience itself.

G: Yes.

J: It's allowing God to experience itself in its infinite complexity.

G: That's correct. That's why it is so important to embrace all aspects of that expression, all differentiated expressions of God, rather than fighting them through separation. God fighting him/herself in separation.

J: I have to embrace everyone? It's harder than I thought.

G: Embrace all of it.

J: Yes. That was helpful, very enlightening.

G: Oh, good.

J: In one of our discussions, you said there are planets in our solar system that we have not detected, and therefore, they do not influence us astrologically. With our telescopes today, we can see things that are millions of light years away. Why can't we detect everything in our solar system that is relatively close? Why wouldn't we have detected these planets?

G: You can see fragmentary masses that are hundreds of millions of light years away. You're not yet able to bring to close proximity certain planetary formations, bringing them close enough to realize their reality, so to speak. You're able to detect in some ways their energies. For instance, several years ago, scientists began to detect the energies of two new planets, the planets that would influence Virgo and Libra because both Virgo and Libra share other planets. So since those planets have been detected, you will now find their influence being felt in your solar system.

This has also shifted the degrees of the zodiac or astrological influence as those planets are coming in. It also brings into awareness the magnitude of influence of both those signs on your planet. So both those signs will be leading influences in this new age. Is it widely known? No. Is it known in scientific circles? Yes. Has it been announced to the public? Yes, it was announced to the public some years ago on television. Was it announced on television in this country? No. The channel and his friend remember seeing it on television in Brazil, for instance. They then came back to this country a few weeks later and realized that nobody had a clue about it. Nobody had been told.

J: Do astrologers know about it?

G: Some do.

J: I would think you wouldn't be able to practice astrology accurately if you didn't know about the new planetary influences.

G: That's right. Those who do not know are still using the old point of reference. But you see, because they don't know, it won't make any difference to them because they remain confined in the reality they have known. It's like the natives in South America that saw the Spaniards coming to shore and thought they were floating or walking on the water. They couldn't see the ships. They had no concept of the ship. Same sort of thing. If you have no frame of reference, then you have no influence. You are what you are conscious of.

J: So you're saying that we're only influenced by planets we're conscious of.

G: That is correct.

J: Were we influenced by planets in ancient times before we had discovered many of them?

G: There has been consciousness of planets in ancient times for thousands upon thousands of years because you have had civilizations that have been very advanced. You have lost awareness of those advanced civilizations and are now only beginning, in some circles, to recover some knowledge of those civilizations, civilizations such as the Atlanteans and the Lemurians that go back thousands upon thousands of years. You are only now beginning to realize and become conscious of those advanced civilizations.

You have held in your mind-set that these were primitive civilizations. They were not. If you look at the configurations they left behind, their pyramids, their buildings, you will find they were highly advanced geometrical formations related directly to the formations of the heavens above them. They took advantage of the influence of the heavens and reflected those influences on the configurations they built on the earth as energetic antennas. One of the most powerful energetic antennas you have today is the Great Pyramid of Giza. It is directly aligned with the Orion and the Sirian systems. It's very significant that it's aligned with the Sirian as Sirius is the doorway into this solar system of all of the star systems that make up this planet.

J: In one of our earlier talks, you seemed to be saying that the convergence of energetic forces we've talked about were being employed by the ascendant masters for the first time because of failed attempts in the past to awaken the soul in earlier civilizations such as Lemuria and Atlantis, etc. When I asked you about this last time I didn't get a clear confirmation that that was so, and I'm confused. I thought this time the ascendant masters had learned from the past and were putting together this new combination of energetic forces to assist the awakening of the soul in this new era.

G: That is true. You see, it was not that they were failed attempts. There really is no failure. There is only awakening or advancement in consciousness. Human beings have been given freedom of choice in their physical awareness. Therefore, it is up to them how far they want to go in any given time in their time/space illusion. And it is up to them how they choose to do it. It will be done. It is evolution evolving in such a way that it realizes all of itself. It is simply God evolving in realization in form of all parts of him/herself, although God has no gender because God has no differentiation.

Therefore, in Lemurian and Atlantean times, as well as even previously and times after that, man has evolved in cycles to certain states, and he has continued to make the same choices. He has grown in his choices to some degree, but he basically has continued to make the same ones, and, therefore in that sense, has impeded the speed of his progress or his evolution. He has repeated patterns of karmic development through cause and effect because of lack of consciousness. Clear choice can only be made based upon conscious awareness. But in the process he has been refining and developing his levels of consciousness in the physical body and refining and developing his chakra system, raising its vibration gradually over time.

Man now enters an evolutionary cycle that has been planned by the ascendant mastery since the beginning of earth time as you know it. Where man is at as he enters this cycle is entirely dependent upon how he has progressed in his own choices. If man as he enters this cycle has shifted all duality in the last age into this cycle, it then becomes a challenge with which he must deal because he has not dealt with the challenge in the previous cycle and integrated it. Therefore, he brings the remains of karma, the remains of cause and effect, into this cycle. And as this new cycle brings its influence, the old way of evolving begins to clash with the new cycle.

You begin to become much more aware of how the old way of evolving no longer serves the new cycle. It comes into conflict with the new cycle, and choices are made based upon that conflict. Therefore, you come to this new cycle having evolved through the consequences of duality you created in the last cycle, and you have the opportunity to realize oneness through the comparison between duality and unity.

J: You said the energetic forces the ascendant masters are bringing together are being employed to help make this a successful awakening.

G: Yes, but remember you still have freedom of choice. You still have the freedom to choose how you want to do that, how you want to embrace the evolutionary blueprint. Do you want to embrace it through holding onto your duality through separation? Do you want to then embrace the cross, the crucifixion, through suffering? Or do you want to embrace the crucifixion through acceptance and surrender to more presence of being, the soul? Do you want it to be a dark night of the soul of experience, a struggle between the lower and the higher self, or do you want it to be an integration, an embracing, a transmutation of the lower self to the higher self? It's entirely up to you because it's through freedom of choice that you get to experience evolvement.

J: As this is the age of unity of mankind, I guess I'm a little confused as to why the ideas of a world government, of globalization, one monetary system, and so on, would be counter to unity when they would seem to embody unity.

G: Because of the motivation, because of the intention behind it. The intention by the few is to control the many. You see, it's not about what you're doing. It's about how you're doing it. If it comes from a soul intention, then you do it for the good of the whole. You do it to support all and the growth and well-being of all. If you're doing it through duality, then you do it to control the whole and keep them in separation, keep them in domination. Do you see? So it's not what is happening. It's always about how it's taking place. What is the intention? What is the motive behind it that gives it the reality? Do you see?

J: So, if it came from the soul, we could still have a world government, but it would come from different motivations. It would be for the good of the whole rather than control by the few.

G: Exactly. It would be for taking care of humanity, for the equality of humanity, for exercising and supporting the individual expression of humanity, not to impair that expression, not to keep you in more separation. Because how is it being done? It's being done through fear, gaining control through fear. Create that war on terrorism. Keep them fearful. Keep them separated within themselves so we can control and dominate them. A few seeking through their greed to control and dominate the many, rather than creating for the many an experience of equality and provision, support, compassion, love, and prosperity, which is quite possible by simply changing the motivation, changing why I'm doing it, how I'm doing it.

J: And I'm supposed to embrace them. That is a real challenge.

G: You cannot change what you cannot accept. If you oppose them, you give them power.

J: I know. You've said we're supposed to create an alternative model.

G: That's correct.

J: And we talked about the fact that we, in essence, already have an alternative model. It's called democracy.

G: Yes, you have it in theory. Now it must be put into form.

J: I guess we, the people, are the only ones who can do that.

G: You have had the model since the beginning of time. You have had the model of democracy as taught by all the major spiritual teachers who have inhabited your planet at one time or another. They all sent the same message: love one another. That is the first form of democracy.

J: Has it ever existed here on earth?

G: Has it ever existed as a whole? No, not thus far. There have been different forms of democracy down through time. The Greeks formulated it into a model. The original intention of the planet Earth is for the success of a democracy, a communion of twelve star systems together as one. A system of democracy is simply a system where the equality of individuality is embraced, where equal importance of all expression is held sacred, where all beings live for the good and the wholeness of one another. What a concept!

J: How much trouble we've have putting it into practice.

G: Yes, because you have so much trouble putting it into practice for yourself. Love begins at home. Love one another as you love yourself. You can only love another as you are able to love yourself. Love is reflected in love.

J: It's hard to keep holding onto that. Yet, it makes so much sense.

G: It's because you're so addicted to separation and because your concept of love somehow has to do with codependency, of sameness. If we join this religion and we all believe the same thing, then we are all the same and we can love one another. If we are all whites living in a certain level of economic development in the cul-de-sac in the suburbs, then we can all embrace and love one another because we are the same. Love has nothing to do with sameness. It has to do with the uniqueness of the expression of being. The love force is the force of the soul, the force of the expression of the truth of being of who you are. And until you can accept and express the truth of all that you are, how are you going to be able to share it with another? How are you ever going to be able to embrace their uniqueness and individual expression that is not the same as your own?

J: Of course, we have to create a place where people are free to express the truth of who they are.

G: Exactly. That is what democracy is about.

Chapter 13:

April 25, 2004: A New Creation Story/ Gnostic Gospels/Jesus and the Early Church/Sacraments and Rituals

J: As I have reviewed the material we've covered, it seems to me that you're retelling the creation story and radically changing our understanding of God and man. Is that what you're doing?

G: Yes, we're reinventing creation.

J: Now that we have almost completed this project, how would you explain your core message?

G: Humanity has never been at one with creation. Humanity has remained separate from creation since its beginnings, since its tribal origins. Its tribal origins and the belief systems and the behaviors those instilled and the primitive animal survival nature of the organism have kept you maintaining that system of separation since the beginning of time as you know it.

On the other hand, we are suggesting that you have reached a state of development where that is no longer necessary as a process of learning. You no longer need to be the child instructed by the dominant father who rewards or punishes you in school if you get the lesson or you don't. You are ready for graduation. You are ready to be the creators. You are ready to be the administrators. You are ready to exercise the power of the God within. But first you must realize that that is so. And the only way you can realize that is by coming to peace with the inner workings of your own being and being able to know that reality is so, within your own heart and with the experience of that heartfelt knowing.

J: That is what this new age is about, isn't it?

G: That is correct. It is the preparation for the coming of God, the awakening in consciousness, in awareness and experience through the revelation of the experiential aspect and individual expression of God called the soul. The soul is the causal aspect of God, God that's all that is. It is the substance and it is the form. It is the expression and it is the experience.

J: As this is about the awakening of the soul, I wanted to ask you about the idea of soul signatures. You've said our first names are the resonance of our soul signatures.

G: Correct. It is the resonance of your particular soul fragment for this lifetime that embodies and involves the particular pattern of learning with which you will come in.

J: So the correct first name somehow gets attached to us?

G: You chose that name before you were born in the physical, dear one.

J: And our mothers and fathers are able to …

G: They are given the name on a soul level. They think they come up with it. They look in a book and say, that name seems to be a good name or whatever.

J: I have always resonated with the name Joel. And I was pleased when I discovered there was a Book of Joel in the Old Testament and that the Prophet Joel prophesized the coming of the Holy Spirit. What can you tell me about my connection with the name Joel?

G: Well, what are you doing?

J: I'm dealing with the issue of the coming of the Holy Spirit [Laughing].

G: There is your answer. If you look back on your life, there has always been a struggle with discernment about what is the truth. And your challenge is to discover what is the truth within you. What is the truth of my needs? What are my authentic feelings? All of that sort of thing. The challenges are set up in such a way as to challenge you as to what you need to look at and what you need to deal with to fulfill that quest to find the truth and to guide the movement towards the discovery of the Holy Spirit, so to speak.

J: You said my life is about seeking truth. As that search appears to be challenging accepted belief systems, would you define the difference between beliefs and truth?

G: Beliefs are frozen ideas and perceptions that are retained because of a collective agreement. The more people who you can get to authenticate that agreement or agree with it, the more solid and entrenched your belief becomes. A belief keeps reality frozen in time. It doesn't allow it to move or to have life, so it immobilizes life and freezes it in time and space as an absolute. On the other hand, truth is living. It is the living flesh of God. It is the living unfoldment of the truth of being. It is ever becoming, ever knowing, ever discovering and ever experiencing more of itself all the time. Therefore, it is not absolute.

There are certain principles of truth that exist within the universe. Those principles of truth are based upon the foundation of the essence of creation or life. Some of those principles of truth are that life is. That means it is. Life is absolute. It is without question. It is, ever was, and will be. That is a given. So that is a foundation of absolute of truth, if you will. But in that is the living truth because that life, that livingness, is, and it is always and ever becoming more of itself, unfolding more of itself. It is ever in movement.

A belief is not. A belief is finite. A belief stands still, immobilized in time and space, frozen and finite and confined in a framework. Anything that opposes it exists outside of its framework. Truth is all inclusive, all embracing, always allowing—it is able to encompass all that is. However, belief is not able to encompass anything except its finite thought form that sustains and maintains the dogma that is an absolute, finite perspective of what it calls reality. With belief systems you must always persuade others of what you call your truth to get them to agree with you. Where truth is concerned, truth has its stability within its own livingness and, therefore, allows for and can encompass and include the livingness of all that is because it is not finite.

J: Several times in the course of our discussions you said the mysteries of mastery would be revealed at the appropriate time, and that we are coming into the time when that was beginning to happen. Recently I have been reading some biblical history including some books about the Gnostic Gospels, which were ancient texts discovered in Egypt in 1945. Apparently, in the first two or three centuries following Jesus's death, a great struggle took place between those who were called Gnostics and those considered orthodox. One of the outcomes was that all of the Gnostic writings were excluded from the New Testament. Not only were they excluded, the Gnostics were also condemned as heretics and their writings destroyed. Apparently, a group of monks in Egypt hid the Gnostic manuscripts to protect them from destruction. Are these some of the mysteries to which you were referring?

G: Yes, they are some of the mysteries we were referring to. And there are others as well. Ancient writings and the symbolism of some of the ancient sacred sites are being translated. They represent the revelations of the mysteries as are the revelations of the true meaning of the hieroglyphics of the tombs and temples of Egypt and the revelation of the Mayan calendar. The mystery we revealed to you this afternoon that you finally to a small degree got on an experiential level, the mystery that is right in your hand at every moment, the mystery of life that is yours to unfold each and every moment, the mystery of life that has been given you freely.

J: You're referring to what you said about breath and breathing?

G: Yes, to be able to sustain and maintain creation. The power of creation is in your hands. It is in your breath. How many people realize that? Almost none. It's the greatest mystery. Those of the East for centuries have realized the importance of this in their yoga practices, the practices of breathing and the alignment of the body's energies through them. All yoga practices are based upon correct breathing.

J: As I studied the historic roots of the Bible, I wrote some questions I wanted to ask you that deal with issues relating to Jesus and the early church. They aren't in any particular order, but I think they are important.

G: Well, we don't mind disorder. We observe it in you all the time.

J: God knows that's true. The first question is, Jesus rising from the dead is evidence to the faithful of his divinity. Did he appear to his followers after he died, and did he appear, as they claimed, in the flesh so that they could touch him, see his wounds and watch him eat?

G: Did he appear in the flesh? Well, yes, he appeared in the flesh, if you will, created as a thought form. In other words, he resurrected his physical body through the strength of his thought form, as we spoke of earlier, through mind over matter. Just as we on occasion have appeared to you as a thought form. We have taken a physical form for you by gathering together bioplasmic matter in the form of a light body and appeared to you as such, so that you would believe. Because you must see everything in your own image and likeness, or think you must, in order to believe it is real. Do you see? So, yes Jesus, the Christ was able to raise up the configuration of the physical apparatus in a vision of reality in order to help his followers see the truth in the illusion of death.

J: That we don't die.

G: Yes.

J: They said they could touch his flesh and see him eat. So we're not talking about a ghostly apparition. We're talking about a dense body.

G: You can make it as dense as you want to, dear one. Bioplasmic matter is just a less dense form of physical matter. That is all. It is held in place by the intensity of the thought form that holds it there. Because, remember, the physical world is a projection held in place by your wishful thinking, by your attachments to your thoughts and feelings collectively. Thus it creates the desired result. But the physical world is no more solid than anything else.

J: So Jesus could have eaten with them.

G: Of course. It's simply the creation of a holographic image he projected for them on the screen of their minds that they then are able to see.

J: The whole hierarchy of the Catholic Church is based on the idea that Jesus told Peter that Peter was to be the shepherd of the flock, the rock upon which his church was built. Did Jesus give Peter that charge?

G: First of all, Peter is symbolic. The symbolism of Peter is the consciousness of humanity. So the symbolism of Peter represents the foundation of a level of consciousness upon which the church will be built. Do you understand? Each of the apostles and each of their names is related to different power mind centers of the body. And those different power mind centers represent different archetypes of creation where the God self or the God being is concerned.

Peter is related to the building of the foundation of spirit in a physicalized reality or form. It is related to manifestation. Therefore, that is its representation or its archetype. It is not so much a personification of a man as it is the personification of an idea that produces the manifestation of the form or the church. What is the church to which the Christ refers? It is the (human) body that is the vehicle for the soul of humanity. It is the body that allows the soul of humanity to awaken and flourish. And so the body becomes the church or the tabernacle of the soul that is awakened and flourishes.

J: Individually and collectively?

G: Yes.

J: So the apostles represent a level of consciousness?

G: They are a level of consciousness. Each is a power mind center of consciousness that maintains and sustains one of the archetypes of the twelve star systems. The twelve archetypes of the twelve star systems are representative of the archetypal experience of the twelve main archetypes of the God experience embodied through the soul in physical reality. And we will at some point be revealing those archetypes specifically.

J: The Gnostic Gospels bear the names of some of the apostles such as Philip and also include the Gospel of Mary Magdalene. What can you tell us about the gospel of Mary Magdalene? Is it true?

G: Is it true? It is as true as your need to believe it. Understand that the Bible, as you call it, is a symbolic representation. Within it is an encodement of the revelation of your history and your time. For instance, the Book of Revelations is a prophecy for and a blueprint for this time, this age, the Age of Aquarius. It gives the steps and stages of the opening and the development of the physical instrument (the body), the tabernacle of the church, of the soul. And it instructs in the revelation of that soul and the awakening of the Christ Consciousness within it. It speaks of Armageddon. It speaks of the end of time as you know it, that is, the end of time from the point of view of cause and effect, from the point of view of duality. A whole new epoch begins based upon resonant causation, the force of the soul, the radiatory force of resonance.

So, is it true? Yes—and no. It is symbolic and it is an encodement. You tend to read things literally as events and say this happened and that happened and she did this and he did that and this occurred and that happened. In reality, what is on the surface is not necessarily what is being said. Just as we have related to you in the past, the symbolism of the Last Supper, for example. Did Christ have a last supper with his twelve apostles? Yes, he did. Is that what is important? No, it is not. What is important is that it is an encodement, it is a symbol, it is a signal, it is a prophecy.

It is a prophecy for your time. As he said, go into the city and find the man with the water pitcher and follow him to the upper rooms and there make ready to feast of bread and wine. The gathering together of the twelve apostles was the gathering together of the twelve archetypes of the twelve star systems, and when that would happen was when they went into the city. Among the masses into the city is moving into the mass of consciousness (of mankind). And as you move into the mass of consciousness and find the water bearer in the Age of Aquarius and follow the water bearer to the upper room. The time of the Age of Aquarius will be the time of the resurrection into the upper rooms, the time when the awakening of the twelve archetypes of God through the twelve star systems will come together and be revealed through the physical matter. So it is all symbolic. Do you see?

J: Yes, I see it more clearly than ever.

G: It is all a series of symbols. The story of the Christ is a set of symbols. You can take the symbols of the Christ story and you can put them in the sky. And you can see all of the symbols of the evolution of the Christ story in the various stars in the sky that reveal themselves at various times and create various awakenings and various archetypes of experience. It's all mirrored in the heavens. As above, so below. As below, so above. For instance, the star system that mirrors the Virgin Mary is a series of stars in the sky that comes into alignment at certain times in relationship to the birth, in relationship to the rising of the sun.

J: I've never heard of that before.

G: Yes. It's all mirrored in the heavens. For instance, if you look at Egyptian cosmology, you will find that the Great Pyramid is perfectly aligned with certain star systems, and at different times those alignments are in exact alignment with various parts of the Great Pyramid.

J: Who built the Great Pyramid?

G: The Atlantean priests taught the Egyptians the powers the Atlanteans had held. After the destruction of Atlantis, many of the Atlanteans fled from Atlantis and others returned to their original planet. Some migrated across the planet and arrived in Egypt. They began to infiltrate the Egyptian culture, and they put together the ancient mystery schools of Egypt, the Left and Right eye of Horus. They trained the Egyptian priests in the initiations, and in that process was built the sacred chamber of initiation, which was the Great Pyramid of Giza. And they taught the powers of levitation, the powers of mind over matter.

J: You said the Bible was encoded. In reading about the early development of the New Testament, I learned a surprisingly few men decided which writings would be included in the New Testament and which material, including the Gnostic Gospels, would be excluded. Was the encoding of the Bible undermined by people who excluded so much material?

G: Yes, which then sets the direction in a certain way. You see, religion has used the teachings of the Bible in a literal manner. The surface stories of the Bible are used to keep the people in control and fear, whereas, the secrets of the Bible are not revealed. Many of the references in the Bible have been removed that were pretty literal in the stories of the Bible. For instance, the references to reincarnation, the references to the original cross, and the references to the practices of the Gnostics who worshipped the divine mother as well as the divine father. All of that was distorted or excluded from the Bible according to the agenda of those in power at the time.

J: Historians have observed that the earliest years of the Christian movement showed a great openness towards women that stopped about the year 200.

G: Yes, and it became a male dominated society. Much of that was cemented in place by Constantine when he chose Christianity as the official religion of Rome. He saw it as an opportunity to have ultimate rule by using what was popular among the people and by embracing it, or seemingly embracing it, and using it to manipulate their minds and behavior.

J: The historical material I read said the church fathers dominant at the time gained the force of law with Constantine; therefore, religion became law.

G: Yes, exactly. You cross my palm, I'll cross yours. You rub my back, I'll rub yours. Do you see?

J: I read that in public, Jesus spoke in parables, but to his disciples he supposedly taught the "secrets" of the kingdom of heaven. Supposedly, he kept the secret teachings private for those who had proven themselves spiritually mature. Paul also claimed to know secret teachings. Did Jesus, in fact, teach secret wisdom to his disciples? If so, what was the nature of these secret teachings?

G: Well, all of the secrets are there in the parables. But people don't understand the parables. They don't understand what is being said. They don't understand the symbols. But all of it is there to see if they choose to see. So that was the way he encoded things, if you will. Because there are those who are not yet ready to use the power of creation. Before you are given that power, you must be at a point of development where you are willing and able to honor the power of creation and hold that in integrity. What man has exercised all of this time on the earth has nothing to do with power. It has to do with control.

Control is the furthest thing from power you will ever find because it is based in fear. Power is based in love. Therefore, love is a requirement of the wielding of power. Until you can love, you will not understand power. As long as you are in fear, you will exercise control.

And to control, you will seek to destroy and eliminate. Through love, you will seek to include, and you will seek to support life.

J: There is some disagreement over who was the first person to see the resurrected Jesus. Some say it was Mary Magdalene; others say it was Peter or James. Some speculate it was Mary Magdalene, but that the story was changed to play down Mary Magdalene's importance.

G: What do you think is the importance of Mary Magdalene?

J: Well, Mary Magdalene, outside of Jesus's mother Mary, is the only major feminine figure among the constellation of people around Jesus.

G: And what do you think she represents?

J: The feminine energies.

G: Yes. You see, the story of Christ itself is the story that harks back to the ancient mystery schools. It reveals the stages and steps of self-mastery and what is required for that self-mastery. That is all. If you look at any cosmology, the Mayans, the Egyptians, you will find exactly the same story. You will find it in exactly the same detail, some with different circumstances, but the same story.

J: You have explained that before. Great significance was attached to who was the first to see the resurrected Christ. Who was the first to see the resurrected Christ? Was it Mary Magdalene or one of the apostles?

G: What does it matter?

J: It seems to be significant to those who have written about it.

G: Well, why do you think that is?

J: They may have an agenda.

G: Yes. What do you think that agenda is?

J: Perhaps to minimize the influence and importance of the feminine and maximize that of the patriarchy.

G: It is again a struggle between the two sides. It is the separation once again, the polarity between the masculine and feminine, the negative and positive, the giving and receiving. Do you see? Because what are the feminine and masculine ultimately about? The feminine is about the inward focus. The feminine is the harbor of the soul, the womb of the soul, the womb of the resurrection. This argument is the denial of the divine mother being the access point of the soul. Until the feminine is celebrated in equal value, until receptivity is of equal value with assertion, until receiving is of equal value with giving, there will not be the possibility of the resurrection of the soul because it requires both in equal value.

In this year [2004], you are moving into that place of receptivity. You are moving into the feminine. And look at what a struggle it is for people to surrender to the womb of the soul, to surrender to the place of unknowing, to surrender to the place where they are out of control, to surrender the domination of the masculine. The masculine is the assertive. It is the energy that focuses the manifestation outward.

For instance, why do you think the male figure has a penis, the outward genitalia? Why the female has inward genitalia, the receptive genitalia? Do you see? And the balance of the two, the two coming together and merging as one in balance with one another, in harmony with one another, produces the communion that is necessary to create the revelation of the soul, the birth of a new child, a Christ child, the birth of a divine child. The child then goes through the seven stages of development that Christ went through and illustrated to come into his divine being— which never happens because it's all disturbed.

J: As you were speaking, I couldn't help thinking about our current foreign policy, which seems to reflect the patriarchy. The only thing our political leaders today seem prepared to do is project power and strength outward. They have given no sign that there is the slightest desire to show compassion, understanding, receptivity, compromise, any of those "feminine" qualities. Meanwhile, the feminine energies that supposedly have been coming into this sphere with the Harmonic Concordance among other things ...

G: Have been creating an upset, an imbalance, an increasing threat to the male energies, to the male identity, to the outward appearance of things. It's creating a greater dissatisfaction in the desire body. It seeks to control the outer.

J: They seem to be trying to control everything they can. They're trying to control the media, trying to limit the photographs of the dead coming home. They're constantly trying to put a nice face on an ugly situation.

G: They're controlling everything that is to be received.

J: And at the same time it all seems to be spinning out of control.

G: That's what happens when resonance begins to shift. You know within yourself when the illusion has been revealed, there are no more ways of denying it. No matter how much you try, it keeps revealing itself again. It keeps revealing the falsity of itself, and it becomes less and less and less able to deny and less and less satisfying.

J: It is a resonance shift, isn't it?

G: Yes, it is. Since 1987, you have been on a quantum movement where the shifting of your planet is concerned, since the beginning of the Harmonic Convergence. You are now in a seven-year cycle that is the revelation and healing of duality for the revelation of the soul.

J: And it is creating a quantum shift.

G: Yes.

J: Is this something that is likely to gain momentum?

G: Of course. That is the idea of quantum shift—it creates a ripple effect. The more it embraces, the more it can eventually create a dominant field. Then, instantaneously, the consciousness can shift. It's the hundredth monkey theory. By the time the hundredth monkey goes down to the water and washes the food, instantaneously all monkeys all over monkeydom create that shift in behavior. All go down and wash their food simultaneously.

J: When we first started talking a year ago, I expressed alarm about the breaking down of economic systems. It sounded scary.

G: Of course. But you're in the governing of the seventh ray of consciousness. The seventh ray of consciousness is the ray that breaks down all old forms that are not based upon equality, equanimity, and balance where the highest spiritual good is concerned. Therefore, it breaks down all that is in duality. You must first let go and make space before you can build a new house.

J: With the extremes of duality that are being revealed during this time, it's very easy for me to focus on the current administration. But it hasn't escaped me that John Kerry is a member of the Skull and Bones and a product of a lot of the same kinds of associations the Bush family has had. So I'm not sure that the Democrats are offering anything but more extremes of duality. I would like to think that with a change of administrations, there would be more justice, equality, evenhandedness, and democracy, so to speak.

G: There will be when you no longer give your power away to a representative to decide your reality.

J: Well, it's hard to function independently of government.

G: That is because you set it up that way. We believe the government was originally put in place of the people and for the people. It is no longer supporting that original intention. Therefore, the people must take control of the government by first of all showing an interest. So what are you doing to pique that interest? What is the person next door doing to pique that interest? What happens if one hundred people pique the interest of ten people each? How many people is that? And if those then, pique the interest of ten more, how many is that?

J: It increases exponentially.

G: That's correct. That's quantum physics. And it all lies in the hands of the power of one. Of the people, for the people. That is democracy. That is not what you have. What you have is what you have allowed through disinterest.

J: Ultimately it's the responsibility of each one of us. I'd like to resume my questions about the early church. I found it interesting how the Catholic Church came to claim papal authority. Pope Clement I, one of the early church leaders, wrote, "God relegates his authority of reign to rulers and leaders on earth who are bishops, priests, and deacons." Then he declared that anyone who "disobeys divinely ordained authority" receives the death penalty. St. Ignatius of Antioch claimed that "bishops, priests, and deacons mirrored the divine hierarchy in heaven." And he warned the laity to "revere, honor, and obey the bishop as if he were God." He claimed God became accessible to humanity through the church, and that heresy included insubordination to clerical authority. The authority of the church grew out of statements like that by the early church fathers. What is your view of these statements?

G: How pompous of them. It is a declaration of absolutism where God is concerned. It has nothing to do with God. It has nothing to do with a relationship with God. You see, religion has very little to do with God. It has mainly to do with man and his struggle with the concept of God and his access to it and his rules about that access are self-created and have nothing to do with the divine.

J: The Catholic Church claims its authority succeeds from the apostles.

G: What authority do the apostles have with regard to your relationship with God? Who was the one who taught the apostles?

J: Jesus.

G: Yes. And what did Jesus say again and again? "Worship not me, but your Father who is in heaven." Where is heaven?

J: Inside of us.

G: Yes, the truth of the connection to your being.

J: You mean by our connection that we are part of God?

G: It's the direct connection.

J: To God.

G: To the Big Guy, the divine mind, the divine plan and your place in it as an individual with your talents and free within him/herself.

J: You have said many times that everything is energy and consciousness. I asked you what is consciousness. I still don't understand it well enough to define it.

G: Consciousness is the awareness of reality in living form.

J: So everything that has ever happened can be explained within the context of energy and consciousness.

G: Yes, everything is energy and consciousness, because everything is life in awareness of itself.

J: So when people try to understand creation, and God and man's relationship to them, they have to understand it within the construct of energy and consciousness.

G: Yes, because that is what it is. You can change the names if you wish. It doesn't matter. They are just names that you agree upon to observe a certain meaning.

J: We understand creation within the limitations of what we understand as matter.

G: Yes. But matter is only one form of consciousness.

J: And it is only a tiny …

G: Infinitesimal aspect of consciousness. It is one infinitesimal awareness of the expression of life in consciousness.

J: So if we try to understand creation by what we understand about matter, we're hardly scratching the surface.

G: Correct. That is why it is folly to attach yourself so conclusively to it because it is not the source of anything. It is merely an expression of consciousness that enables you to experience an expression of consciousness.

J: And that is why it is just an illusion.

G: Correct.

J: It is so hard for me to stay with that. I keep forgetting that it's all an illusion, and I get caught up in my personal dramas.

G: You are caught up in your desire body, your astral attachments.

J: Let's talk about martyrdom.

G: All right.

J: It played such a big role in the early years of Christianity when Christians thought that if they suffered and died like Jesus, they would be redeemed or "saved."

G: Yes, somehow the concept of suffering brings about redemption.

J: So martyrdom has no value?

G: All martyrdom will do is crucify you.

J: We're seeing a rebirth of fervor about martyrdom right now in the Middle East where so many people believe they will meet God and be rewarded for sacrificing their lives by turning themselves into bombs.

G: How is that different in the West? When people join the military, they put themselves in a position of possibly destroying another or being destroyed. That is the same thing as martyrdom. It is a useless waste of life.

J: When they die and move into the astral plane, is there a sudden understanding of that?

G: None whatsoever.

J: They're still under the illusion that they have achieved something?

G: The astral plane is the plane of illusion.

J: Where they are in life is where they are in death.

G: That is correct. They will carry on from the same moment that they left the physical body. Nothing will be resolved.

J: They have to move through the seven sheaths to the causal plane, the soul plane, before they begin to understand the truth.

G: That is correct. That is when they begin to connect with the truth of the soul. The soul begins to interpenetrate the illusions of the astral plane. But you see, in this stage of evolution you are being given an opportunity to do that in the physical. You don't have to wait till you leave the physical body in order to do it. You can do it right here, right now. You can transcend the need for death. You can allow the soul to resurrect and to awaken in the physical body without the experience of the suffering of the cross, but rather welcome the experience of the surrender to the cross.

J: And that is the Light Ascension process.

G: Yes. It is the process of conscious awareness, of conscious choice. It is freedom of choice exercised consciously.

J: I am studying Light Ascension, and I'm attempting to grow in consciousness.

G: Then there is no problem.

J: But I don't feel I know what I'm doing.

G: No, you don't have control over what you are doing. You are choosing and in choosing, you are exploring the realm of faith, the realm of the soul's truth revealed that moves beyond the need for safety, security, and assurance of the lower self that must always be in control.

J: So I have to give up control.

G: Yes.

J: And just be?

G: Be in charge instead by making conscious choices whenever you have awareness on any level. Choose consciously to move towards life, to move towards the expansion of life, towards the awareness of life, towards acceptance of life rather than resistance to it. Then you will be choosing life. You are the truth, the resurrection, and the light. The truth shall set you free.

J: Well, part of the truth you're helping me understand is that much of what we've been taught, that we accept as truth, is really little more than brainwashing. For example, when someone is made a saint, I guess it is just a title the church bestows that has no meaning outside of the church. What about the sacraments, such as baptism? Jesus was baptized. What is the meaning and value of baptism?

G: First of all, the ritual of baptism is not the act of baptism. The act of baptism is the second stage of spiritual development, the awakening to the realization of the self as a spiritual physical being. That is the baptism.

J: Is that something that happens through the church?

G: No, it is something that happens within you. The church may recognize it, may ritualize it, may sanctify it. It does not make it so.

J: What makes it so?

G: The experience of it. So now you are going through on your planet the baptism initiation. You're going through all seven levels of it. You're also going through all seven levels of the birth initiation, all seven levels of the transfiguration initiation, the renunciation, the crucifixion, the resurrection, all of it, you see? The baptism is the process whereby you transform the emotional body, and in doing so you come to the realization of yourself as a spiritual being by awakening the soul. Because the emotional body becomes the vehicle of the soul once all of the feelings are accepted and the emotional body becomes still. There is no further duality. In the emotional experience, it has been purified. It has been baptized, and then it becomes the intuitive knowing of the soul.

J: Is that what Jesus experienced when John the Baptist baptized him?

G: Yes, the symbol of baptism was simply the recognition of—the ritualization of—that level of awareness.

J: So all these rituals and sacraments performed by the church have no intrinsic meaning.

G: That is correct. What makes them real and what gives them power is the belief in them.

J: A child who is baptized can't believe anything. The child is totally unaware of what is going on.

G: That is correct.

J: So at what point might it be possible for the baptism to take on its real value?

G: When human beings begin to take charge of and responsibility for their own emotional body.

J: Which has nothing to do with a religious ceremony.

G: Nothing whatever. It has to do with the spiritual unfoldment of the being.

J: Jesus said eat this bread and drink this wine, and some Christian churches replicate that in the communion service. Does that have any value and meaning?

G: It is symbolic. It is symbolic of the flow of the life force of the soul through the body. The bread is representative of the true higher vibration of the physical body realized so that the soul may be hosted in the physical body. This is why it is called the host. When the physical body has reached a place of flow of the life force where it is no longer encumbered by its armoring and its belief systems and its emotional conditioning, when it is able to flow freely with the life force and raise its vibration, then it can be used as a vehicle through which the soul expresses, experiences, and has its spiritual being in the physical form.

J: Catholics are required to confess their sins in preparation for receiving Holy Communion. Are you saying confession has value if you think it does, or does it intrinsically have value?

G: Everything has value according to what you think and your emotional attachment to it. That's what creates your version of reality that is basically an illusion. The illusion you have been living through your myths are your ego defense. It is a myth. It has no reality. Yet, you have been living it as though it were reality. That is a ritual you serve every day. Your ego mask. It is a ritual you observe with holy sanctity and commitment every day of your life. You even insist that everyone around you observe the ritual of your ego mask by validating you as a nice person, as a good guy. And you insist they allow you to fulfill their needs and their feelings at the sacrifice of your own. That is your daily ritual.

J: I was oblivious to that.

G: Of course, as most people are oblivious to most of the commitments they make where their religious beliefs are concerned. They do as they are told, like children, like sheep.

J: So is there anything sacred in the sacrament of communion?

G: It depends upon how you are using it. It can be a point of focus. For what purpose? It depends upon how you see God, how you see yourself in relationship to God. If you see yourself always as demeaned and less than and of no importance and as sinful and deserving to suffer and be punished, then that is the relationship you are having with your version, your idea of God. Does it have anything to do with the reality of God? No

J: So I would guess the value of communion has something to do with your personal intention for it.

G: That's correct. It has to do with what you believe it is. Like anything else.

J: So if you believe it is honoring God, then it honors God.

G: Yes, except that God doesn't need to be honored because God is the very experience of honor itself.

J: So it doesn't redeem you in any way, and doesn't save you in any way.

G: No. The only redemption is to act honorably. Then you act as God.

J: So it is a ritual constructed by the church as part of its control over people.

G: Exactly.

J: As is confession and all the rest of it.

G: Yes, to give you something to do. And to keep you in a place of seeking redemption, and to keep you in a place in your psyche of being sinful and wanting and less than and separated. You're in a constant state of redeeming yourself until you are honorable enough to be given permission to be connected with God. But that permission lies in the hands of your priests, doesn't it? God is created in your image and likeness. Therefore, you are worshiping a graven image. You are worshiping the golden calf. And it has nothing whatsoever to do with God.

J: Many people are likely to be upset by what you're saying. What would you say to them?

G: We're not interested in harboring your sacred cows to make you feel good. It is not our job to make you feel good. It is not our job to support your vanity. It is our job to reveal the truth as it is. Ye shall know the truth, and the truth shall set you free.

J: That statement has more meaning for me now than it ever did before. I truly understand a great deal of what we have been taught has been made up by man.

G: That is correct. You have been living a fairy tale.

J: Have we ever lived truly?

G: Consciously? No.

J: How about when we first came here from the twelve star systems? Was there consciousness then?

G: There was the consciousness of each star system that brought its archetype into being. And then all of those archetypes have been melded together to create an overall experience of God remembering itself.

J: But there never was a time when man had the consciousness of unity we are talking about now?

G: No. Your evolutionary process is the experience of God knowing itself experientially through all the various facets of its beingness. To do that, it has had to separate all of its beingness from its unity to be able to experience them all individually. Thus the use of a device called the soul or causal reality.

J: For our experience here on earth.

G: Yes.

J: And He has used the entire universe to experience all of His parts.

G: Yes.

J: You said that in these times the mysteries would gradually be revealed, as we noted before. One historian who has written about the Gnostic Gospels observed that if these gospels had been discovered a thousand years ago, they would probably have been burned as heresy. But in these times, of course, quite the opposite happened. They have been used as resources for scholarship and research.

G: Because humankind is ready in their consciousness to embrace the reality of truth rather than the illusion of nontruth.

J: The Gnostic Gospels seem to speak of an internal transformation and internal resurrection quite similar to what you discuss as opposed to the outside physical.

G: All reality begins on the inside. All reality is sustained and maintained on the inside.

J: That seems to be what the Gnostics were teaching. And those teachings were eliminated.

G: Because the outside wanted control of the inside.

J: Will more sources of information such as the Gnostic Gospels be found?

G: There are other sources that have already been discovered but have not yet been revealed. They will be in time, as man is ready to let go of his sacred cows.

J: Are they intentionally being withheld?

G: Yes.

J: Will they be revealed in our lifetime or some future time?

G: That is completely arbitrary.

J: What does it depend on?

G: You.

J: All of us.

G: Yes. You are in control. You are in charge of the reality you reveal to yourself by your readiness and your willingness to accept it and to see it, and your readiness and your willingness to let go of illusion and your attachment to it. One involves the other involves the other. One is a requirement to reveal the other to reveal the other to reveal the other. You must dispel illusion to reveal the truth. You must reveal the truth by dispelling illusion. As you dispel illusion, you reveal the truth, and as you reveal the truth, you dispel illusion. As you give, you receive. As you receive, you give, and thus the eternal round.

Chapter 14:
October 21, 2004: Redemption/World Management Team/Ecosystem Imbalances/God's Messengers

J: Your description of the original mission of the United States to bring equality, justice, and unity to mankind had a powerful impact on me. I believe everyone needs to hear how you claim that mission is being distorted and those ideals are being undermined.

G: Rather than righting wrongs, approach it from the point of view of redemption. The human soul is an experience of redemption. When there are challenges—rather than things that are wrong—when there are challenges to consciousness, challenges related to ignorance, to unconsciousness, which is simply the inability to deal with and face reality, then it produces challenges and problems. Those challenges and problems then seek redemption.

Redemption is about bringing things into conscious awareness and responding and from that receiving the learning it offers you and uncovering in that greater parts of yourself. You see, that is the whole purpose of challenge. Challenge is not something to defeat you, to create pain for you, to create suffering for you. That is what you do with challenge because you look at it from the point of view of judgment based on a system of morality that says this is wrong and this is right. This is good and this is bad. Nothing is good or bad—it's just a journey of choices. In those choices something called evolution takes place. Evolution brings about higher levels of consciousness, more expansion of awareness and presence of being. That is the purpose of challenges.

Challenge is not to create pain or suffering. When you approach it from the point of view of trying to get rid of the problem, then you have conflict. And then you have a challenge that seeks to defeat you. Rather, look at it from the point of view that everything you see that is negative or that frustrates you is there to reveal something you are unconscious about that needs to be uncovered, revealed, that you need to be inspired about in some way in order for you to transcend a present limitation of ignorance, of unconsciousness.

J: So you're suggesting we should look at problems and challenges as opportunities to learn, to develop greater awareness and consciousness?

G: Yes. Look at the history of the human experience as one of coming into awareness and consciousness that allows you to see and experience reality in a conscious way. That then allows you to use that reality to discover and to grow and become more of the potential that you are. Challenges reveal your potential. They reveal those places where potential is blocked or thwarted or unconscious. In what you call the negative experience or the frustration of the challenge lies the redemption because in it lies the answer to what you're looking for. Behind every negative experience is redemption, revelation, and inspiration.

You see, every challenge needs to be seen as an inspiration and a revelation of life because the negative aspect of it, the part that is unconscious, is simply the part of the self that has not been revealed. Those things that are the most challenging, the most frustrating, that have caused the most pain and suffering, offer the greatest redemption, transformation, revelation, and inspiration when you go into them from the point of view of what they offer you, what is underlying them, what they are covering up. Because that which causes you challenge and pain is simply something that is unconscious, something of which you're unaware. Therefore, you don't know how to respond to it. You feel threatened by the unknown of it, and you resist that reality. You create conflict. Then it becomes a fight, a struggle, a battle.

J: As you were explaining how redemption can be achieved through meeting challenges, I thought of Christopher Reeve who died last week. He is the actor who played Superman in the movies who became paralyzed in an accident several years ago. He seemed to turn his personal affliction into sort of a world mission.

G: Yes, he used it for world service. Here is an example of a soul inspired to its place in the revelation and inspiration of life and humanity.

J: I would guess that was a soul choice before he came here.

G: Yes, but he had to be able to realize, be awake enough, to exercise that soul choice. How many people would use their affliction for that purpose and thus redeem and transform the challenge? This is a perfect example of what redemption is. He redeemed his condition by using it to serve and to inspire.

J: He certainly did inspire. The response to his death was quite amazing.

G: This is what is inherent in all negative experience. What, for instance, does the challenge of the act of war reveal to you? It reveals to you an alternative. It reveals to you the great and dire need to preserve life and to preserve the right to individuality. Despite what countries and leaders will tell you or the frenzy of crowd consciousness that causes a country to back a war and its leaders, no war has a noble purpose. But in this case, there was no real backing. It was manufactured by those few who have an agenda, where the world management is concerned.

J: As you just referred to the World Management Team and the Iraq War, I've wanted to ask you this. You have said the WMT was distorting the original intention of the United States, which was unity of mankind. Of course our president is elected to enforce all our laws and the constitution. The question that raises, it seems to me, is this: is President Bush consciously connected with these global forces, or is he an unwitting accomplice?

G: Yes, his family has been for years. The Bush family goes back to Ramses II of Egypt who was involved in the New World Order and was a part of the secret societies.

J: You have said several times that the Bushes go back to Ramses II. What is the significance of that?

G: The significance is that the consolidation of the various mystery schools began during Egyptian times, which led to the creation of the intention of a New World Order for the future of the world. These ancient mystery schools have been working on this for thousands of years. It didn't just happen in the last one or two hundred years.

J: I thought the original intention of the mystery schools was self-mastery.

G: It was. But then, you see, certain people get into the organizations and the temptation to use the power they learn for manipulation and control becomes too great for them. This is a test of all initiates. When they are given the understanding and the power of the secrets of the universe and the power of creation, their temptation many times will be to misuse it in some way.

J: So you're saying George Bush is consciously seeking to achieve the goals of the World Management Team.

G: Yes.

J: He is elected to support our constitution and the laws of our democracy.

G: It doesn't matter what it says on a piece of paper. What matters is how it is enforced and demonstrated.

J: So if the World Management Team is undermining the constitution …

G: Then the constitution is being held up as a facade—like the magician who keeps you busy over here while over there he is doing the trick, so that you don't see the trick.

J: So, in essence, you're saying we have a president who is a traitor to the constitution.

G: Basically, most of your presidents have been traitors to the constitution.

J: That's pretty scary.

G: Because the behind-the-scenes agenda has always been to gain control of the people to create this New World Order. That's why the Council on Foreign Relations was created to begin to bring it together and make that happen. That's what the Council on Foreign Relations is all about. NATO is the first inception of an international military system. Get the people used to the idea. For instance, you have a flu scare. All the news headlines announce that there's not enough flu serum. Why do you suppose that is? Do you think that is an accident?

J: How is the scarcity of flu vaccine connected to what we're talking about?

G: Your government since 9/11 has been trying to pass laws through Homeland Security to make it mandatory for everyone in the various states to be vaccinated or inoculated when it comes to certain public diseases. And they've been trying to bring that into the acceptance of the various states. Most states have rejected it because most people still believe they have a democracy. Therefore, it would be against the constitution to institute that you have no choice as to whether or not you want to be inoculated. Do you see? Enforced inoculation will then enable them to begin to install in the general populace the little radio transmitters or microchips into the body with all the information needed to control the mind and the nervous system through electromagnetic frequencies.

Great Britain began chipping babies at birth a few years ago, saying to the parents your babies will be safer if they disappear, if they are snatched away. This is why they created the whole concept of missing children. Put all the missing children on your milk cartons so that you can be constantly aware and build fear throughout the country about losing your children. They're offering many reasons, missing children, medical records. They're doing it in the military under the guise of people being able to be located and rescued if they are lost in battle or captured.

J: There was another story in the news I wanted to ask you about. There appears to be a massive die-off going on with amphibians around the world, frogs and lizards and so on.

G: All species of animal life are endangered at this time. You have created a ripple effect in the imbalances you have created in the ecosystem. The ecosystem is like the nervous system of the planet that holds all the aspects of nature in balance and in relationship with one another. You create a distortion in one area, and you affect everything else. As we have said, everything affects everything else. That is the basic theory of quantum physics, the basic theory of resonance and of entrainment. If you create an aberration in one part of the universe, the whole universe will adjust to that aberration and be aware and conscious of it, and it creates a ripple effect. The fact you are altering the gene structure of your food is creating a genetic disaster, a mutation in the species' gene pool, in the species' DNA. You're creating an ecosystem alteration in the DNA structure of physical form that will alter it for all time.

J: What are the consequences of that?

G: A distortion in the balance of your physical environment, the ecosystem of your physical being. You can't do one thing over here and not have it affect everything else. As we always say, when a butterfly moves its wings in Japan, the air moves in New York—and it does.

J: As everything is connected to everything else, I shudder to think of what the implications are of a massive die-off of something such as amphibians. They're such a vital part of the ecosystem.

G: Well, your oceans are dying. They are heavily polluted. They are being polluted not just as dumping grounds for industrial waste and all kinds of other things, but with frequency waves that are creating toxic destruction in the balance systems, particularly in the whales and in the dolphins, the original Sirians.

J: Dolphins are the original Sirians?

G: Yes. The dolphins hold the Sirian consciousness of the earth.

J: Do dolphins have a developed consciousness?

G: Yes. They are a relay system for the archetype of the Sirian. It is the way in which their ships communicate with the earth and send out their information signals through the dolphins.

J: Are dolphins sophisticated beings in the way that man is a sophisticated being?

G: Yes, in some aspects they are far more sophisticated. They have taken their shape so that they may have great influence in the bodies of water of the earth. They use those bodies of water as the best possible way of sending out the most powerful aspects of their informational frequencies.

J: To whom?

G: To the planet, particularly to unlock the instructions enclosed within the Sirian archetype that contributes to the planetary ascension.

J: Are their efforts being overwhelmed by man?

G: No, you are seeing the extremes of duality. You are seeing the imbalance of one side because your universe has been evolving through an out breath, an out breath into form (matter) that has divided it from source (God), creating a tremendous duality from source by its expansion of the universe into form. That form has been the main concentration of reality in the evolution process of the out breath. The out breath is the process of evolution.

You now come to the midpoint where you become consciously aware of the extreme imbalance between the form and the source. You are now informing yourselves through the central part of the cycle, which is where the shift takes place, through the integration of the physical world with the spiritual world. Your planet and the entire universe now begin their devolution. The universe begins to collapse upon itself and go back to source. Now this will take many millions of years in your sequence of order of time.

J: Probably billions of years, wouldn't it?

G: Not necessarily. If all souls in your universe made a conscious choice together to accept ascension directly, then your entire universe would collapse in upon itself instantaneously. The process would be accelerated. They would create a quantum shift.

J: Scientists believe the universe was created about sixteen billion years ago through the Big Bang. And you're saying we have reached the furthest expansion from the Big Bang?

G: Yes.

J: The expansion of the universe has stopped?

G: It has reached its maximum point of expansion. Therefore, it now moves into the shift. The shift is the interval. The interval in all cycles is the moment between the in breath and the out breath. That place is the place of the void. And it is also the place of chaos. It's the place where the scientific principle of chaos rules because what happens when the in breath and the out breath meet, and that shift takes place, is you have an integrative process. You have one side, form, meeting the other side, source, that does not have form. And you then come to a meeting of the two, the inner and the outer, as above so below, the physical and the spiritual.

J: If the universe has stopped expanding, does that mean at some point it is going to implode?

G: Yes. It will begin to implode in the year 2012. This is when the shift will take place. This is the eight-year cycle that brings that about.

J: So you're saying the whole process will take billions of years to happen just as it took billions of years to expand unless the consciousness of all beings shifted.

G: That is correct because, you see, you have consumed your planet. So far you have consumed more than half of its natural resources. That means you have created a tremendous imbalance in the biological functioning of the planet. You have created a mutation there. It had those things before to keep its frequencies in balance to maintain and sustain its progressive change. That progressive change has now been mutated because you don't have the resources that you had that maintained the balance.

J: I'm confused. We seem to be jumping between the earth and the universe.

G: They're one and the same because the earth is contained within your universe. This galaxy contains your solar system.

J: Why would anything that happens on earth affect the universe? The earth is such a tiny speck in the vast universe.

G: No. This involves the whole spectrum of holograms that you must begin to understand. This is the spectrum of cause and effect that nobody takes seriously. When you create an action, you create an effect. That effect resounds endlessly, infinitely, into the universe and affects every aspect of creation. When you create effects that are extreme, that have to do with the unbalancing of the system, you immediately create a runaway process of resonant causation, quantum shift.

J: So you're saying what we're doing to earth affects the whole universe. It's like the butterfly wings in Japan affecting New York.

G: That is correct.

J: I want to ask you about some other recent events here in the United States that relate to what we're talking about. You have said that everything is energy and consciousness and that we create our own reality. This summer our southeast has been battered by massive hurricanes. What if any role does our consciousness play in generating those kinds of storms?

G: Well, first of all, weather is the expression of the emotional body of earth. When certain areas of the earth are disturbed or altered by mutation, the weather patterns of the earth mutate, and they have and they are. That is one of the reasons all species of animals and plant life are endangered. The ecosystem's imbalance is creating such a rapid quantum effect of change and mutation that those life forms can't respond to their regular patterns of evolution. Instead, they are responding through an evolutionary pattern based upon new movements of the emotional body of the earth, the weather patterns. So these species cannot catch up. They cannot maintain themselves as a part of the resonance.

J: How does that play out in weather? Florida was hit by four hurricanes this year [2004].

G: Florida is what we call a transient area. It is very densely populated in many areas with a consciousness that has to do with a deeply blocked emotional body. Therefore, you have what? You have storms. You are creating a mutation of weather through what you are holding inside.

J: So consciousness is creating the weather?

G: That's right. Consciousness has created disturbances in balances in your emotional body. The disturbances in the collective emotional body of all humanity then create an overall emotional body experience for you or for the whole universe because of the ripple effect. The more people who embrace the consciousness, the more influence they have over the emotional memory, the emotional conditioning, of the planet. Where Florida is concerned, there is a lot of emotional blockage, resistance to feelings.

J: What do you mean by emotional blockage? Their feelings aren't being expressed?

G: Yes.

J: Why would that happen in Florida?

G: Because Florida is a state where people escape to when they can't find an answer for themselves anywhere else.

J: So they bring a lot of emotional turmoil to the place?

G: Yes, and also the Atlantean vortex is held near there. Florida is just the southern tip of it. It is more closely related to North Carolina. And it is also the location of the Bermuda Triangle. The Bermuda Triangle is a dimensional doorway where you can move through different dimensions.

J: You alluded to the Bermuda Triangle once before. You said that when planes and ships disappeared, they went through a doorway in time and space. What happens to them?

G: They shift into another dimension or another dimension of time where their history is concerned. They may shift into a past century.

J: That exists concurrently?

G: Yes. This is the conceptual understanding of resonance related to holographic awareness. You are the hologram of your entire universe. You contain within your physical body the holographic imprinting of all that is in the universe. You contain within one cell of your being the microcosm of the macrocosm, the entire hologram of all creation. It is all contained within one cell of your being. You contain within your DNA the embodiment of all of creation related to organic form, emotional form, and mental form. It's all recorded in your DNA. Your DNA also contains all of the elements of all the other dimensions and of all the star systems, which are directly connected to the functioning of your endocrine system, to the immune system. The endocrine glands produce the chemicals to sustain and maintain a physically based consciousness.

J: If I am a hologram of the universe and I do something constructive, can I benefit the entire universe?

G: Yes.

J: For instance, if I go through the initiation process, will it have a ripple effect?

G: Yes. That is why you are sent on these journeys, those who choose to go. By focusing in a sacred site that is a combination of an overall resonance and a focus of several energetic vortexes, you can take advantage of those energies and conscious awareness to determine, dissect, figure out, whole aspects of creation in the universe.

J: You have referred to young souls. I was under the impression that all souls were created at once. What are these young souls?

G: The infant souls are those who are just beginning their incarnational experience on the earth. Those who are more mature souls or old souls or even teacher souls have had many many thousands, even millions of incarnations. So their experience of life is more complete, more transcended, more experienced, simply because of the time and effort they have spent through so many lifetimes. The infant soul is related to the first chakra, which is related to learning how to survive as a physical being.

At this time on your planet there are very few baby infant souls developing because it has no reason or need for it. The planet's present process is in the final stage of development where physical matter is concerned. It would be of no import and it would not serve the progress of this stage of development of the planet's oversoul to begin introducing new souls when you are at the final stage of your soul level development. Infant souls would not contribute. It doesn't do you any good to know survival. You're moving out of survival. Therefore, you will have more souls at higher levels that are incarnating.

At this time you have the highest resonance of higher soul levels incarnating in the physical. There are many of them, but for the most part they are dormant because they haven't been activated. They haven't been inspired. All you have to do is inspire them, and they will become activated and they will respond. And they will respond faster than ever before because they have created and maintained a resonance of a certain vibration. They will move right ahead from there because they are operating at a very high vibration as opposed to when they came in at previous cycles when the earth was at a much lower vibration.

J: I wanted to ask you about Osama bin Laden, who seems to have vanished. You said in one of our earlier discussions, "We would venture to say he is being protected by the CIA somewhere in the world undercover." What do you know about him?

G: He is being protected. That is all that we can say because anything else, to identify location, that sort of thing, would interfere with your freedom of choice.

J: Protected by whom?

G: By the American government.

J: That's a definite?

G: Yes.

J: Mr. Bush knows that?

G: Oh yes. The whole Afghan thing was just a ploy, as was Iraq.

J: I wanted to ask you about the presidential challenger, John Kerry. As a young man when he came back from the Vietnam War he challenged the government officials who kept sending more men to fight and die there. I was impressed to see this relative youngster stand up to the Senate committees and challenge U.S. war policy. That gives me hope that he is not a part of the World Management Team alliance. Would that be a correct assumption?

G: No. It's just a better disguise. Bush is less subtle because he is operating through a different set of defenses. Therefore, he is easily angered when he feels he is being made wrong. So his weaknesses are more apparent. His desire to be stubborn and dominate from his point of view is greater as well.

J: So are you saying no benefit would come from a Kerry presidency?

G: That is not what we are saying. There are benefits from all of it. All it's doing is mirroring your commitment. What would you say is your commitment, your responsibility, that you are not taking which is why what is taking place is taking place and getting out of hand?

J: Well, I guess we're not standing up strongly enough to say no.

G: And not having the interest. You see, the fact your government has run away with your freedom is simply mirroring back to you how easily and effortlessly you have given up on holding sacred your individuality and being able to contain your space in reality. That's all it is mirroring back to you.

The very fact, dear one, that in your country during an election year less than 50 percent of the population shows up to exercise their right of choice is a good indication the overall attitude is listless, without passion, without involvement and without caring—an indication of a docile society that has become self-satisfied and at the same time is rendered powerless in believing it has no influence whatsoever on reality. Think about it. Not even half your population is taking responsibility to exercise its freedom to choose how it is governed!

J: As I was editing this manuscript, I made a connection that was such a light bulb experience for me that I wanted to address it with you. I connected your definition of love with the idea that God is experiencing himself through all of us. One of your definitions of love was, "learning to awaken, realize, accept, express, and experience in the fullest way possible the experience, expression, and potential of your being as an individual." Obviously, the best way for God to fully experience itself would be through all of us learning to love— to awaken, realize, accept, and express in the fullest way possible our being as an individual. It makes perfect sense. I got it!

G: Got it, get it, good.

J: That is what it's all about, isn't it?

G: Yes. That is your unification. That is your place in the role of God. That is how you are God's messenger and at the same time you are God. You are the discoverer and the uncoverer for God of all the parts that He, Her, They, It—because God has no gender—gets to experience itself through. The fact you've been given freedom of choice is not without a purpose where the divine is concerned. It is a brilliant choice where infinite consciousness is concerned because through freedom of choice, God gets to experience and gets to experience itself, its fulfillment of its beingness. It gets to experience it as if it were itself going through a process of evolution and discovery, which is what creates experience.

Chapter 15:

November 29, 2004: Election 2004/2012/God and Religion/Two-Thousand-Year Cycles/Root Races/Polar Shift

J: This is our first discussion since the 2004 U.S. presidential elections. I'm concerned that Bush won because of the connections you said exist between the Bush administration and the World Management Team.

G: What you are experiencing is the unfolding of the final stages of a plan that has been in inception ever since the beginning of the creation of what you call the United States. If you examine the roster of presidents and their bedfellows, you will find that without exception every single president you have had was either a member of the Masons or a member of another secret organization such as the Knights of the Templar. There has been a plan since Egyptian times.

J: Are current political developments undermining the mission of the United States, which you have referred to as the New Jerusalem?

G: They are not undermining that [mission]. They are doing what they do. Is the other faction doing what they do? Or are they waiting for permission from the faction that is? That's the question to ask yourself. Because from that place of questioning is where I can take responsibility for my participation, how I participate, how I don't participate. I have the right and the freedom to create the reality I want.

J: Most people would believe your warnings are just wild conspiracy theories.

G: Unconscious most of the time.

J: In our last conversation, you seemed to be saying it didn't make much difference which candidate was elected because, essentially, it was just a different mask.

G: Yes, but you don't want to come in condemning another belief system or condemning the people who institute that model of reality because by opposing them, you empower them. Then the reality that I have for myself is always based upon what I am opposing.

J: You have said the more effective way is to create an alternative.

G: That is correct, and that alternative grows until it becomes of such magnitude that it builds to millions of people who are beginning to consciously seek the light behind the form. When that takes place, you begin to build a resonance. Then when others come into contact with you that are not of that resonance, it begins shifting them.

J: I would like to move to a subject of change on a much larger scale. You said last time that the contraction of the universe would begin in the year 2012. I speculated that would take billions of years, but you said it could happen in the twinkling of an eye.

G: But most likely it will take billions of years.

J: You added that a polar shift was one occurrence that could change the time frames. Some metaphysicians were predicting a polar shift would occur around the end of the last millennium.

G: It's already taking place as you speak. The polar shift you are experiencing now is less damaging and dangerous and less extreme than it has been in the past. In the past, it has happened instantaneously, within a few hours. The planet is a thousand years overdue for a polar shift if you look at it in terms of past evolutionary cycles. However, a polar shift is very dependent upon magnetics and gravitational pull and the energetic force of friction produced as a result.

When you are dealing with energy and transformation, you are dealing with fire. The element of fire creates transformation from the point of view of death and rebirth, destruction and construction. That which was is consumed by the fire and is alchemized. From that which is destroyed or broken up is created the new reality.

You are starting the process leading to the year 2012 of the fire, the burning away of the dross, the alchemical moment of the transformation of lead into gold. The lead is the old reality of duality. And that is being transformed. That changes and shifts you into the next millennia, the millennia of quantum shift and transformation from the destruction of the old. This process is the process of transformation that is now taking place.

J: The process will be completed in 2012?

G: It is the completion of the cycle that marks the synthesis of the out breath and the in breath, which then brings about the awakening of the new force, the solar force—the soul beginning to radiate from the inside out and reality shifting for all time from the reference point of its meaning and its purpose lying outside of myself.

J: So the polar shift is not a sudden shift of the earth, but is rather happening gradually?

G: It is happening, but it is happening less and less because the north and south poles are gigantic holes in the magnetic fields of the planet. For several years now scientists have been observing a gradual shift in the poles of the planet. It is happening in slow time so that the shift will be experienced in two ways. One, it will be experienced from a place of fullness, a place that comes from you as the source. On the other side it will be experienced as a tragedy and disaster—no matter what I do, I cannot get away from death

J: Are you talking about a worldwide physical disaster?

G: Well, that is a possibility. Everything lies in potential. Because of the shifting, the polar ice caps have broken away and are melting. This is creating a radical mutation in all of the life forms in the northern and southern hemispheres of the earth. Because of the shifting climactic conditions, all of the animal and plant species residing in those areas will begin to become extinct.

J: So the melting of the polar ice caps has more to do with the polar shift than it does with global warming?

G: Global warming has accelerated the patterns that produced the polar shift. It has accelerated the shift. It is not the source of it.

J: Wouldn't a gradual shifting of the poles affect navigation?

G: It does. It causes navigators to adjust their instruments. True north is no longer true north. They are adjusting their instruments. This also affects the alignment of the heavens in your solar system and the influence of the other planets. Astrology also needs to make adjustments. We said years ago that consciousness has shifted reality. So the slowing down of the polar shift is an affirmation of what you have been doing as individuals and the power you have to create radical change, because that is radical change.

However, you may ask, if we can do that, Gabriel, why can't we do it with George Bush? Why? Because you don't have the same attachment to the earth that you have to George Bush. You're not trying to get rid of anything where the earth is concerned. You're concerned with balancing. You're concerned with maintaining it as a harmonious experience. With Bush, you would just like to get rid of him. Therefore, you set yourself up as an antiforce. And in doing so, you strengthen his position. More people were [voting] in opposition rather than voting to move toward what they wanted because they don't know what they want unless it is to oppose something that affects them. Their extreme opposition is the height of the experience of duality.

J: You said last time the souls that were "incarnating now at the highest resonance levels for the most part are dormant because they have not been activated. What you have to do is inspire them and they will become activated and they will respond." What would it take to activate them?

G: What did it take for you?

J: It has been a lifelong pursuit of the truth.

G: What was the key thing? What caused you to suddenly desire to wake up? You didn't suddenly wake up, but you opened the door. Something triggered it.

J: The Conversations with God books helped open me to new ways of understanding.

G: Yes, so you see you were not open to the truth from the beginning. What you were open to from the beginning was finding and discovering things that you could attach to in different ways that would absolve you from responsibility and put you in a place of feeling safe. So you could give your power to a God who would take care of you and you didn't have to take any responsibility as long as you just obeyed the rules and did the right thing. That is not the truth.

J: And that didn't feel good any more.

G: That is correct. And why did you think that didn't feel good any more?

J: I didn't believe it.

G: And why do you think you didn't believe it?

J: Because there was a new rationale that made more sense to me.

G: That's correct, and that initiated the awakening of the new possibilities, a new level of your development where your soul's awakening and its consciousness is concerned. Do you see?

J: So perhaps this book, like the Conversations with God books and others that come along, will be a catalyst for the awakening of others.

G: Exactly. And also keep in mind what you do not want to do. You do not want to create the information of Gabriel as a dogma. You do not want to create it as something that is imposed upon anyone. You want to make it available to those who resonate with it, and they will find it. That doesn't mean you don't do everything you can to get it out there to as many people as possible. You see, it contains its own level of consciousness. Anyone who does not resonate with that level of consciousness won't go near it. They won't even see it. They won't even find it.

J: I want to ask you about the Antichrist. There are so many references to it in Christian literature.

G: If you are in resistance, you're in fear. If you're in fear, you are opposing or anti-love. Christ is love. Love is soul. Soul is Christ. Soul is love. Anything that is not of love is in opposition to life, and, therefore, it is the Antichrist.

J: So it's not some figure, some powerful person.

G: Again, you see all your different stories and myths in your Christian theology about your relationship with God were all created by men. Let us repeat this as we have said many times: religions are made by men. The Antichrist is simply resistance to love, to the movement of life. It is unconsciousness. It is the destructive force of fear.

J: Is this another example of the misinterpretation of scripture?

G: Yes. Understand, people create religions. God did not create religions. God has no use or need for religions. God does not have to explain itself. People create religions based on their own agendas. You look at every single religion, and you will find the construction of the religion, every one of them, is based upon a patriarchal system, a tribal system, a system of: You're Superdad. I'm the bad child. If I don't do as you say, I'll be punished. If I do as you say, I'll be rewarded.

J: I can certainly see how that perspective comes out of the patriarchal system. But it is harder for me to understand why some things are not intrinsically good or bad.

G: No, they are not. That is a judgment of experience based upon something you have created called pain and pleasure as a measuring stick of experiences that come about through resistance to movement, resistance to change, resistance to life. That is all. That's all you are experiencing when you have, for instance, a Hitler who kills several million people. All he is doing is mirroring your commitment to your resistance to life, not being good enough to live it. Fighting the feeling of not being good enough. That is all. That is all that is taking place. All the rest is judgment. That's wrong. That's bad. It's simply people reacting to their wounding.

J: You said that mankind evolves over two-thousand-year cycles.

G: Yes, two-thousand-year cycles that are astrologically based and ray-based. In the evolutionary process of the planet, those two-thousand-year cycles create a process that relates to the evolution of humankind through specific archetypes. Those archetypes of influence are the archetypes of your particular astrological sign, which is the influence of a particular star seed that is exerting its influence and teaching the population about itself in that two-thousand-year cycle. It's how the star seed has the opportunity to be on the "lecture circuit" for two thousand years and speak to the whole population to educate them as to their people, their customs, their experiences of life, and their challenges where their soul growth is concerned. So that humanity as a whole, through these cycles, can contain the awakening of the experience of all twelve star seeds.

J: Your references to root races seem to be tied into two-thousand-year cycles. But when you refer to root races, you only talk about the Lemurian, the Atlantean, the Ayrean, and now the Spiritual. That is only four. We have had many more than four 2000-year cycles.

G: But you see they are not singular in nature. In other words you have carryovers of integration processes. In a two-thousand-year cycle you will have the influence of the previous root race working through the influences of a new root race. There is a whole complexity of influences. A particular star seed of astrological influence teaches and trains its archetype of consciousness in two-thousand-year cycles depending upon the dominance of the particular star seed such as the Age of Aquarius and the Age of Pisces. But root races operate and manifest over thousands of years.

But time and reality have been accelerating in the quantum physics process. That is why there was more progress in the last one hundred years than in the previous five thousand. Now progress is doubling every decade. That is quantum shift. The same thing happens with the influence of cycles and the progressive learning process the cycles contain. They are able to handle more. They are able to move more quickly. Now does that mean that in this two-thousand-year cycle the entire root race of spiritual man will form and develop? This two-thousand-year cycle will introduce the birth and the inception of this new root race into the physical. Will it go into light during this two-thousand-year period? It could, but not likely. At the present rate of progression, we do not see that. We do not see the manifestation being that rapid where the quantum aspect of it is concerned.

Now look at the earth and the shift of the poles. The shift of the poles is largely influenced by electrical friction, so it's the realm of creation through opposition. The more opposition there has been, the more rapid the polar shift took place. As you progressed, there has been less opposition and less friction. As change takes place through less resistance, the earth becomes less susceptible to instantaneous movements and shifts. That is an indication you are moving out of cause and effect and into resonant causation.

In resonant causation, shifts are instantaneous and almost imperceptible even though the shift itself may be extreme. All of a sudden all human beings everywhere on the planet one day will drop their guns. There is no more desire for violence. You may say, well, that's dramatic. No, it's not dramatic because the dream we're referring to is the dream of dysfunction created by resistance. On the other hand, the quantum shift happens out of love

J: There seems to be such a gap between where we are and where we want to be.

G: That is because there is still so much resistance. What percentage of people embrace life with divine love? How many people embrace the teachings of Christ? Take a guess. What percentage would you say?

J: I would guess a very small percentage.

G: About 2 percent.

J: I have been wondering about this next question for a long time. When you announced to the Virgin Mary that she would give birth to Jesus, you said she would give birth to the Son of God. Why did you use that phrase when we are all sons of God?

G: Because Jesus the Christ is the Son of God, the son of the soul. He is a man who demonstrates for you what you are and what you have always been. You are the Christ and the Christ is you. You are the Son of God, the sum of God, the solar force of God. You are the ensoulment and embodiment of a living God, living and moving and having the experience, the individuated expression, of God's being.

[The tape was not decipherable from this point. We scheduled another appointment to complete the interview on December 10, 2004.]

Chapter 16:

December 10, 2004: Duality Versus Unity/Secret Orders–Modern Organizations/Power Of Consciousness And Intention

J: We began our discussions on April 11, 2003. You said at that time that the timing of this book was good because we were entering a new two-thousand-year age to bring about the unity of mankind. Here is what you said then:

"The spiritual development of the past has been based on duality, the separation between the divine and the physical. Spiritual practices and religions have been based more or less on the idea of the division between man and God, and that man must in some way make himself worthy of that connection." You said that was a fallacy, and it was important for us to "allow mankind to see that they are not separate, that they are a part of all things, that nothing is divided from anything else, nothing is separate."

I believe we have clearly addressed that idea in so many ways under so many different topics. Have we addressed it as clearly as you would like?

G: How do you feel? Do you feel you understand it?

J: I believe I understand it thoroughly.

G: OK. Explain it to us in two sentences.

J: We are all one. Everything is a part of everything else, so nothing is divided from anything else.

G: Very good. And what appears to be divided is what?

J: Is not.

G: Exactly. It is an illusion of division and separation because human beings fight for their isolation rather than sustain their individuality.

J: As I have tried to understand and accept the unity of everyone and everything, I realize that when I'm disturbed, when I hear statements that are painful or upsetting to me, it almost always relates to the idea of separation and disunity. Some individual or group is being defined as undeserving or less than or is being demonized.

G: It's very simple really. The universe is a unified whole. Nothing is separate. Yet, human beings defend their separation, fight for their separation because they haven't become attuned to their individuality.

J: When you say not attuned to their individuality, you mean?

G: Their individual needs, their individual feelings, their ability to contain their own sense of self, to be autonomous on all seven levels of their being, all seven stages of self development of childhood. Each level of consciousness is united with every other level of consciousness. Separation is something that can only be understood from the perspective of the reality that embraces it. From the God force, it cannot be understood. It cannot be understood that I have to separate myself in order to experience myself as an individual. The God force cannot be understood from the ego perspective in that sense. The ego force cannot understand how individuality can be sustained and maintained without a strong independence or separation. And that is because they (human beings) have been unable to see being as it really is and that is at one.

J: As this is likely to be our last interview for this book, I wanted to ask a final question about the U.S. elections last month. You said it really didn't matter which presidential candidate won because they were supported pretty much by the same powerful forces.

G: Yes, more or less. You see, contrary to what you believe and to what you are told in your publicity machines, governments are not ruled or run by government leaders. Governments are ruled by the money people, as for the most part they always have been. Particularly as populations divided into groups and civilizations, it became a necessary part of the process. However, corruption also became a natural part of the process, even though that shouldn't be so. Corruption is an interference with the process, a disfigurement or a distortion of the process or system.

So government leaders in this day and age are tools. They're implements, figureheads if you will, who carry out the directions of those who rule behind the scenes. They are the bankers, the oil brokers, the pharmaceutical companies, and all the very large organizations. The powers that be more or less rule or run the world. They run the economy, the governments. They even influence the major religions, which will last as long as they need to be used for the advantage of those who wish to control.

J: They control religions too?

G: Yes. When in their estimation, a religion gets out of hand or is not serving their purposes, they will do something to shame the religion or shame the people in it in some way. Just as you had the first real attack on the Catholic Church when you had all the articles in the news. All of it happened at once, lasted for a few months, and then kind of disappeared. Curious, don't you think?

J: What are you saying?

G: Curious they would suddenly create sound bytes about the corruption and sexual politics within the Catholic Church and reveal those things at this time.

J: So you're saying those news reports about alleged sex scandals were the product of some planned strategy?

G: Yes, it is a strategy. They are seeking to render each group powerless so they will be under their control. Each religious group, each political group, each and every individual state of being, they are seeking to render powerless. They are already set up for a one-world economic system. The meetings they've been having around the world that many people protest, particularly those who met in Seattle, Washington last year, are for the purpose of creating international trade and a one-world economic standard. And that will not float in a system such as this, which calls itself a democracy.

So you have within your world a split that is based upon those in control and power who want to control everything, control freaks who want control over the earth. The same people who pollute the atmosphere, who use up all the resources, are in secret meetings throughout the world. These various organizations, these secret orders, if you will, have basically been grooming people for thousands of years.

J: What do ancient secret orders have to do with what is happening now?

G: All of these organizations (ancient secret orders) have been turned into modern organizations. They are now functioning in these modern organizations with the practices of the ancient ways and with the rituals. So the power of that which is ancient is brought in and creates a tremendous solidity of intention in the astral world. Because the astral world, after all, is strengthened by your thoughts, how you think.

J: You were saying there were two forces. Those who want to control everything, but you didn't define who the other side was.

G: Those who want to control everything, and those who want to create a new world of oneness and unity for humankind.

J: Are those looking to create unity in power anywhere, or do they just show up in protest groups?

G: They are organized in various groups. They are joining together in their soul groups. They are active in starting new businesses, new forms of teaching, that sort of thing. So these are taking place before your very eyes. The world order, from the economic perspective, the enslavement of the human species from the point of view of money, has already more or less been accomplished.

J: There doesn't seem to be much of a balance between these two forces. The control of the various corporate empires is pretty complete. That's where the power lies. You have said the people should wake up. But I have no idea how people would take back control. It would be very hard to turn that around.

G: Perhaps. It depends upon what you are moving towards and what you are moving against. If you are against something, you'll have a tremendously hard time because you will be opposing something.

J: When we were talking about Bush winning last time, you said voters who had voted to oppose him had only strengthened him. Now you're linking that idea to how we change the course of the earth. It's not about fighting or opposing. Could you explain that again so we can understand the concept?

G: When you are in opposition to something, you are trying to stop the movement of its life force. When it tries to move, it will feel your opposition, and it will oppose you. Therefore, the more pressure you place upon it, the stronger it becomes because the harder it has to work to oppose you. What you resist persists.

J: So what do we need to do?

G: Say yes. Say, show me. Demonstrate to me a new system, a better system that functions in different ways.

J: To whom are we saying this?

G: People like you who are embracing a level of conscious awareness of healing the world's soul and serving the divine where your soul is concerned, taking your place in the divine plan.

J: So you're suggesting we say to those who want to map a new course for the world, show us a new way, a healthier way, a more desirable way.

G: An alternative that celebrates the formation of, the honoring of, the integrity of the individual.

J: And our home, our planet.

G: Yes. So, it's up to you. You are the brave new world. You are the mapmakers and the dream weavers. You will unfold the future of your earth. And so, as the dream weavers, you must entertain the dream. You must dream the dream. What appears to be taking place now is to prevent you from dreaming the dream. What must you do to dream that dream, to explore it, to cause yourself to be activated, to be stimulated, to live a dream through your independent, individual self, self-contained, self-empowered, making choices based upon your contributing your life force to something greater, to something that includes you but is not all about you? It's something that is about the whole of humanity, the whole of the world, something that is going to create a new world, where the questions are different and so are the answers.

J: That's very inspiring, but we're dealing with powerful forces that are very well organized to stop all of that from happening.

G: Yes, remember that consciousness wins out. Any focus of energy that maintains and sustains itself as a resonant field, a dominant field of vibration that operates at a high frequency, will begin to entrain itself to the higher vibration, not the other way around. That's the advantage you have if you're working at a higher level of vibration. You have a greater influence. Therefore, you have the capability of changing your reality at will once enough people embrace a cause, causing a resonant effect, a resonance,

J: This will occur when enough people have a change in consciousness. Is that what you're saying?

G: Yes. You see, you create a place of critical mass. When you create a critical mass, the whole harmonic shifts. When the whole harmonic shifts, it shifts because of the integration of that critical mass rather than its separation.

Your Christian Bible speaks of the 144,000 who will enter the Kingdom of Heaven. What they're talking about is critical mass. It relates to the quantum leap theory of quantum physics, of instantaneous change. You also know from your human experience that when enough people entertain an idea about something and other people grab onto it, it becomes a part of the reality you embrace. It becomes the critical mass that now shifts instantaneously. This is also the principle behind healing. It is critical mass. It is quantum leap.

J: So you are saying this is working in our favor because we can focus our intention and develop critical mass.

G: Yes, and you can build it at a high vibration.

J: And that starts an entrainment process.

G: Yes.

J: And it begins to shift all consciousness.

G: Everything is going to operate more and more through quantum resonance as everything is beginning to operate at a higher vibration because higher vibrations have been raised on the planet.

J: So, in essence, the wind is at our back now.

G: Yes, you might say that. You are moving from the electrical force to the solar force. You have not accomplished it yet. That is what the eight-year cycle is for to 2012. That's why it is called the end of the world, the end of history, the end of time, because the soul does not exist within history, time, and space. It exists independently. Energy is independent of all other laws from the point of view that energy responds according to how consciousness is directed. And it manifests instantaneously. In the last century, you progressed more in one hundred years than you did in the previous five thousand. Now that's critical mass. That is quantum physics. Now every ten years consciousness doubles. So what normally would have taken four times now will take much less, one quarter of that.

J: You frequently have talked about the acceleration of the quantum physics process.

G: Yes. That is what the solar force activates. It activates a resonant field, a high vibration. It activates the soul signatures, the essence of each person, throughout the planet. That is the highest point of frequency of energy of that person. Within that is contained all the memory of people's lives as souls and instructions on various kinds of tools and that sort of thing they manage to squirrel away.

J: So what is it activating in each one of us?

G: It activates a quantum leap. A quantum leap has actually been taking place. When a quantum leap takes place—let's say it doubles through one experience—in the next experience after it has been integrated, all of a sudden it doubles again within a shorter period of time.

J: That is producing all of the advancement we've seen. And that is just an indication of what is going on in consciousness?

G: Yes.

J: In the past, you've tied that in with resonant causation. You've said, "With resonant causation dramatic shifts can happen instantaneously but imperceptibly." And you gave the example, "Human beings everywhere can suddenly drop their guns." That seemed very profound to me, that resonant causation could cause massive shifts in consciousness so that suddenly mankind might drop its guns and stop using violence to address human problems.

G: Yes. As you start to attract your soul groups, each soul group resonates at a certain vibration. Each soul group has within its group all the different layers and levels of soul awareness. But the main vibration at which the group operates is determined by consciousness. And how consciousness shifts causes physical reality to shift.

In the past, it has taken a long time for things to change. You can see that is no longer true. You see rapid progress in medicine, in technology, the interconnection everywhere through the Internet. It is all progress. They all seem to have suddenly leapt out of thin air. Where lower levels of soul consciousness are concerned, change is less perceptible. Changes are still taking place, but the resonance is different. It doesn't include as vast a field of influence.

J: So when I express discouragement about the power of these international organizations and wonder how we can ever change the direction of the earth, you're saying the hopeful signs are the enormous changes and advances that have been happening over the last hundred years or so because they are really signs of shifting consciousness. This new era of resonant causation and all the energy fields we have talked about are powerful forces that are, in a sense, harnessing and speeding up these changes in consciousness.

G: Yes. That's why we send you to sacred sites. It's a focus of energy. It's like taking a gigantic powerful quark, focusing your intention in a certain way and having it appear over here instantly where you focused. That's how rapidly the energy moves. Energy of a high vibration moves more rapidly. It creates a greater influence over a greater distance from the point of view just of movement. It's not that it's traveling somewhere dependent upon distance. Its distance is measured in vibration.

Therefore, it is also located in vibration by the way in which vibration seeks the harmony of its own environment. That means that when you sustain and maintain yourself in a field of higher vibration, you create a quantum effect, a quantum field, and the possibility of quantum movement, and you create a quantum mass experience. But the critical mass and the manifestation will be confined to those who consciously embrace the process and are serious about it because you need their focus. You need their similar point of view.

J: And vehicles like this book can help. What can you tell us about pulling together intentions and having soul grids coming together?

G: Focus on intentions of a high vibration that have to do with the highest good of all concerned, that honor everyone's individuality, everyone's right to be different, to express differently, to have his or her own reality, to feel the way the person wants to feel, to be able to say no, to be able to say yes, the connection to others within a cycle of similar belief structures. As individuals you will find yourself no longer just a member of the crew. You will be mixing soul vibrations. So if you have people from older soul groups coming together, you will come together for the purpose of activating the ashram of that soul group. When that takes place, it can immediately create an acceleration of energy.

J: And that relates to resonant causation where energy draws to itself?

G: Yes.

J: That is really the path we will follow as we move into this new age.

G: As you move into this new age it is the path, the pattern you will follow because it is the pattern and path that has been evolving since time began.

J: You have said Jesus demonstrated the path and the pattern of self-mastery we are to follow in this new age. We're entering the Christmas season, which of course celebrates the birth of Jesus. But it has become a vast economic industry. What might you say about how we celebrate Jesus's birth?

G: What conflict do you have with the way it is now?

J: Jesus had a great spiritual mission. We're celebrating his birth by decorating Christmas trees, buying gifts, and holding office parties. The real significance of his birth seems to be lost.

G: Yes, that's true. But at the point of critical mass, all the symbols that you have had and used come into question. What was once meaningful may become meaningless. This is how quickly everything is moving and shifting. The ritual of Christmas, for instance. For more and more people, it seems the meaning of Christmas is lost. They are caught up in the world of form and they find it increasingly disappointing each year, but they continue doing it because that's what they do. However, there are those who begin to question and who begin to do it differently. They begin to volunteer their time somewhere, some children's organization, or they go to soup kitchens, etc. It's just a change of choice. They're all just choices that celebrate a level at which they can relate.

Those who celebrate Christmas with a tree and gifts, that is the level of celebration at which they can understand and relate. Others who remember the story of Christ and dress appropriately and listen to someone telling the profound story and do some rituals or whatever it is they do, that is how they remember and that's how they celebrate. Someone else in another place is saying in their language, "It is Christmastime—let the tribe celebrate." And they start dancing with the drums beating around the campfire.

All of these different things are simply ways of focusing intention. What is at the basis of your intention? No matter what you are doing, the basis of the intention is to focus celebration. So, if you are focusing celebration, and you are buying gifts and setting up trees and exchanging a lot of love in the family and remembering others and caring and taking a moment of reflection for that purpose, then it serves the purpose of the intention. You see, the form itself does not create the reality—the intention creates the reality. It's all symbols. It has no more or less meaning than you give it.

A ritual does not make something powerful. What inevitably matters is not what you are projecting onto a symbol, but rather what you are containing within yourself that is ongoing, that cannot be taken from you because it is so precious, because it is life in all of its symbolism in all of its different areas expressed in every way. This is why religions are all dogmatized into separation. We've got God locked up in our church down here because we believe it this way. And you'd better come to our church because we've got it right and they've all got it wrong. And they're all going to hell. And we're the only church that's going to heaven. Do you see? And the other church down the street, they're claiming the same thing. It doesn't matter if it's a church, if it's people playing with Santa Claus. It doesn't matter what it is. It's the intention behind it that gives it the power.

J: Ultimately the intention is about love, isn't it?

G: Yes, it is. And what is love about? Acceptance. Wow. This church can have God, and that church can have God, and all those people who don't go to church can have God too if they want. And those communists, they can have God too if they want, or they can do without Him too because He's present anyway whether they need to make Him important or not. He does not need to be important because He is.

J: He does not need to be important because He is.

G: That is correct.

J: You've told us that God does not need to explain himself.

G: Heavens no. It would be redundant.

J: It would be redundant because?

G: Because it is. Everything is. That's like embarking on a fool's journey to explain everything that is rather than take the easy way. Embrace everything that is. Give everything that is space to live, move, and have its being, in God, in you.

J: Embrace it all, you're saying, embrace it all.

G: Yes.

J: That's very powerful. It's a wonderful way to end our conversation. This is the last interview for the book. Would you make a statement to our audience about what you see as the value of the book?

G: We would say it is a series of questions and answers conveyed in a conversational manner so people may feel they are a part of the different aspects of the present reality they're living in, to change their fear and suffering into a reality of joy, freedom, and love.

J: Thank you very much, Gabriel. It has been a wonderful journey with you.

G: We thank you for allowing us to be in your divine presence. We hope we have been sufficient unto the day where you are concerned for your purposes. So we will close, then with a blending as is our custom. And we ask that you simply indulge us for a moment by closing your eyes for the purpose of imagining as a child would imagine and see us, Gabriel, as a pinpoint of blue light in your mind's eye, and see it grow to an elliptic of light that encompasses the height, depth, and breadth of all that you are as we lend our energies of love and light to support you on your journey of the soul. We say, so be it. We thank you for allowing us to be in your divine presence at this time. And as we take our most joyous leave, we ask always, as you are able to remember, to love one another.

Afterword

Three years have passed since I conducted the last interview with Gabriel (December 2004) that appears in this book. Before publishing the manuscript, I decided to get Gabriel's perspective on a number of events that have taken place since the last interview and scheduled a series of talks with Gabriel through Robert Baker beginning in October 2007.

The weekend I began preparing my questions a huge double-page ad appeared in the Sunday New York Times. It was placed by the John Templeton Foundation with the giant headline, "Does the Universe have a Purpose?" That question was posed to twelve "experts" from various scientific, religious, and academic disciplines, including the humanities. Their answers were: Unlikely, Yes, No, Not Sure, Perhaps, Very Likely, and I Hope So. Not much different, perhaps, from what any group of nonexperts might come up with.

Though Gabriel addressed this question early in the book, I decided to begin our interview with it. What follows is an edited version of our discussions about a host of topics conducted during three interviews in October, November, and December 2007. When I asked for his response to Templeton's question, Gabriel responded: "The purpose of the universe is to learn to love." I asked him to expand on my statement in the book's introduction: "God uses the vast universe to discover and experience its infinite diversity through all the countless expressions of creation, including us."

Gabriel responded that all of creation is a vehicle for God discovering itself:

"God gets to experience all parts of itself, and each creation of God gets to experience the whole. So one serves the other serves the other. That is the force of love. That is learning how to love. By learning about all the different infinite aspects of possibilities of creative expression of being of which God is made up, man gets to experience himself as God, and God gets to experience all that He is made up of. And that is why God is love. For the purpose of creation is to love."

J: Why does God need or want to experience itself in all its infinite complexity?

G: It doesn't need to. God has no needs. God is complete within itself. But by the very nature of its creation and the exploration and evolution of that creation, it gets to experience all parts of itself by default, by the very nature of how it is set up. The fact that God is all that is and by each and every aspect of creation fulfilling the task of being its individual expression of that being, it fulfills the task of its place in the divine plan that allows God to know all that it is. And it allows each expression of God—through its exploration and in its evolution of realizing its wholeness—to know itself as God.

J: So the mission for every expression of God is to experience itself.

G: Yes. All that is necessary for each and every part of God is to know itself.

That, essentially, is what Gabriel has told us is the mission of every human being on planet Earth—to know ourselves by awakening to the realization of ourselves as divine, to evolve through the seven stages of soul evolution to achieve the self-mastery that Jesus demonstrated. That is the Second Coming, and this is the age when it begins.

Our collective soul awakening needs to be understood within the vast evolutionary context that Gabriel has revealed. We are all on a soul journey that takes us from the darkness of separation to the light of unity. That journey, Gabriel tells us, has been played out countless times in countless worlds that today we number as stars—planets that have completed the ascension process and have gone into the light.

But mankind's soul journey of awakening on earth is an unprecedented divine experiment. Our seeding by twelve star systems created the "ultimate challenge in the universe," an unprecedented extreme of duality because "only through the extreme nature of duality can you know oneness." Man's conflicts and challenges on earth are all about moving from separation (duality), working through all the diversity represented by the twelve star systems that seeded us, then embracing our oneness as individual expressions of God (unity).

Gabriel has explained we are being helped on our journey of soul evolution by the ascendant mastery and other divine influences that are bringing in high frequency energies to the earth plane to help raise our consciousness. I asked Gabriel what effect these energies were having on mankind since out last discussion:

G: The planet is in the greatest crisis it has ever been. With the photon belt moving through the solar system, it makes it a thousand times what might have been because everything is accelerated by its high vibration and it brings everything of a low vibration into like vibration and into awareness. With all the energetic shifts and all of the preparation that has taken place where the ascended mastery and the planetary hierarchy who work with the consciousness of souls behind the scenes are concerned, it is surprising how mankind still clings to the last possible breath of his old reality with every bit of struggle he can muster. It is unfortunate because it makes the transition so much more difficult for the masses who are unaware, first, that change is taking place on an unprecedented evolutionary level; second, that the photonic light is influencing that change; and, third, that they have any say in it.

If they were aware and were to consciously work with their own energy bodies and their own physical energy fields, they could lend so much amazing and joyous experience to this transition of evolution. But man as always goes kicking and screaming as grace is not his middle name— resistance is, and drama. This is the preparation period for when the soul energy force will begin to awaken beginning around the year 2012. This is the time of all the behind-the-scenes work—the photonic light, the ascended masters, and the planetary hierarchy—to establish these energies in a way that they could be taken full advantage of if at all possible.

If they (the ascendant masters) were the ilk of the frustrated, they would be frustrated. But it's like water rolling off the back of a duck. They're not concerned with man making the "right" choices. They're concerned with evolution and all that's affected by it, what those effects are, and how that initiates and fulfills this most important portion of the divine plan in that evolutionary process.

J: I'm disappointed because I expected the energies coming into the earth plane would be raising our vibrations and our consciousness so that we would begin to be more enlightened about the choices we make.

G: Well, it will eventually as the entrainment process takes place. But in the beginning the entrainment process creates chaos. Eventually, it will create balance and well being and a conscious connection to your spiritual being. When the entrainment starts to happen, it brings about chaos because all the old forms and everything of a lower form comes into awareness and comes crashing down around you. So it becomes transmuted and transformed to a new form. As everything comes into awareness, the old starts to lose its charm. This will, for example, bring about the extreme downsizing of religions where their influence is concerned, their pastors, that sort of thing.

This is the time when you really begin to see the acceleration of that process we speak of when we say your planet is dividing into three groups. One third will leave the planet. One third will carry on as they were before, struggling and resisting and fighting, because they love war so much and they basically have little wisdom. But they have the capacity to make world-changing decisions and the capacity to fight. Then the third group are those who are bringing about that golden light of the soul.

Gabriel and I discussed climatic and other changes occurring on earth, including reports that approximately one third of the world's bees had vanished, raising questions about the pollination of fruits and vegetables.

G: It's a reaction to the imbalance in the ecosystem that was bound to happen. Not only the bees but approximately fifty thousand animal and plant species are becoming extinct every year because they can't adjust to the damage that has been done to the ecosystem. That will only increase as it moves into quantum time as the acceleration of the planet takes place with the photonic light and the consciousness of humanity. You can slow that process down, but it can't be reversed because it is too close to critical mass.

J: How could we slow it down?

G: Act consciously in every way where your ecosystem is concerned. Be careful with the uses of energy and pollution. Organize groups to get on the backs of corporate czars who are doing more than anyone else to destroy the ecosystem. They poison the oceans and waterways by dumping more toxic waste than any other beings and then have the audacity to buy up the water rights of the remaining reserves of water that have not been polluted so they can then sell it back to the people. Now that is arrogance.

J: We're dumping so much carbon dioxide into the atmosphere, which is contributing to global warming. We're hearing alarming reports that Arctic ice and glaciers are melting at much faster rates than predicted. With the rapid economic growth of China and India and other emerging economies adding to this problem, I can't see how this can be slowed, let alone reversed.

G: Why do you think the United States is declaring wars to control the remaining oil reserves? Because of rapidly changing climates and the reduction in the availability of the hydrocarbons necessary for the production of fertilizers and insecticides, if things accelerate along the same lines the ability to grow food will diminish by 50 percent within the next twenty-five to thirty-five years because the changes are creating droughts in some areas, freezing temperatures in others. So it is going to take some massive rethinking and new actions and structures.

This is the time when all of the old forms that are in duality fall apart and/or are exposed for what they are doing that disturbs the life cycles. On top of that, they (scientists) are splicing the genetic structures of the three kingdoms of nature, particularly the animal and plant kingdoms. One example is using fish genes from fish skin to make tomato skin more resilient. When you mix different kingdoms of nature and their genetic structures, you are doing what the Atlanteans did in their experiments, their scientific alterations that produced terrible mutations. You're creating a situation that can't be reversed by mixing gene pools. Man knows so little about the ripple effects he is creating.

J: You have referred to the photonic belt a few times in this discussion. What is the photonic belt, and what is its influence on the solar system and the earth?

G: Photonic particles are the highest dimension of light particles that move beyond the speed of light. They are penetrating the entire solar system. The outer planets have been penetrated by the photonic light, producing an entrainment, which is beginning to raise the vibration of all matter. As the photon belt penetrates the outer planets of the solar system, it begins to radiate to the earth and raise earth's vibrations. As the photon belt moves further into the solar system and eventually penetrates the whole solar system, there will be a complete shift in consciousness, an instantaneous shift in reality.

We have been working with humanity to try to allow humanity to experience this shift without leaving the density of form [our bodies] so that it can be experienced. In previous shifts when a planet moves into its ascension process, it moves into etheric reality and out of physical form or density. So by attempting to raise the vibration of the body, you are raising that vibration so that it is possible to experience this ascension and this amazing movement into multidimensional reality with the full presence, awareness, consciousness, and direction of the soul in physical form—as in the example of the one, the master Christ, who embodied the physical body of the one, Jesus.

J: Is that why you are predicting that one third of the population of earth will be leaving the planet— because their bodies will not be able to deal with the photonic energies raising their vibrations?

G: Yes, because they are not able to raise their density. But they will operate in the etheric form.

J: Will the photonic energy arrive in full force around 2012 to 2020?

G: No, it will not have penetrated the entire solar system by then, but it will be close. And the influences will be such that it will create a mass shift in consciousness.

J: What will be some of the symptoms of that shift?

G: The breakdown of the old, which is already happening as we have discussed.

J: People are starting to notice. There seems to be a growing unease about the changes we're beginning to experience in climate and such things we've talked about as the die-off of various species such as amphibians and bees. There is also increasing concern about the stability of the world economy and the volatility of the world's securities markets, which are bell weathers of economic health.

G: All systems that are in duality must find the balance in the middle to bring about the cohesion of the expression of the truth of being of the one soul. That involves the unified field of all consciousness. You see, duality is an aberration. It is something that human beings have created. It is not a natural part of the nature of things where the universe is concerned. It is a tool of learning and exploration through extremes. As long as you are embracing one side or another, you are opposing the other side.

J: After Bush was elected in the last U.S. presidential election, you said it was an example of the "extremes of duality." As the Bush administration approaches its final year, I was wondering what observations you had about how this presidency represented the extremes of duality.

G: Look at the extremes where the wars of the world are concerned. You see, war no longer involves just separate countries because nothing is separate. As man has become interdependent where his systems are concerned, he realizes that everything is dependent upon everything else. Therefore, it is not a war between the United States and Iraq, it is a war between different factions of ideologies that have to do with a world view. War is an opposition that involves the embracing or resistance to one side, like all opposition, all resistance, all pain. When mankind is no longer at war with himself as an individual, he will see that reflected in the world around him. The terrorist is the inner terrorist. Of course, mankind doesn't want to take responsibility for his choices and has not yet been able to embrace the power of the freedom of choice, nor has he learned how to. He continues to blame external sources. There is nothing out there.

J: That is probably the hardest principle to understand, the idea that the real terrorist is inside, that there is nothing out there.

G: "Out there" is simply a form of manifestation of the reality that is created from the inside. All reality is nonphysical.

J; To me, that points up how critical it is to love one's self. How else do you address it?

G: How can you care about another if you cannot care about the source?

J: You have warned about attempts to turn the United States and, in fact, the world into a military dictatorship to maintain the hidden power structures of the world and to protect duality. I have a growing list of books by very credible journalists and former government officials that document how there has been an almost stealth attack on the U.S. Constitution by this administration. They document the eroding of our constitution's checks and balances by building the power of the presidency at the expense of the courts and Congress. Meanwhile the military has come to dominate our federal budget while the true costs of the war are kept off-budget, much like they tried to hide the war dead by banning photographs of their returning coffins. Many people are frightened by this administration's efforts to restrict our civil rights and its ability to conduct wars despite the opposition of the majority of American citizens. To me, the greater danger lies in the precedents it creates for the abuse of power by future presidents. It sounds like a scenario for creating the very thing you warned about.

G: Yes, this is so that people will hopefully wake up and start to take responsibility for themselves. You must become self-governing.

J: Is the Bush administration helping us to see that?

G: It is serving as a mirror.

J: Showing us the extremes of duality?

G: The terrorist is at home in your backyard. The terrorist is the inner child who is wounded. That is the terrorist. Why do you think you have children taking each other's lives in school? It is coming closer and closer and closer until you cannot ignore it. The mirror is coming closer because it is showing you that there is no separation, that you are your brother's keeper. Do unto others as you would have them do unto you. Love one another as yourself.

J: As I reviewed the manuscript, easily the most challenging material had to do with your charge that the U.S. government perpetrated the 9/11 attacks as an excuse to invade Afghanistan and to expand access to and control over Middle Eastern oil.

G: Yes.

J: Though that is one of the big conspiracy theories out there— millions of people, especially in the Middle East, believe that—it still remains a challenge for me. It seems too incredible.

G: Why do you think that it was able to happen? Because enough people think like you do. They can't imagine it could happen.

J: You told us it happened because we don't have control of our own government. We haven't exercised our freedom of choice.

G: Of course.

J: You said the U. S. government was hiding Osama bin Laden. Is that still true?

G: Yes. Who was allowed to leave the day after the event? The only family that was allowed to leave the United States was the bin Laden family. What were they doing here in the first place? Interesting isn't it?

J: What were they doing here?

G: Time, the great revealer.

J: We have a presidential election coming up in 2008. The candidates of the Democratic Party have more diversity than we're used to seeing.

G: It doesn't matter because it's all rigged.

J: Some of the candidates appear to be speaking a more independent line than usual.

G: Yes, to make it seem more real.

J: So you're implying that they're all products of the same forces.

G: More or less.

J: A couple of years ago you said that Kucinich was different.

G: Do you think he is going to be allowed to take a position of power? He is an amusement that is allowed to happen to lend a modicum of reality and legitimacy to the operation so it doesn't seem too one-sided. It doesn't matter who becomes the puppet representative because that person is controlled.

J: Don't we get different kinds of policies out of a George W. Bush than from say a Clinton or …

G: No. They are told what to do.

J: Well, here we are supposedly entering a new two-thousand-year age of spiritual man, the unity of mankind.

G: Yes, and all of the corruption must come to the surface, which is what it is doing.

J: So the revelations we have been seeing are all about revealing the duality, which is going to be destroyed.

G: Yes, it's the healing crisis.

J: In the process, our civilization may go with it, but from the ashes would come a new age of unity and oneness?

G: That is to be decided. It's all up to you. It's always up to you because you have freedom of choice. And you are yet but children who are just learning what that means. You have never utilized your freedom of choice because you've lived in a system of herd consciousness. The idea of freedom of choice scares you because it requires total responsibility.

J: You have said so many times that we have to take personal responsibility for our spiritual understanding and growth. And that's what it's going to take for each one of us to create this new age.

G: Everything in nature takes total responsibility for its place in nature and its effect. Man is the only creature that does not.

J: Though man has not responded enough to the energies coming in to the earth, there seems to be a shift in consciousness taking place. The feminine energies seem to be more powerful, taking a more assertive role in the world. And we've talked about the growing awareness of the dangerous changes occurring in the weather and the ecosystem. People are starting to wonder, what is going on here?

G: That is the healing crisis. That is the awakening.

J: What can each of us do to make this a better world right now?

Gabriel responded with twelve things each of us could "initiate in your lives that will change things for the better and will inspire others. Everything you do has an effect on every thing in creation. That's how powerful and important you are. That is how one person has within their hands the ability to change the world."

1.   Man must grow up and take responsibility for his reality, for himself and for others. He is acting as though life is happening to him as opposed to his acting on life.

2.   Give up duality. Give up a system of right and wrong, good and bad, reward and punishment that produces fighting against one another. Allow space for all that is. Don't judge one side as good and the other as bad. Embrace both and create a state of neutrality.

3.   Give up the herd consciousness. By embracing the herd, you give up the self. Understand the celebration of the middle road. Embrace neither one side nor the other. Allow both to be included. That is how you let go of duality.

4.   Embrace the nurturing of life, all forms of life. Nurturing all forms of life develops intimacy, sharing, and communication, particularly with families.

5.   Give up judgment, which creates shame and condemnation.

6.   Exercise forgiveness for yourself and others.

7.   Develop a conscience. Recognize there are many choices in all situations. Choose, and if you make a mistake, forgive yourself and others. Developing a conscience allows for your mistakes and the mistakes of others. It allows you to explore many possibilities. The possibilities of choice become endless, and that allows the creative force to be expressed.

8.   Do unto others as you would have them do unto you. Look at each choice that you make and know that choice has an effect not just on you, but resonates endlessly into the universe. So always ask yourself, if I were to be affected by this choice, would I want that? If the answer is no, then reevaluate your choice. If the answer is yes then by all means make that choice.

9.   To thy own self be true. This involves connecting to the soul self, to the truth of being. It contains three lessons:

The first is your life lesson that involves your talents, abilities, and qualities of being that bring about the realization and the fulfillment of self. By honoring that which is inherent within you, those talents, abilities and qualities are uniquely expressed through you. Even though they may be similar to others, it is important to express them because they carry within them the unique signature of the soul sound that is you. From this comes fulfillment because you are honoring the truth of who you are. So look at whether you are indeed honoring the truth of who you are by honoring your talents, abilities, and qualities of being because that is what you have to give and to share with your fellow souls that contributes to all creation or the God body. Who you are is absolutely unique and must be honored as such. Who you are is of value in its uniqueness.

The second lesson is the soul lesson, which is the ability to experience everything that life has to offer with acceptance—acceptance of your feelings, allowing those feelings to be felt, experienced, and completed in each moment. This brings about a depth of meaning to life that reveals your unique needs. If you are not able to experience life through your feelings, then your needs cannot be revealed because it is feelings that reveal a need. When you know how you feel, you reveal what you need. And those needs are unique to you, even though you share some common needs with every human such as the basic needs of health, wellbeing, shelter, food, etc. But from the unique perspective of your creative self, your needs are unique and they must be honored. When your feelings and needs are honored that brings about the fulfillment of the third lesson, which is your life purpose.

Your life purpose cannot be fulfilled without your knowing your needs and understanding the meaning those needs have for you. The conscious direction of your purpose involves the choices that you make and your ability to choose freely. Freedom of choice only becomes freedom of choice when you know your value and you are able to fulfill your meaning by being in touch with your feelings and your needs so that you may act upon your talents and abilities and exercise your qualities. Then you are able to direct your choices and your actions with a purpose that fulfills the truth of who you are.

10.   Heal the emotional body. Accept all your feelings without shame and realize the highest aspects of yourself. This has to do with releasing yourself from living out the myth of the past and being present in the moment of now—being able to respond to what is rather than to what is not without projection of the past as the past has been completed because you allow all feelings. You allow each moment of experience to be completed by allowing the feelings.

11.   Heal the mental body. Free the mind of all thought so that you have the direct pathway to the soul's knowing, so the soul can take charge of directing the personality, the ego self. Through that knowing there is a connection between spirit, soul, and matter. The soul is the joining point. That is the Christ Consciousness. That is the resurrection. That is the life. The soul is always present in the here and now. The personality, which is confined by the mental body and the emotional body's busyness and noise, is not able to be present with the soul because of all the noise. The soul is ever present whether you are or not, and the soul operates through the love force. Therefore, when

the emotional and the mental bodies are healed, when you are present in reality, you are present in the experience and the expression of the creative force of love.

12.   Love one another as you love yourself. This involves realizing that you are your brother's keeper, that your choices are not separate, and the choices of others are not separate from you. Everything is connected. Look at nature to realize this. The divine plan is laid out in nature. But has man looked to see the divine plan and its teaching in nature? No. Instead he has tried to conquer nature, conquer and divide as he does everything else. Therefore, he has created himself separate from nature and sought to destroy nature—thus the problems of the ecosystem.

Man must know himself as the source, that the source is not outside himself, that the world of form is simply a world of manifestation. It is not the source and substance of anything. It is simply a manifestation. The source of all reality is the invisible exercised through the exemplification, expression, and action of the creative force of love. Therefore, man must take responsibility not just for himself and for his fellow man, but also for the manifestation he has created and what he has done with that manifestation in order to come into harmony with the love force. That must be done not only by honoring himself as an individual, but honoring others in their individuality.

Loving one another involves many things. It involves, first of all, honoring the truth of being of all individuals, their needs, their values, and their purpose. Loving one another also involves taking responsibility for the environment and what you have done to it and correcting that, stopping any further destruction. It also involves releasing yourself from all opposition to differences and embracing all differences because love makes space for everything, for all individual expression of its truth and its infinite possibilities of being.

J: Thank you, Gabriel.

G: You are very welcome, dear one.

December 2007

Energetic Exercises

Preparing ourselves for the awakening of the soul involves much more than simply doing a series of physical exercises designed to "raise the vibratory rate of the body to match the vibratory rate of the soul." Gabriel addresses this issue in many places in our dialogue.

In chapter 13, he tells us that the church Jesus refers to is the "human body that allows the soul of humanity to awaken and flourish. So the body becomes the church or the tabernacle of the soul that is awakened and flourishes."

Later in that chapter he says the "bread in communion is representative of the true higher vibration of the physical body realized so that the soul may be hosted in the physical body. When the physical body ... is no longer encumbered by its armoring and its belief systems and its emotional conditioning, when it is able to flow freely with the life force and raise its vibration, then it can be used as a vehicle through which the soul expresses and experiences and has its spiritual being in the physical form."

So preparing the human body as a "host" for the soul involves the mental (belief systems), emotional (emotional conditioning), and physical (releasing the body's armoring and raising its vibrations).

For me, changing belief systems involved accepting a different understanding of God and creation as revealed in books such as the Conversations with God series and Gabriel's teachings, including Reiki and Light Ascension, which are programs of self-mastery.

In chapter 3, Gabriel explains what he means by dealing with emotional conditioning. He tells us we have to create peace and harmony and acceptance within ourselves before we can do that (love) with others. "It is important that you integrate you first, that you do your internal process to be at peace with you and awaken the soul in you. Then you can love one another. You can only love one another as you love yourself. If you cannot love yourself, you cannot love one another because you're only having one relationship and that is a relationship with yourself." We see, then, why Gabriel defines the Awakening of the Soul as "giving up the separated self, the fight of separation and acknowledging your unity within."

Of course, we cannot acknowledge our unity within if it doesn't exist. "If you are in duality with yourself and not in full acceptance of yourself, how can you possibly be in full acceptance of others? If you are not able to integrate the wholeness of your individuality and respect and honor it and experience the integrity of it, how can you ever possibly expect to do that with the individuality of everyone else?"

When I asked Gabriel how we can learn to fully accept ourselves, he responded, "By dealing with all of your past history. Dealing with all the traumas and conflicts within you. Dealing with everything within yourself that divides you from loving yourself and accepting yourself unconditionally and completely. And being able to separate, reveal, and share every part of your being without reservation and without judgment. How many parts of yourself are you able to accept? What are the parts of yourself that you hide that you are ashamed you cannot accept? What feelings within yourself do you find difficult to embrace and accept and respond to? These are all parts of yourself from which you are divided, all parts of yourself you have disowned or suppressed or judged or shamed. All that needs to be owned, to be brought into integration. All that needs to be healed."

So all the parts of us we've disowned, suppressed, judged, or shamed need to be integrated, owned, and healed. Some of us can heal ourselves, but as Gabriel says, "It's better to take advantage of people who already have a process that you can utilize, who have tools that can teach you so that you have a tool kit."

Of course, Gabriel is talking about therapy. My therapy sessions with Robert Baker over the past several years have helped me to begin to accept, heal, and reclaim myself, as they have scores of others on the same path.

Dealing with the body's energetic armoring is a key part of preparing the body for the awakening of the soul. As Gabriel explains in chapter 4, "The exercises are at the heart of the process of awakening the soul consciousness or Christ Consciousness because until you can clear the vehicle that holds the soul in conscious awareness, no matter how much the soul attempts to waken, it will be blocked by the unconsciousness of the vehicle receiving it. So the physical body must be free flowing without blockage and without the density and pollution of lower vibrations. Your body is the temple of worship, the temple of your being, the temple of God. Therefore, it must be maintained at a vibrational level of awareness and presence of being that allows you to evoke the conscious awareness of what is passing through it. The only thing that prevents you from accessing the soul right now in total awareness is that your physical body has become so dense and blocked that it is barely living."

The physical exercises presented here are designed to release the energetic armoring, the "pollution of the lower vibrations," that is blocking the life flow in our bodies. They begin with the breath. Breath is life. Before you do any of these exercises, practice inhaling the breath by breathing deeply into the body, expanding the solar plexus. Hold it for a short time. As you begin to release the air, drop the jaw with your mouth open at least two fingers wide, making a loud aahh sound. Feel the opening in the back of the throat, and you should feel a connection of energy that activates a sensation all the way down to the base of the spine. Breathe in, drop the jaw, and then aspirate the breath six times before you do the exercises. As you do the breathing exercises, get in touch with your feelings and allow the sound of aahh to vary in its expression and loudness according to what you're feeling. Connect what you're feeling to the expression of your sound and release with aahh anger, rage, sadness, joy, happiness—anything that you're feeling through that sound.

Exercise 1:

Lie on a mattress or an exercise pad with pillows around to catch your blows. Make fists and begin lifting your arms one at a time as high as you can, then bring them down pounding the pillows or mattress. Then add the legs, kicking them scissor like, pounding them into the mattress. The legs and fists don't have to be synchronized. Get in touch with your feelings, expressing them with the sound of aahh. Begin to attach words to your feelings and replace the aahh with them. Phrases like: "No, No, No, No. I won't. Leave me alone. I love you. I hate you." Express whatever you are thinking and feeling with statements like these. Do this for up to ten minutes or until exhausted. This is an effective exercise for generating energy throughout your entire body and beginning to loosen the layers of energetic armoring.

Exercise 2:

Lie on your back and bend your knees with your feet flat on an exercise mat or mattress. Do the breath and sound. Lift the pelvis as high as you can and let it drop on the mattress, continually raising and lowering the pelvis at a fairly rapid rate. This will loosen the layers of armoring in the pelvic region and allow the life force to move down the legs into the feet. As you do the exercises, get in touch with your feelings and begin to verbally express your feelings with phrases that reflect your emotions. As you verbalize your emotions, trust that phrases or statements will come from your subconscious into conscious awareness. Do the exercise for ten minutes or until you are exhausted.

As you release the armoring, different feelings and memories may begin to surface. You may begin to have memories of childhood experiences. Strong feelings may suddenly overwhelm you. Allow, honor, and feel the feelings and they will change.

Exercise 3:

Most of us became frozen emotionally at a certain stage of child development and build up armoring in the upper back, arms, shoulders, and chest. That armoring is usually related to receiving and/or giving. The child frequently believes it is unsafe to receive because of a lack of nurturing and emotional support. Consequently, a child's nervous system is constantly preparing for pain, distorting the child's relationship with desire. Desire is a yearning that is produced from a loss of connection to our authentic core self as a child. We then constantly seek fulfillment outside of ourselves. This exercise helps release armoring related to our feelings and resentments about a lack of nurturing and helps us unlock our assertive energy, enabling us to be self-motivated, to fulfill our goals, and to manifest in the physical world.

Stand in front of a sofa or pile of pillows. Once you have connected with your feelings, begin the breath and sound. Bend your knees and raise a plastic toy baseball bat high over your head (get one that is fairly hefty and plump). Bring the bat down with as much force as you can, repeating the motion over and over. As you beat the mattress or pillows, express whatever you are feeling. Give yourself permission to fully express whatever feelings come up. It is an excellent exercise for releasing anger and rage. Don't force a feeling. By accepting where you are, you can move towards where you want to be.

All this expression of feelings helps us connect with our authentic selves. As Robert Baker says, "The expression of feelings and the movement of the life force through the body are simply preparing the way for the expression of your divine being in your physical body, your soul. So you are really doing soul restoration, soul reclamation. Through that reclamation and restoration you will still and heal the mind and the emotions. When that takes place, you open your relationship with your divine self at the core of your being. You are now in touch with your soul. Your emotions become the inspiration of your intuition. And your thoughts become the doorway for your soul's knowing. So you are then operating through intuition and knowing. And it's all coming from inside you. You are the source, for you are a soul. You are an expression of God. You have a direct relationship through the soul's connection to spirit expressed in the physical body."

The exercises do not need to be done in any order or frequency. However, in the first week you might do three sessions with a day between. Monday, do exercise 1; Wednesday, exercise 2 and Friday, exercise 3. Do that for two weeks, then mix them and begin doing one a day. The bat exercise is effective when you need to release anger or aggressive energy.

Finish each exercise session by sitting quietly with your legs crossed yoga style and meditating for about five minutes. Breathe in and out deeply, focusing on the breath. If thoughts or feelings come up, allow them and let them move on. At the beginning of the meditation, ask your higher self, your soul, if it has any advice for you. At the end of the meditation, ask if it has an answer for you. Listen with your heart and your mind for the answers. All the answers are within. Everything that you need is in your physical body. The body has the ability to restore itself endlessly, but you must begin to honor it as the sacred tabernacle of your being. Treat it with gratitude and joy. End your meditation with thanks to God and God's guardians for being present with you in your time of surrendering and healing of your past experiences, and ask for the assistance of all beings of highest good, love, and light to serve you on your path.

Glossary

Age of Aquarius

This two-thousand-year age of spiritual development that is governed by the Aquarian star system.

Akashic Record

The complete record of all the evolutionary cycles of the living organisms of the earth, including humankind.

Antichrist

Anything that is not of love; unconsciousness; the destructive force of fear.

Armageddon

It is within. It is the conflict between the ego and the soul, physical and spirit, as the soul seeks to imbue the personality with its light and soul consciousness or Christ Consciousness and takes over its direction.

Armoring

Rings of blocked energy chronically impacted in the muscle tissue that prevent the movement of energy and in time can manifest as disease in different areas of the body.

Astral Plane

The place consciousness goes when it leaves the physical body at death. It is composed of seven levels of bioplasmic matter through which the soul moves as the soul gradually releases from physical experience back into the soul plane, which is the home of consciousness. It is the intermediary plane between the physical and the soul plane.

Awakening the Soul

Giving up the separated self, the fight of separation, and acknowledging your unity within. Bringing the soul into conscious awareness so that you have a connection through your intuition and knowing.

Beliefs

Frozen ideas and perceptions that are retained because of a collective agreement. A belief keeps reality frozen in time.

Book of Revelations

The map of evolution for this age as written by the Apostle John.

Causal Plane

The soul plane.

Christ Consciousness

Soul consciousness. Your realization of yourself as divine and your ability to channel that connection to the divine. The Christ Consciousness is the ascendant master who awakens the awareness of the soul in physical matter. Jesus was the physical embodiment of the Christ Consciousness and became Jesus, the Christ, man of the soul. He embodied the teachings of mastery of the Christ Consciousness.

Dark Night of the Soul

The struggle between the lower and higher self, the physical and spiritual.

Democracy

A system where the equality of individuality is embraced, where equal importance of all expression is held sacred, where all beings live for the good and the wholeness of one another.

Desire Body

Body of the lower will, the physical.

Desire Elemental

Your emotional, physical, and mental desires that are attached to the physical world as the source of your sense of self and reality. When we free ourselves of attachments, we can use the world simply to grow, to gain experience, and to learn.

Devil

Ignorance, unconsciousness. The shadow that lies within the subconscious that rules you and governs you without your knowing it. Things you're trying to suppress that never become integrated or dealt with based upon your unconscious traumas that cause you to react and to defend.

Duality

Anything that is divided against itself, good and bad, right and wrong, etc. The split or schism between the physical and spirit.

Equality

Embracing and honoring the individuality of all things in acceptance and love.

Energetic Grids

Grids of intention that generate energetic forces that gradually bring consciousness into matter and influence evolution. Jesus developed the energetic grid of the seven levels of spiritual initiation that awakened soul consciousness in matter during his lifetime.

Enlightenment

Being in the now, fully present.

God

Creation, universal mind, universal consciousness, undifferentiated consciousness.

Harmonic Concordance

Initiated by a planetary alignment forming a six-point star on November 8, 2003. It brought about the initiation of ascension into the physical, an awakening between the unconscious and the conscious. It initiated the opening of the doorway of the soul in the heart into the lower self, the physical.

Harmonic Convergence

A five-year period beginning in 1987 in which the consciousness of the earth was blocked from the development of the consciousness of humanity. Humanity was able to develop and raise its consciousness without influencing the movement of the earth, thus preventing humanity from destroying the planet. It entailed a great awakening in human consciousness, the beginning of what is sometimes referred to as a New Age.

Heaven

The awakening of the consciousness of your being. Your connection with the soul within. The freedom from the duality of self.

Hell

You trapped in your desires and your separation and fighting for it.

Immaculate Conception

The connection of two souls, the soul of the child with the soul of the mother. Every birth is the product of an Immaculate Conception. It has nothing to do with the absence of sexual intercourse in conception.

Spiritual Initiations

Seven stages of soul evolution: the birth, baptism, transfiguration, renunciation, crucifixion, resurrection, and ascension. They represent a process of self-mastery involving the mental, emotional, and physical bodies preparing and raising the physical body's vibration to a vibratory rate where the physical body and the soul body can awaken as one within each other, where the vibratory rate of the physical body matches the vibratory rate of the soul.

Birth—birth of man's knowledge of himself as a spiritual being

Baptism— purification, the release from all personal history, emotionally, mentally, and physically in order to set you free to respond to the moment of now.

Transfiguration—time when the lower self and the higher self are introduced to one another and the soul takes over and transforms the lower self.

Renunciation—when we renounce the lower will (ego) completely and surrender fully to soul consciousness in a place of purpose and service to the world. This is when the Christ began his service. "Thy will, not mine be done."

Crucifixion—matter surrenders to spirit and spirit surrenders to matter. The place where the divine plan is revealed to the soul, and the soul takes its place in the divine plan for service to humanity.

Resurrection—the soul being born fully in its light. It completely takes over the physical being. It is then ready for the ascension.

Ascension—transcends matter as an individual experience of separation, isolation, and duality. He then becomes the Christed one. He becomes the living, breathing light of the soul consciousness guided by the God force in every moment of his life. He then has the power of God in his hands to transform all mankind.

Oversoul

A dimension of being that contains all of the soul fragments that make up the whole of you as a physical being in your evolution through all of your incarnations, your physical experiences from first to last. It acts as an intermediary between your soul fragment and the unindividuated force of God. It governs your overall connection with the wholeness of you that is fulfilling your purpose in the divine plan.

Physical Body

A vehicle through which life expresses itself in individuated form for a period of time.

Physical World

A state of consciousness used to experience the evolution of the soul— how the soul grows, expands, and deepens its consciousness and awareness of itself.

Piscean Age

The last two-thousand-year cycle represented by two fish swimming in opposite directions, which is representative of the higher and lower self or the physical and spiritual in opposition to each other.

Planetary Logos

The soul plan of evolution for this planet including this two-thousand-year cycle of soul evolution.

Planetary Monad

The band of energy, of DNA, surrounding the planet Earth that holds the Akashic Record of the Earth.

Purgatory

Souls trapped in the first two levels of the astral world, usually waiting to be rescued by the Christ. They are caught between the physical and nonphysical worlds because of their beliefs.

Reality

Created in nonphysical realms by the direction of energy by the mind and the emotions.

Root Race

Represents a major development of soul evolution and consciousness in humankind.

Soul Signature

The resonance of our particular soul fragment for this lifetime that embodies the particular pattern of learning we come to this incarnation to achieve. Our first names hold the resonance of our soul signatures.

Spirit

All consciousness combined, undifferentiated, all inclusive, infinite.

Soul

The individuated personification of God that lives within the physical and makes it possible to experience God as a physical being. A fragment of the consciousness of God that is used to express and experience an aspect of God's consciousness that becomes enclosed in a physical body and animates the purpose of that experience.

Rays of Consciousness

Divine rays projected by the sun that produce a particular level of vibration.

Second Ray

Ray of love wisdom. Governs the awakening of the planetary soul and soul consciousness in this new two-thousand-year age. Enables us to experience and use more consciously the wisdom of the divine plan and put it into operation in the physical.

Sixth Ray

Governed the last two-thousand-year cycle, the Age of Pisces. The ray that celebrates the pairs of opposites, duality, represented by two fish swimming in opposite directions.

Seventh Ray

Spiritual ray that transforms all physical structures that are in duality. Creates an entrainment process that raises all consciousness to its higher level, bringing humankind out of duality into unity. Governs this new two-thousand-year age of spiritual unity.

Redemption

What we receive by discovering and developing who we are for the fulfillment of our potential as a human spiritual being.

Reiki

Life force. When the body is fully available to the life force, that is Reiki. It is a perfectly balanced state of being in physical reality. So the purpose of Reiki is to help balance the life force in the physical body and its flow.

Resonant Causation

When humanity evolves through knowing by being able to sustain a certain vibration and frequency to shift evolution consciously rather than through unconscious choice. The law of attraction based on the laws of quantum physics that when an energy of a certain level maintains a field, it begins to create a resonance that attracts things of similar resonance into its field.

Second Coming

The awakening of the soul in all mankind replicating the awakening of God consciousness and self-mastery that Jesus demonstrated through his life.

Shoemaker/Levy Comet

The crashing of this comet into Jupiter in 1994 represented the birth of this millennium, the birth of the Christ Consciousness in mankind's awakening through initiation into the knowledge, experience, and expression of himself as a spiritual being of God. The collision in time began raising the vibrations on earth for man to begin the awakening of the soul. It initiated the development of a new level of evolutionary consciousness in our solar system.

Solar Logos

The divine plan for the evolution of this solar system, which radiates from our sun.

Star gate

A dimensional opening in time and space where incoming space ships can change their frequency to come into a different vibrational space such as the earth.

Synchronicity

Coincidences that come about through the law of the universe that like attracts like based upon its energetic frequency.

Truth

Truth is ever becoming, ever knowing, ever discovering, and ever experiencing more of itself all the time. Therefore, truth is not absolute. A belief is finite. It keeps reality frozen in time. Truth is inclusive, all embracing, ever becoming more of itself. It is ever in movement.

About the Author and the Channel

JOEL ANASTASI has been a news reporter, magazine editor, officer in a large financial services company, and management consultant for many large and small organizations. He has been a student of metaphysical, spiritual, and religious subjects for many years. Joel began studying Reiki, an energetic healing art, in 2002 with Reiki Master Robert Baker, one of the great trance channels of our time. Joel holds a BS in Economics from Syracuse University and an MS in Journalism from Columbia University. Additional information is available through **GabrielSecondComing.com** and **ChildrenOfTheAwakenedHeart.com**.

ROBERT BAKER has been a trance channel bringing through the teachings of the Archangel Gabriel since 1990. He is a Reiki Master, counselor, and healing practitioner. You can learn more about Robert and Gabriel's teachings and current readings at **ChildrenOfLight.com**.

Printed in the United States
130367LV00005B/88-273/P

9 780595 494057